THE BEATLES UNCOVERED

**1,000,000 Mop-Top Murders
by the fans and the famous**

by Dave Henderson

FIRST PUBLISHED 2000 BY THE BLACK BOOK COMPANY LTD

PO BOX 2030, PEWSEY, SN9 5QZ, UNITED KINGDOM

ISBN 1-902799-04-6

DESIGNED BY KEITH DRUMMOND n REPROGRAPHICS BY RIVAL COLOUR n COVER BY DAVID BLACK

Black Book Company Ltd

"Across the universe."

"I WROTE THIS..."

DAVE HENDERSON is a music obsessive. He can seek out record shops with specially-prepared vinyl-diviners and is often to be found in shadowy cellars with dusty fingers. The first record his Dad bought him was a copy of Help! which cost £39/11d. He wore it down.

He saw Yellow Submarine and didn't understand it and once organised an event for Q magazine which resulted in Sir Paul McCartney walking out in the middle of a speech by Phil Spector. He became obsessed with Beatles' covers two years ago and has an enormous pile of worthless vinyl by amazingly dodgy people as a result.

His favourite Beatles song is Within You, Without You as covered by Rainer Ptaceck and Howe Gelb of Giant Sand. Through researching and writing this book he's rediscovered his love of Jellyfish, discovered Klaatu's back catalogue and come to the conclusion that Cilla Black was actually once not a bad singer at all – especially her version of Tim Hardin's Misty Roses.

His favourite Beatles song by The Beatles is Rain and if, in a strange cosmological, time travel type of way, he could be a member of The Beatles at any point in time, he'd almost certainly like to be Ringo in Help! or John during the filming of the video for Penny Lane. Paul during the filming of Strawberry Fields Forever or George when he bought his first sitar.

He is currently publishing director of Mojo and Kerrang! and Creative Director of the Q Awards.

"THE HENDERSONS WILL ALL BE THERE..."

WHEN I FIRST GOT sucked into the world of record collecting I had no idea what I was doing. Thankfully now I still remain vaguely innocent and a little bit confused.

I'm still attracted like a drunken moth to sleeves that look "really interesting". I often buy albums that look good or that have an interesting line up of instruments or a ridiculous track title included purely because I'm desperate to hear what they're on about.

I'd love to be a completist but I've never been able to catalogue things. There's still a thrill when I go through the record rack at home and pull out something I've not heard for ages. In fact I've often been so enthusiastic about an album that when I've seen it again for next to nothing in some bargain bin I've snapped it up so that I can, at some point, pass it on to someone who I think will like it.

This isn't meant to be a confessional, it's just a way of explaining how I've ended up with a huge box of albums that are either completely full of Beatles' songs or are memorable only for the fact that they feature one Beatles song which is either:

a) absolutely corkingly strange
b) ridiculously terrible
or
c) hopelessly average.

Whatever, I couldn't bear to be parted from any of them. They're locked in. Under beds. In cupboards. Here, there. Everywhere.

A couple of years back I was discovered that I'd started, quite by accident, picking up Beatles' covers. Firstly I already had a lot that I really liked but, as is the way with these things, I became fascinated with how people would interpret a set of songs that were quite finite and specific in their detail. Add to that they came in some

really peculiar sleeves and the rest is history in the making. It started as a joke - of course. But now, well, I suppose it's not so funny.

I was an instant enthusiast and almost immediately Kenny Ball And His Jazzmen's version of When I'm 64 attained a new relevance. The

Long And Winding Road by Cissy Houston became a minor classic to my ears. A real hairs on the back of your neck job. And Keely Smith's lagubrious All My Loving plucked at all the right heartstrings.

And I wasn't alone. It's plain to see that The Beatles' music affects people. It moves them. Often in mysterious ways. How else do you think someone could create a whole album of Beatles songs delivered in the Baroque style? Joshua Rifkin did. And in the excellent Phil Bowen book Things We Said Today, David Santer even wrote a poem, The Only Record Of The Beatles I Have Is The Beatles Seasons Played Baroque, about how that album affected his world view. It goes:

Early 60s
And from the back of my Bantam
(me, square tie on square bike)
Carl shouts, 'They're good,
They're going to be great,
Great with a capital G.'

They'll not go far', I scream
and think
Bach's Great
and Beethoven
Da da da dum
and the Good Life
with Geese and a Goat
and my Grandfather a Jones
and the Great View
From Lleyn.

Hey, that's rock 'n' roll. If not quite Keats. And it fully backs up Tim Rice's comment that, "The Beatles were the Mozart of popular music." Well, almost.

Obviously their catalogue is unique, full of standards set in time. But, it's when those structures and formats are eroded that their music attains new dimensions. Sure, a lot of the stuff I've come across is piss poor, emotionless drivel but there are even sweet moments in the worst of covers. And in the best, there's much, much more.

In Beatles Uncovered, I've listened so that others don't have to. I've suffered the slings and arrows of Stu Philips' outrageous Hollyridge Strings. I've gone head to head with Russ Sainty. But I've also reclined with Sergio Mendes, plumped up a cushion for Claudine Longet and let out a hearty laugh for David McCallum, Kenneth McKellar and The Big Ben Banjo Band.

These pages are filled with exotic extremes. There's heavy metal howlers, Latin rhythms, French sensuality, psychedelic nonsense, punky tirades and enough lush strings to moisten a whole desert. The Beatles gave a little bit of something to everyone. And whether it's a straight cover of one of the classics or a convoluted collection of songs that they gave away, then they all have merit. Everyone has a different take on The Beatles. For example, take The Beatnix album It's Four You. The Australian Beatles-a-likes concocted a collection 19 songs that the Fabs gave away and delivered them in the style of the band of the day. In doing so they recreate the vibe this album might have had if it had ever existed. Complicated? Mad? Crazy? Actually, the album sounds pretty good.

Hopefully you'll find something in this book that will change your preconceptions of The Beatles' oeuvre. Or maybe just something to add to your collection. Something to complete the surround sound. If not, at least you'll be able to marvel at the sheer wonderment of some of the people who tried to be Fab. Failing that, you could always burn the book in memory of the Beatle bonfire that took place in Georgia back in 1966. It's your choice.

The Beatnix
It's For You
RAVEN RVCD 45. Released: 1994.

I'm In Love; Nobody I Know; If You've Got Your Troubles; It's For You; Hello Little Girl; Like Dreamers Do; Step Inside Love; Woman; That Means A Lot; I Don't Want To See You Again; One And One Is Two; Bad To Me; Tip Of My Tongue; I'll Be On My Way; World Without Love; From A Window; I'll Keep You Satisfied; Love Of The Loved; Goodbye.

The story: Australian would-be Fabs The Beatnix go in for a bit of passing off sleeve-wise but create something of a neat oddity along the way. Highlighting 19 songs which The Beatles gave to other acts – Cilla, Cliff Bennett, Billy J Kramer, Peter And Gordon, etc – The Beatnix adopt an early Cavern stance and produce an album's worth of tunes that might have become comprised an early Beatles' platter had they not been busy doing the albums they did. In reality its fuzzy logic makes it quite a tasteful collection, jangling all the way to the jukebox and sounding pretty darn leather-clad and sweaty into the bargain.

LET US TAKE YOU DOWN...

Paul: "Once we've done it and it's published then anyone can do it."
Who do you think does The Beatles' songs best?
John: "Us."

THE ACT YOU'VE KNOWN FOR ALL THESE YEARS

WHEN I WAS GROWING UP I never understood the vagaries of the music business. The concept of published songs. That Cliff Richard didn't write all his own material. Or that The Beatles would give away theirs. It was all rum stuff when the truth came out.

As The Marmalade careered to the number one spot with Ob-La-Di, Ob-La-Da, a careful perusal of the label revealed that the song's chirpy international feel wasn't the creation of the floppy-haired Scotsmen but that of Paul McCartney and John Lennon. How odd, I thought. And much odder it was to become.

Several years later I'd made the move from liking football to liking music and my taste had been affected by my mate's cousin who introduced us to a whole raft of West Coast bands, from The Byrds and Flying Burrito Brothers through to Grateful Dead. Granted, it didn't help my social skills when potential girlfriends were keen to converse to a backdrop of Motown. I'd be cranking up The Dillards' wild mandolins and be enthusing about their fusion of psychedelia and bluegrass, as they scrabbled for their coat.

The Dillards were great. They'd started out as straightforward banjo and mandolin pickers, who'd fallen into the Newport folk scene and impressed the likes of Bob Dylan. But they were always experimenting and their albums Wheatstraw Suite and Copperfields became cornerstones of my collection. Both boasted orchestras, traditional bluegrass sounds, folky strums and highly-melodic songs and they also both featured covers of Beatles' tunes. I've Just

Seen A Face and Yesterday were delivered in a unique and very soulful way and were nothing short of unique.

Nearly 30 years later, in 1998, I dug out the same two Dillards' albums after I met the group when they reformed to play the Cambridge Folk Festival. I talked to Rodney Dillard about those Beatles' covers and he introduced me to an even earlier source of cross-cultural revolution when he told me about The Charles River Valley Boys, Elektra labelmates who'd knocked off a whole album of Beatles songs as Beatles Country. Amazingly I found the album for about eight quid within a week and was struck by the awesome playing but, perhaps more importantly, by the ability of The Beatles' songs to travel so easily into a very well-defined setting.

Sure, I was a Johnny-come-very-lately, but I was impressed by the Beatles' repertoire and how fresh it sounded "done" country. I realised that there must be hundreds of versions of Beatles' songs in all manner of styles out there. Wouldn't it be great to start collecting them? Flicking through my own collection I turned up 20, 30, 40 Lennon and McCartney and George Harrison songs by artists as diverse as Rainer Ptaceck, Jose Feliciano, Richie Havens and even William Shatner. Yeah, this might be fun.

Investigating The Beatles' sections in record shops it was evident that there was already a small industry of Beatles' collections by other people and, of course, there

was the exceptional Exotic Beatles series. Lovingly prepared by Jim Phelan, it collated fairground organs, flustered opera, sitar orgies and all manner of Beatlisms into one flowing stream of consciousness. Volume Three also then led me on to The Beatles Covers List, a highly-informative, ever expanding list of thousands of covers at www.wmin.ac.uk/~clemenr/covers/covers.html.

Even a light perusal lodged two things in my brain.

One: I have quite a few of these songs lurking in my collection and I hadn't even realised. The Beatles were already working their way under my skin.

Two: I'd really like to hear The Beatle Barkers.

The Beatle Barkers is an album of Beatles songs with vocals supplied by dogs, sheep and various other animals. Several tracks are featured on the Exotic Beatles series and, yes, it is as odd as it sounds. If the Dillards' covers were some way from Merseyside, then this must be, well, if nothing else, a few constellations further out. Of course, I couldn't find the album. I've been looking for two years now, but no luck.

But I have found a website, Frank's Vinyl Museum at http:// franklarosa.com/$spindb.query.new.vinyl, where you can actually hear a couple of tracks from the album and read what Frank thinks about it.

Frank: "I've listened to hundreds of Beatles covers over the years in just about every style and format you can possibly imagine. I've got Beatles covers by groups trying to sound just like the Beatles and groups trying to sound like anything but the Beatles. Covers sung by celebrities, TV stars, musicians, and nobodys. Musical styles ranging from Country to Jazz to Classical to Acapella. Just when I thought I'd heard everything, along comes this treasure: The Beatle Barkers. On it are 12 of The Beatles' most popular early songs, done up by a traditional rock 'n' roll band with the vocals supplied by dogs.

"I don't get it. Beatles songs with dog and cat noises is supposed to be entertaining? Cartoons of dogs playing guitars with Beatle haircuts is funny? Am I missing a chromosome somewhere or is this the stupidest idea for a recording since Edison cranked out the first wax cylinder?"

Hey, it's only music. Or is it? That someone has gone through the process of recording Beatles material and releasing it to the general public vaguely suggests that they want people to buy it for its own merit. The Beatle Barkers are no different. Whether they wore dog outfits when they were doing it is a completely separate issue. The album exists, even if it is a dog. (Arf. Arf)

Unless of course, they were intent on just passing themselves off as The Beatles – or at least The Beatles' dogs. Maybe it was just an effort to make a fast buck. In Cool And Strange Music magazine issue ten, Jim Yoakum examined a handful of Beatles' cash-in albums from the '60s. But The Beatle Barkers, he claimed, falls outside of such rudimentary shindiggery. Instead he spends the article highlighting The Manchesters' A Hard Day's Night, The Bearcuts Swing In Beatlemania, The Merseyboys' The 15 Greatest Songs Of The Beatles, The Buggs' The Beetle Beat, The Ripoffs Play A Golden Age Of The Beatles, The Liverpools' Beatle Mania In The USA and The Liverpool Kids' Beattle Mash, Jim concluded that these albums go beyond sheer novelty, that they possess a certain degree of skullduggery and deceit. "It's a cloaked attempt to lure you, the

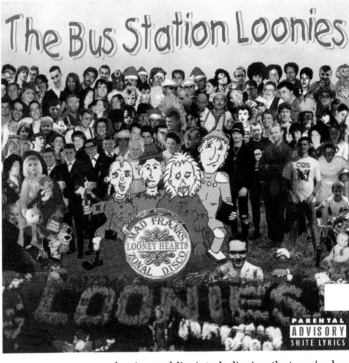

buying public, into believing that you're buying one thing when you're plainly getting something else."

Indeed, the line between passing off and paying homage is thin. Check out the selection of sleeve pastiches that exist of Sgt Pepper's for example. Fans or fogies? The culprits include Frank Zappa's Mothers Of Invention's We're Only In It For The Money, The Exotic Beatles Volume Two, The Bus Station Loonies' Mad Frank's Zonal Disco,

RED ROCKET 7

by
MIKE ALLRED

Makem Music's The Sound Of Sunderland and the compilations The Moonlight Tapes and A History Of Punk. It doesn't stop there either. The 100th issue of Q from 1996 had a fold-out Pepper's pastiche, Mojo's 1995 100 Greatest Albums Ever Made issue did like-wise, and the comic Red Rocket issue seven delivered the Pepper concept sketchily, while the millennium special issue of Rolling Stone used the format for inspiration. And, as Peter Blake will surely confirm as he does every time he's quizzed about it, that very concept netted him less than a 100 quid.

As the '90s drew to a close, I realised I was hooked on this one. Digging around in junk shops and at jumble sales, I was turning up a host of Beatles' material, a lot of which attempted to illustrate their bond with the Fabs through strange illustrations, the use of wigs and other such ludicrous Liverpudlian ideas.

And as my collection bulged I realised I was giving house space to music by military marching bands, mad keyboard players, strange psychedelic combos, Scottish nut-cases and even groovy character actress Dora Bryan. Dora's gorgeous 1963 single wasn't a Beatles' cover at all. But it had cap-tured the excitement of the British public when it was released and in my clamour for Beatles-related material it produced a warm feeling. On its release, amid crazed Beatlemania, Dora schmoozed, "All I want for Christmas is a Beatle" and, indeed, at that time who on earth could argue with that? It's a gem.

Having dug out all the Beatles' albums too, I was fast becoming consumed by their wares. Like collecting Pokemon cards, I had a number of cover version targets to seek out and I had to get them all. It just became a fascination. How did Liberace deliver The Beatles? What was The Silkie's best Beatles moment? How did Petula Clark sing Please Please Me in French. And wouldn't it be great to hear Siuoxsie And The Banshees' version of Dear Prudence again? And, why else, for instance, would a grown man be seen skulking around the Acker Bilk section in record shops. It had to be done.

Hand in hand with this enormous research project, my personal tastebuds had become spiked with power pop from the likes of

American bands like Myracle Brah, Cotton Mather and The Shazam, each one a direct descendent from The Beatles, through Badfinger, Klaatu and Jellyfish.

It seemed that everywhere I went there were Beatles' songs and everything I heard was on a dotted line back to Lennon, McCartney or Harrison. Even Ringo was in the news, with talk of a compilation of cov-ers of Ringo songs which came with a free Ringo single too. Weird.

Amid this miasma of melody, the BBC decided to gather together some disparate souls from the entertainment world, all of whom would cover a Beatles song for no other reason other than they could. It

was Saturday night TV and with members of the UK soap opera fraternity, newsreader Anna Ford and boy band A1 all in attendance the collected works of The Beatles were plundered and eventually cut to ribbons. On a string of heartless readings, perfectly underlining the magical powers that these songs contain by exposing these would-be crooners as the ham-throated thesps that they were, there was little joy on display. It seemed crazy that this crew of ne-erdowells were making the likes of Joe Pesci sound entertaining (but more of that later).

The Beatles were (and are) everywhere. On the radio it was Earth Wind And Fire's Got To Get You Into My Life, at the cinema it was Elliot Smith closing American Beauty with an a capella version of Because. And even at the fair ground on the revolving tea cups with my four-year old daughter, there was Lucy In The Sky With Diamonds piped into our spinning vessel as I got ready to throw up.

And, in the wonderful world of power pop? Well, what could be better than David Grahame's Beatle School Graduate Class

Of '70 on the wonderfully-named Dog Turner label. A White Album sleeve pastiche and an opening sample from the soundtrack of Help!, with those immortal words, "Go to the window". How fab is that?

The Beatles and their once-removed output became an obsession. And, so, the search for yet more bizarre Beatles goes on. I still haven't located the Berlin Cellists, or the soul compilation Rubbered Soul, not to mention Ramsey Lewis's whole album of Lennon and McCartney. But there are a couple of thousand tracks that I have dug out and over the next 100+ pages I'll clue you in on the good, the bad and the plain ugly.

We start with The Beatles' catalogue and look album by album at the monumental string of covers. Then it's whole albums of Beatles' covers, from Chet Atkins, Booker T and George Benson through to The Big Ben Banjo band. Next up it's the tributes and compilations, followed by the best of the odd songs that are wandering about almost of their own free will and concluding with a look at the power pop legacy.

Go to the window…

LOVE ME.DO

The Beatles released 12 albums if you include Yellow Submarine, which was really half an album, and you don't include The Magical Mystery Tour - which was really an EP that became an album when a bunch of singles were added to it. So, you could say it was anywhere between eleven and a half and 13, depending on how pedantic you want to be. In fact, if you add the numerous territorial variations in title, sleeve and format and phasing, then it just gets ridiculous. And if you think that the White Album was a double...

So, for the sake of clarity, this section looks at the chronologically released UK albums - Please Please Me, With The Beatles, A Hard Day's Night, Beatles For Sale, Help!, Rubber Soul, Revolver, Sgt Pepper's Lonely Hearts Club Band, The Magical Mystery Tour (the soundtrack), The Beatles (White Album), Yellow Submarine (the soundtrack), Abbey Road and Let It Be.

Here we examine the hundreds of versions that have been committed to vinyl, CD or cassette. And, when we've finished with the albums, we round up the tracks that never appeared on any albums but just ended up as singles or flipsides..

So, prepare to be immersed in the strange and the psychedelic, the plainly ludicrous and the absolutely amazingly gorgeous world of Beatles' covers. Some of the things you'll encounter simply won't be good for you. But some will be just plain lovely. Be careful out there.

Please Please Me

Parlophone CDP 7 46435. Released: March, 1963. Number one in the UK.

Singles released

Love Me Do (Reached 17 in the UK, 1962)
Please Please Me (Reached two in the UK, January 1963, number 3 US, January 1964)

The first album, the classic effervescent sparkle that Brian Epstein converted from the Hamburg clubs and those wild days and nights at the Cavern into a recordable sonic slew that the "experts" predicted would be hit and miss and gone before you knew it.

You know the stories. Decca say they weren't very good in the studio. They passed on them. But they signed with Epstein. Got haircuts. Suits. EMI got in quick. The rest is... whatever.

What the sleeve says: "This brisk-selling disc went on to overtake all rivals when it bounced into the coveted number one slot towards the end of February. Just over four months after the release of their very first record The Beatles had become triumphant chart toppers."

What Q said: Please, Please Me was more raw than any other Beatles album until Let It Be. Understandably it's also their least confident.

What Jimmy Saville said: After playing it on the radio for the first time, he intoned, "Well, I hope it pleases someone."

The Best Of The Covers

I Saw Her Standing There

Famous interpretations: The Merseybeats? Well, almost, it could have been them or The Beatles who reaped mass success, fame, fortune, the girls and… Well, at least The Merseybeats had a hit.

Celebrities in the house: Little Richard, Cliff Richard, Elton John with John Lennon, Hank Williams Jr and Maggie Bell.

Infamous covers: The Pete Best Band's 1995 reworking and The Pink Fairies' ham-fisted stab.

The ones to cherish: The Jerry Garcia Band's simple acoustic strum from the Run For The Roses album and the late lamented Bar-Kays from the Stax soul archive.

And some of the others: Johnny Hallyday (in French), popette Tiffany making it 'Him' instead of 'Her', punk glam dropouts The Tubes and Botulisme.

Misery

Celebrity doings: Comedian, show man and tap-dancing thesp, Kenny Lynch, come on down with the first-ever Beatles cover…

Kenny: "John and Paul told me they were thinking of going up to the microphone and singing 'ooooh' at the same time, I said, 'You can't do that, people will think that you're poofs'."

The good guys: The Flamin' Groovies' homage to all things fab in the midst of the punk '70s explosion was something to marvel at. Their version of Misery from their 1976 album Shake Some Action is ace.

Anna (Go To Him)
Written by Alexander

Chains
Written by Goffin/King

Boys
Written by Dixon/Farrell

Ask Me Why

Not a lot of covers at all, but classical composer George Pehlivanian, whose name you'll see a lot in this book, wove it into one of his many Beatles Symphonies.

Please Please Me

Infamous interpretations: Petula Clark's bi-lin-gual capability was tested to the hilt as she assaulted the track in French as To Perds Ton Temps.

Even stranger goings-on: There's The Leon Young String Chorale's churchy ambience, Keely Smith's cabaret sugar and David Cassidy's teeny bop canoodle to name but a handful.

The ones to hear: Red Kross's power pop churner still rings the jangle and Santo And Johnny's strange Hawaiian strumalong is an epic experience.

And some more: Barnes And Barnes' bizarre worldview and officially "zany" delivery on their album Voobaha is frightening. Elsewhere spare a few seconds to remember Bob Leaper (orchestral), Francois Glorieux (almost classical), Los Mustang (with one of many international franchises), Los Chicos (even more so) and Les Felins (ditto).

Love Me Do

Shoeless wonder: Sandie Shaw, the Eurovision bare footer gave it her all on her Reviewing The Situation album in 1969.

Eccentrics: US wunderkind pianist Daniel Johnston took the song back to its naïve base in the '90s, as did Floyd Domino, Chris O'Connell, and Maryann Price's version from their Beatles Favourites For The Very Young some decades before.

Loveable rogues: Lovers of the absurd need look no further than the Portuguese approximation by Renato And His Blue Caps. Whether you'd actually cherish it is something else altogether though.

Drawn and quartered: There's also the cartoon tomfoolery of The Chipmunks (they did a whole album of Beatles' songs in 1964), The Beatle Barkers (showing that any animals can woof their way through a Lennon and McCartney song), not to mention the swishing Hollyridge Strings and harmonica-toting Billy Lee Riley.

PS I Love You

A Starr by any other name: Kay Starr, that old light programme crooner with some gusto.

Jangle and indeed jingle: The Rattles' early 60s live version recorded at the Star Club in Hamburg is officially "interesting" but it's Santo And Johnny (again) who really give it the funky lounge gloss it deserves on their album The Beatles Greatest Hits. Never before has a Hawaiian guitar sounded so wholeheartedly, er, Hawaiian.

Anyone else out there: There's not a lot of takers here, but Pink Sapphire, The Vogues and Les Missiles all have their moments.

Baby It's You
Written by David/Williams/Bacharach

Do You Want To Know A Secret?

Chart toppers: Billy J Kramer And The Dakotas had the hit.

Billy: "I had been the first person to cover one of their songs. Paul actually said, 'Thank you for believing in our songs before anyone else did'."

Famous friends: Count Basie gives the song a silky sheen, laced with lead saxophone and complimentary tootling brass for moody popability on his album Basie's Beatles Bag. There's also a wicked organ break too.

Infamous liaisons: Russ Conway takes some beating in the mundanity stakes. And beating might have been the way to go in retrospect.

The ones to cherish: Mary Wells from her album Love Songs Of The Beatles is succinctly soulful, and Eddi Reader's delivery on Fairground Attractions' version is worth digging out.

And some oddities: It's those Chipmunks again! And, there's even an album of Beatles songs played on toy instruments which includes Do You Want To Know A Secret?

A Taste Of Honey
Written by Scott/Marlow

There's A Place

It seemed like a good idea at the time: Keith Richards and Andrew Loog Oldham vaguely directed the Aranbee Pop Symphony Orchestra back in 1966 and created something of a gem with their instrumental version.

Other guys having fun: The timeless versions from The Kestrels (1964) and The Flamin' Grooves (over 20 years later) are always worth consulting.

And the strangest things: Les Surfs (all enthusiasm, little presence), Bob Leaper (big band), Los Idolos (delivering Hay Un Lugar, no less) and White Flag (neo-punkily).

Twist and Shout
Written by Medley/Russell

With The Beatles

PARLOPHONE PCS 3045
Released: November 1963.
Number one in the UK. Meet The Beatles with similar track listing released in the US, reached number one.

With the album topping the UK charts, The Beatles were big news. They played their Christmas show at the Astoria in Finsbury Park, lining up alongside Cilla Black, Rolf Harris, The Barron Knights and Tommy Quickly. Phew! Showbiz. If Please Please Me had brought hysterical screams of delight, then With The Beatles rounded out their sound and let them rock it up with a cleaner, sharper polish.

What the sleeve says: "Fourteen freshly recorded titles - including many sure-fire stage-show favourites - are featured on the two generously filled sides of this record. The Beatles have repeated the successful formula that made their first Please Please Me LP into the fastest selling album of 1963. Again they have set eight of their original compositions alongside a batch of "personal choice" pieces selected from the recorded repertoires of the American R&B artists they admire most."

What Q said: With The Beatles is their finest early work and probably their best pure pop LP of all time.

What Paul Weller said: "My first Beatles' memory was at this time. I saw them on the Royal Variety Performance and I realised 'This is what I want to do'."

The Best Of The Covers

It Won't Be Long

The twang's the thang: The old-man of bluegress, Lester Flatt in full souped-up mode is unstoppable. Alison Moyet gives it a fair flogging too.
And some other oddballs: Indie twee pop gliteratti Heavenly did it, as did Red Kross. They both stayed true to the original, while less obvious versions come from the slightly less underground Bugs Bunny And Friends.

All I've Got To Do

Infamous covers: Part Four used their strangely-atuned arrangement skills to re-align the song for their own means.
And one more from the oddpile: And for composition and danceability? Dirsten Grandahl gave it the full reggae rhythm.

All My Loving

The famous: One of the few Beatles' tunes that rat packer Frank Sinatra deemed to cover. Who were these new fellah's, anyway? And, following in Frank's footsteps don't forget the loving, caring rendition that Scouse comedian Jimmy Tarbuck offered on All My Loving. And who could forget Max Bygraves? Even if they tried really, really hard.
Max Bygraves: "I got on really well with the Beatles at the Royal Variety Performance. They wanted my autograph for their aunties."
Celeb action: Actress Annette Funicello (various beach movies and former Mickey Mouse Club hostess) turned to music in the early '60s and covered the song on the album Something Borrowed. Then there was Duke Ellington and Herb Alpert, Count Basie, Matt Monro and don't forget Pinky And Perky.
Infamous covers: German metal monsters Hellowe'en mulched the melody for an Iron Maiden-styled caricature, almost as bizarre as The Chipmunks and their tree-bound tirade. Weird, but perhaps not as strange as Francois Glorieux whose arrangement in the style of Tchaikovsky takes some beating.
The ones to cherish: Nick Heyward, from Haircut 100 covered the song with passion on his Hard Day's Nick EP. Suzy Boguss and Chet Atkins teamed up for some country soul 'Loving' and, as you might expect, Mary Wells' homage to Lennon and McCartney sounds superb.
And some of the oddities: There are all manner of genres that have tackled this one. There's those soul-less troubadours The Brothers Four, then the one-upmanship of The Frivolous Five and the mariachi movements of The Mexicali Singers. The song also exists as an easy listening swayer from The Sandpipers, not to mention the intense acoustic salvo of Neil Hogan, the Spanish rumba of Los Fernandos and, indeed, All My Loving's part in Angel, a Beatles concerto by The Royal Liverpool Philharmonic Orchestra with pianists Peter Rostal and Paul Schaefer.

Don't Bother Me

Just the one, then: The I-Tones reggae version of this George Harrison song is, well, rock steady.

Little Child

Jazzman cometh: Wes Montgomery's jazz exploration almost goes back to the melody line when needed. Occasionally.
Sixties stylists: There's single cuts from Jackie Lynton and Nino Tempo and April Stevens, along with The Newbeats and the more recent, but still authentically time-tunneled Inmates.

Till There Was You
Written by Wilson

Please Mr Postman
Written by Holland

Roll Over Beethoven
Written by Berry

Hold Me Tight

Famous classicists: Joshua Rifkin's Baroque Beatles album was one of the first Beatles' covers album that utilised a completely alien musical style and their Hold Me Tight is fine stuff. Forsooth. Hey nonny nonny, etc.
Crazy people: When in doubt, there's the mid-'70s lunacy of Stackridge to fall back on. Virtually everything the fiddle-wielding bowler hat wearing student combo did was collapsable fun anyway.
And another thing: Swing-meister general Count Basie let his brass beg to Hold Me Tight on his Beatles Bag album.

You Really Got A Hold On Me
Written by Robinson

I Wanna Be Your Man

The big one: The Rolling Stones' had the chart hit in 1963, then the covers just flowed.
The large ones: There's Count Basie again. And the usurped Adam Faith. The former 'British Elvis' added a beat group to his backing band following the arrival of The Beatles. It was the only way that he felt he could compete. Then he covered their songs too.
The crazy guys: Art critic Brian Sewell's be-

plum-mouthed talk-through takes some beating for quirkiness. And don't forget Francois Glorieux in the style of Gershwin and the shaky Japanese run-through from '90s jangle merchants Shonen Knife.

The pop gods: The Rezillos devil-may-care punk assault on the song is rivetting and Suzi Quatro's gregarious glamming is top notch.

And the less commercially-viable: Rotgut, The Rockin' Ramrods, The Purple Helmets and The Privates all "do it" too.

Devil In Her Heart
Written by Drapkin

Not A Second Time

Not much of a cover story here, although Robert Palmer included it on his Looking For Clues album and The Pretenders have played it live but never recorded it as yet.

Money
Written by Bradford/Gordy

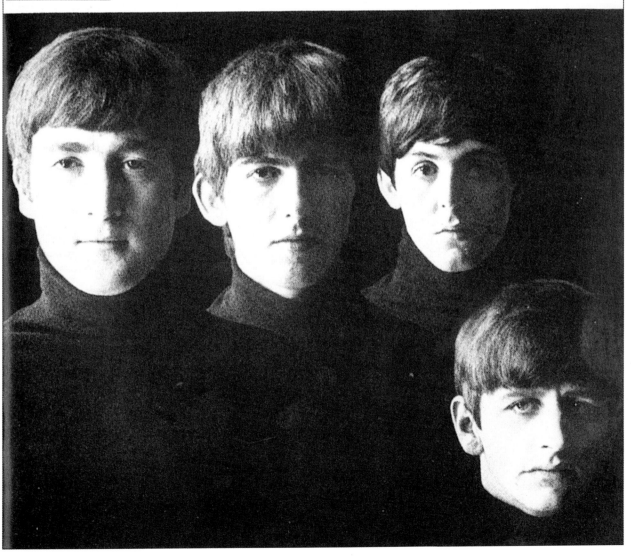

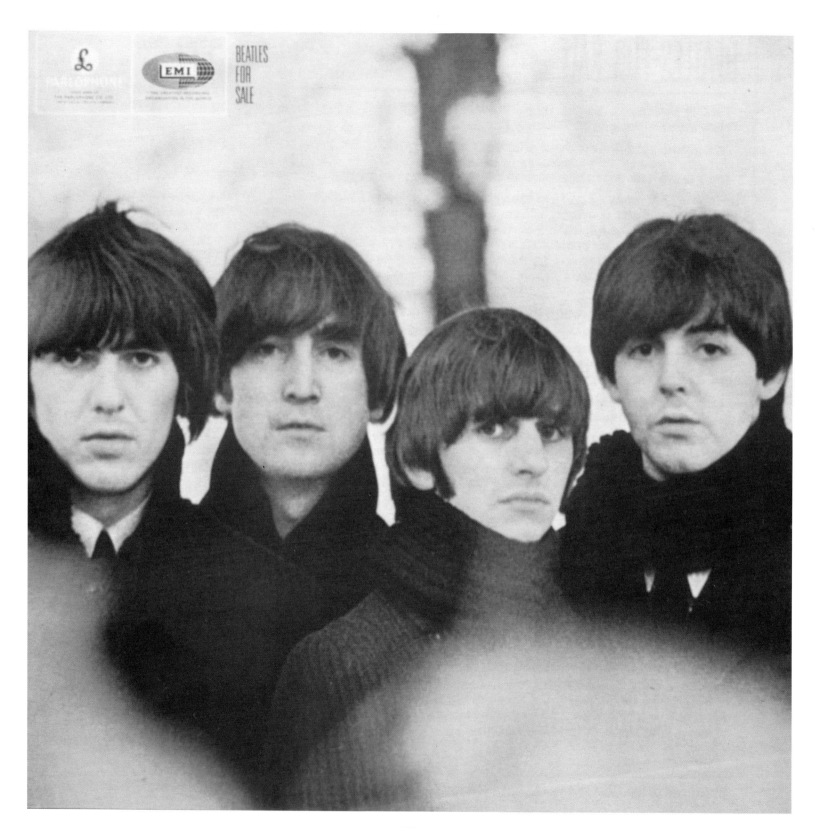

Beatles For Sale

Parlophone CDP 7 46438 2.
Released: December, 1964. Number one in the UK.

Singles released
Eight Days A Week (February 1965, US number one)

Amidst the banning of Beatle haircuts in Indonesia, the outbreak of Beatlemania in the States and the ever-increasing UK Beatles fan base, Beatles For Sale saw something of a departure for the group. Eight originals were surrounded by seven covers, including a couple of songs from Carl Perkins, and one apiece from Chuck Berry and Buddy Holly.

The international success of A Hard Day's Night and their excessive touring and recording schedule meant that they were strapped for time and beginning to look to self-parody their success. Northern wit ruled and the potential for people to take that dry charm and make it their own was not easy.

What the sleeve says: "This is the fourth by the four. Please Please Me, With The Beatles, Hard Day's Night. That's three. Now Beatles For Sale. "The young men themselves aren't for sale. Money, noisy though it is, doesn't talk that loud. But you can buy this album - you probably have, unless you're just browsing, in which case don't leave any dirty thumbprints on the sleeve."

What Q said: There's a weariness in their fourth album, from the cynicism of the title, and the unfamiliar note of sourness and doubt in new songs I'm A Loser and Baby's In Black.

The Best Of The Covers

No Reply
Leave it to the old faithfuls: The Hollyridge Strings from the Beatles Songbook Volume Two, Floyd Domino, Chris O'Connell, and Maryann Price from their kids version of The White Album, which this wasn't on.

I'm A Loser
Celebrity performances: Marianne Faithfull from her eponymous 1965 album, back when everything was just sweetness and light.
The international brigade: Vince Guaraldi and Tufano Giammarese.
And, hey, I'd really like to hear that one: Tony Trischka on his 1992 album Solo Banjo Works.
They're back: The Hollyridge Strings, surprisingly.

Baby's In Black
The other Elvis: Costello with Nick Lowe in tow.
And the country cousins: The Charles River Valley Boys' austere bluegrass on their great Elektra album Beatles Country.
And the also rans: The Hi-fi's.

Rock And Roll Music
Written by Berry

I'll Follow The Sun
On the organ: Floyd Cramer on his Class Of '65 gives it a run for its money on the 88's.
On three legs: The Roger Kellaway Trio from 1965 sound like three guys having fun.
On the usual: Chet Atkins, The Brothers Four, The Hollyridge Strings, The Kings Singers and Floyd Domino, Chris O'Connell, and Maryann Price.

Mr Moonlight
Written by Johnson

Kansas City/Hey Hey Hey
Written by Leiber and Stoller and Penniman respectively

Eight Days A Week
Winsome: Alma Cogan's single from 1965 heralded a new age of musical celebrities recognising that The Beatles could actually do them some good. It's a monumental mix, a walloping big melody and a glorious version.
Love some: Procol Harum, oblivious to tradition or the times, covered it in 1975 amid the rising tide of punk rock on their album Ninth.
Lose some: Joemy Wilson (who?), Don Costa (jazz-lite), Lou Gramm (MOR-lite) and the wonderfully named Tiny Yong (lightweight) all gave it a go.
Not forgetting our friends with the cash-in: Dr. Fink And the Mystery Band, George Pehlivanian, The Baroque Chamber Orchestra, Francois Glorieux, Joshua Rifkin and The Royal Philharmonic Orchestra

Words Of Love
Written by Holly

Honey Don't
Written by Perkins

Every Little Thing
Love it to death: There are three main contenders here. Three diverse outfits who have taken this song to a new musical plateaux all of their own. Let's hear it for The Simon Gale Orchestra, Yes - who did it as a single back in 1969 - and The Spencer Davis Group.

I Don't Want To Spoil The Party
No-one wants to spoil the party. Do they?: Only The Savoys and Tom Hartman have been brave enough so far.

What You're Doing
And it gets worse: The comedy duo Wallace and Ladmo and John Calabro being the only people to give a hoot about this one.

Everybody's Trying To Be My Baby
Written by Perkins

A Hard Day's Night

Parlophone PCS 3058.
Recorded: January 29-June 3, 1964.
Released: July 1964.
Number one UK and US.

Singles released

Can't Buy Me Love (Released March 1964, reached number one UK and US).
A Hard Day's Night (Released US July 1964, reached number one).
I'll Cry Instead (Released August 1964, US only, reached number 25).
And I Love Her (Released August 1964, US only, reached number 12).

Hits aplenty and for many people the first opportunity to see what all the fuss was about with the film of the same name. Richard Lester had previously worked on shorts with the Goons and a lot of humour of that kind sneaks into A Hard Day's Night to elevate it above being a series of songs that have been thrown onto the screen. Strangely, in isolation they sounded even larger than their cinematic counterparts.

Where did the name come from, George Martin: "The title came from Ringo. After a particularly strenuous session, he said, 'Oh, it's been a hard day'. Then he looked at the clock and saw it was midnight. He said" 'It's been a Hard Day's Night'."

What the sleeve says: "Creating and perfecting completely new compositions for the soundtrack of A Hard Day's Night presented John and Paul with one of the greatest challenges of their pop-penning career. In the past their songwriting had been done at a more leisurely pace. Now a shooting schedule had to be met and the entire collection of fresh numbers had to be compiled during a season of concerts in Paris and a now legendary trip to America."

What Q said: The years have robbed nothing of its freshness, nor its infectious delight.

What Mojo said: They may have been, as John Lennon later said, "shoving some sounds together", but no-one else could do it quite so serendipitously.

The Best Of The Covers

A Hard Day's Night

Famous interpretations: It's a soul revue staple, as has been presented with some swaggering grace in the past by Otis Redding, and later Dionne Warwick.

Celebrity alert: Talked through by Peter Sellers in his best Richard III voice, de-crooned by Max Bygraves, and in full jazz swing with Ella Fitzgerald.

Infamous covers: Would you like it unstylishly bonged by The Mighty Fire Steel Band? Or out of tune at the piano of Mrs Miller? Maybe you'd just like it daintily jazzed with Peggy Lee? Or perhaps Take That's interpretation on their 'pop' opus Everything Changes is nearer the mark. Beyond that, there's the crazed psycho-rant of Shockabilly.

The ones to cherish: Two years after its release it turned up twice courtesy of two soulful keyboard players. The Ramsey Lewis Trio released it as a single and latter day Beatle, Billy Preston included it on the album The Wildest Organ In Town.

And a full and frank list of also rans: Drummer Sandy Nelson, The Kelly Family, Gary McFarland, Beatles-obsessed vibes and guitar duo Santo And Johnny, Anita Lindblom, Rainbow Red Oxidizer, piano man Billy Joel, psyche-monsters The Hoodoo Gurus, Sonny Curtis, Johnny Tedesco, Ten Tuff Guitars, Les Beadochons, veteran producer Quincy Jones, and bluesman John Mayall.

Plus the usual suspects: Chet Atkins, Count Basie, The Boston Pops, Al Caiola and Enoch Light.

I Should Have Known Better

The surfing specialists: Jan And Dean on the album Live In Person and The Beach Boys from Beach Boys Party! go tube city with the tune.

The one to yearn for: Amon Duul! Surely the German art terrorists can't have included this on their 1973 album Disaster. They did? Cripes.

Hey, that's even more weird: It was delivered in a folk protest style by Phil Ochs and Eric Anderson and given full reggae dubbery by Sly And Robbie.

And the rest: Both The Naturals and The Rattles attempted to cut in on Fab-success in the early '60s by covering the song. Then there was Johnny Rivers, Los Mustang and Renato And His Blue Caps among others.

If I Fell

Effortless celebs: Not many songs in the history of the universe can claim to have been covered by Peter And Gordon and Peters And Lee. But If I Fell not only satisfied the '60s pop duo but also the '70s Opportunity Knocks and cabaret circuit crooners.

And some other X-File like participants: Indeed, any song that can bring together disparate talents like noodling guitarist Adrian Belew, tortured nightclub crooner Lou Christie, countrified Brits Southern Comfort and jazz bohemians like Gerry Mulligan and Sonny Curtis, takes some beating. What is the power of If I Fell?

I'm Happy Just To Dance With You

Pop moments: Beehived '80s popster Mari Wilson and '70s country star Anne Murray both celebrated the dance, while The Johnny Mann singers sang it somewhat simple too.

The one to be concerned about: The Cyrkle's psyche-pop dalliance from their Neon album is worth harking back to 1967 for in all its dysfunctional strangeness. Undoubtedly it's one of the oddest songs you'll ever here with scant regard for the way it should scan or carry the melody.

And the McOther one: Maureen McGovern from her Greatest Hits?

And I Love Her

Famously covered by: Nottyash comedian and bad-toothed crooner Ken Dodd. Well, he's sort of famous.

Lovingly massaged by: Bob Marley And The Wailers. It was early days.

And let's hear it for the soul brothers and sisters: Smokey Robinson And The Miracles, Bobby Womack Sonny Curtis, The Detroit Emeralds and Esther Phillips all loved it madly.

And the jazz chops: Roland Kirk, Nancy Wilson, Xaviar Cugat, The Count Basie Orchestra, Sarah Vaughan, The Ramsey Lewis Trio and Lena Horne.

Plus the nightclubbers: Santo And Johnny and Pucho And The Latin Soul.

THE BEATLES

A HARD DAY'S NIGHT

And the instrumentals: Chet Atkins, Peter Nero, Enoch Light, Boston Pops and Ferrante And Teicher.
Not forgetting the folkies: The Lettermen and Jose Feliciano.
And finally, so, if they're doing it, then so can I: Georgie Fame, The Sandpipers, Gary McFarland, Mark Wynter, Shirley Horn, Los Diablos Negros, Julio Eglesias, Neil Diamond, Connie Francis, Jack Jones and Roger Williams.

Tell Me Why

Not so many takers here. In fact if it wasn't for those Wilson brothers and their 1965 album Beach Boys Party! This would be a lonely one.

Can't Buy Me Love

Not so for this one. The roll of honour is long and indeed winding... Here's the best half dozen.

1 Beatles-friendly goon **Peter Sellers.**
2 Jazz crooner and scat queen **Ella Fitzgerald.**
3 The groovily lounged **Henry Mancini**
4 The oddly grand pop singer who lost her footing when the Fabs appeared, **Brenda Lee.**
5 Jazz legend **Stanley Turrentine.**
6 Country rock and roller **Johnny Rivers.**

And some more: Angelically The King's Singers, Los Idolos and the one who sounds like he's a soccer star, Thierry Vincent.

Any Time At All

Famous swingers: Frank Sinatra.
Old rockers who died in mysterious circumstances after a fling with someone from the mob's girl: Bobby Fuller.
People with guitars: Nils Lofgren and Dweezil Zappa.

I'll Cry Instead

Lots of people with "J" in their name attempted this one. Including: Joe Cocker, Billy Joel, Jerry Inman and Johnny Rivers.

Things We Said Today

The famous Brit: Cliff Richard. Only famous if you're English. He's had more than 100 hits .
The infamous others: String Driven Thing in all their folk rock, acid folk finery. With wild scenes just out of camera shot.
The ones to hum along to: Jackie DeShannon's '70s single version and, more recently Dream Academy.
The annoying one: The King Singers' austere a capella from their Tempus Fugit album.
The country one: Dwight Yoakam on his Under The Covers album.
And the other ones: The Sandpipers, Os Vips and Trubrot. Anyone?

When I Get Home

It's all been left up to Billy Joel I'm sorry to say.

You Can't Do That

Famous interpretations: He would later go on to drink himself silly, be mates with John Lennon and cover Badfinger's Without You, because he thought it was a Beatles' song. But back in 1967 he made a great album with Pandemonium Shadow Show on which he covered You Can't Do That.
The other ones to cherish: Brit power pop from Ian Gomm. Psychedelic tomfoolery from The Godz and poppy jangle from The Standells. Not to mention The Pretenders.
And some: The Bobs and The Blenders. Honest!

I'll Be Back

Strange bedfellows indeed. Including: the neo-metal of Golden Earring, the under-rated pop of The Buckinghams and the rounded harmonies of The Johnny Mann Singers.

Help!

Parlophone PMC 1255; PCS 3071
Released: August, 1965.
Number one in the UK and US.

Singles released

Ticket To Ride (Released April 1965, number one in the UK and US).
Help! (Released July 1965, number one US and UK).
Yesterday (Released US, September 1965, reached number one).

The second film and the "thing" that launched The Monkees, the art form of the video, and eventually MTV. Help! has got a lot to answer for. If the film was fantastic - and it was - it was also the only way that the world could get close to the group at that time. My earliest recollections of going to the cinema involved things like Mary Poppins and The Jungle Book, when Help! was released you couldn't even get in. People would see it four or five times in a week. They'd go every day.
And the album? It was the first album my Dad bought for me. It cost 39/11 and it eventually had to be retired. It was worn down. For me it contained the greatest Beatles' songs ever, including the tremendous melancholy of You're Going To Lose That Girl and You've Got To Hide Your Love Away. Who could ask for more?

What the sleeve says: Songs from the film Help*. (They're all on side one.)

What Q said: There are minutes of brilliance, like the radiant Ticket To Ride, but also hints of writing on auto-pilot.

John Lennon: "Help! Was where we turned on to pot and we dropped drink, simple as that."

The Best Of The Covers

Help!

Famous versions: Peter Sellers in best thespian style for his 1965 single. The Damned as the flip-side of their debut Stiff single New Rose, Tina Turner on the album Private Dancer, Dolly Parton singing in the shower, crooner Buddy Greco giving it full tuxedo and pop combo The Newbeats thrashing it out.
Infamous troubadours: Deep Purple on Shades Of Deep Purple, The Carpenters on their album Close To You and Bananarama, wherever.
The inevitable: Count Basie, Jose Feliciano, Andre Kostelanatz, Peter Nero.
And the rest: Alma Cogan, the streakin' Ray Stevens and the quasi metal Extreme.

The Night Before

They're the US Fabs: Gary Lewis And The Playboys with the poppy US alternative, which just sounds quite like them actually.
He's a wild and crazy guy: James A Gardner on recorder.
It's them: The Hollyridge Strings.
And: KGB.

You've Got To Hide Your Love Away

The good: The Beau Brummels, The Grass Roots with PF Sloan in tow, The Silkie, Tim Rose, Jan And Dean, Joe Cocker, Elvis Costello and The Beach Boys.

The bad: Gerry Marsden (he used to be a mate) and Dino, Desi And Billy.
The regulars: Floyd Domino, Chris O'Connell, and Maryann Price (for kids), Francois Glorieux (classical), The King's Singers (polite vocals), Madam Cathy Berberian (opera), Joshua Rifkin (baroque) and Percy Faith (strings).
Their mates: The Kentucky Headhunters, The Apples.
And two Michaels and an Eddy: Michael Parrish, Michael Borkson and Eddy Mitchell.

I Need You

Not a lot on this one, just Yukihiro Takahashi and The Beatles Revival Band.

Another Girl

Similar. It's just The Kingsmen. Wonder how it fits with Louie Louie.

You're Going To Lose That Girl

And the sad ballad? Its roll of honour boasts the jazzily named Chris Martin Manifesto, The Beatles Revival Band, The Cornell Glee Club and that bloke Joshua Rifkin again. I loved it though.

Ticket To Ride

Those strange bedfellows in full: Alma Cogan (ridiculously overblown but sweet nonetheless), The Bee Gees (nostalgically), Madam Cathy Berberian (operatically), The Carpenters (weepily), Frank Chacksfield And His Orchestra (sort of poppily), Natalie Cole (soulfully), The Fifth Dimension (doop doop doopingly), Dr Fink And the Mystery Band (heavy handedly), Francois Glorieux (as usually), The Hollyridge Strings (slushily), Husker Du (grungily), The New Seekers (harmonically), George Pehlivanian (symphonically), Joshua Rifkin (baroqueily), The Royal Philharmonic Orchestra (stringily), Sonic Youth (experimentally) and Vanilla Fudge (groovily). **And who?** Henry Robinett, Jeff Grottick, The Shakers, Dick Rivers and The Katzenjammers.

Act Naturally

Done with cellos by Ofra Harnoy And The Armin Electric Strings and in mad hillbilly mode by The Squirrels. Ringo would have loved it.

It's Only Love

For America: Gary US Bonds, Eddy Arnold, Roy Drusky, Ella Fitzgerald and Tommy James And The Shondells.
For the Brits: Ray Price.
For the Geordies: Bryan Ferry
For the jazzheads: The Music Company.
For God knows who: Mr Curt's Camaraderie and Herbert Rehgbein.

You Like Me Too Much

Possible Frenchmen alert: Les Faux Freres.

Tell Me What You See

Possible trouble: Jacob's Trouble

I've Just Seen A Face

Country gentlemen: The Dillards and The Charles River Valley Boys, both on Elektra, both mandolin-fuelled.
Crooners: Would-be teen sensation Jordan Christopher, jazz soulstress Holly Cole and Arlo Guthrie.
Crazies: Calamity Jane, Free Beer, The Paperboys and Tater Totz.
And Leon Russell.

Yesterday

There's quite a few of these.
Let's look at the first 50.

1 **Matt Monro** with the 1965 hit single.
2 **Cilla Black,** relegated to a 1966 flipside.
3 **Marianne Faithfull** in her wispy folk period.
4 **The Supremes** from I Hear A Symphony (1966).
5 MOR jersey wearing **Perry Como.**
6 Blue-eyed soul singer and mod icon **Chris Farlowe.**
7 The sons of Jerry Lewis and Dean Martin: **Dino, Desi And Billy.**
8 **The Charles River Valley Boys'** bluegrass take.
9 The gloriously poppy **Beau Brummels.**
10 Surfer's pals **Jan and Dean.**
11 **Ray Charles,** need we say more?
12 Direct from the Stax soul revue: **Carla Thomas.**
13 The gentle sound of **The Sandpipers.**
14 The mutha of rockin' chair folk **Val Doonican.**
15 Keyboard-handed **Floyd Cramer.**
16 From the Motor City, **Smokey Robinson And The Miracles.**
17 From Haight / Ashbury **The Head Shop.**
18 The one and only **Marvin Gaye.**
19 Sir **Elvis** Of **Presley.**
20 The former Righteous Bro **Bill Medley.**
21 Original country rockers **The Dillards.**
22 Jazz pianist **Oscar Peterson.**
23 **Dr John** the gumbo priest.
24 Smooth jazz expert **Benny Goodman.**
25 The singalonga "sensation" **Max Bygraves.**
26 Close harmony soulettes **En Vogue.**
27 The bald cheek of **Michael Bolton.**
28 R&B harmonies of **Boyz II Men.**
29 Scottish pop toppers **Wet Wet Wet.**
30 Silver hipped Welshman **Tom Jones.**
31 The double-breasted harmonies of **David And Jonathan** (that's King).
32 Jazz tooter **Herbie Mann.**
33 Cabaret schmoozer **Al Martino.**
34 Pianist **Peter Nero.**
35 Bacharachian **Dionne Warwick.**
36 Often exhumed country crooner **Tammy Wynette.**
37 Dixieland jazz combo **The Village Stompers.**
38 Clarinetist and shore stranger **Acker Bilk.**
39 **Gladys Knight & The Pips.**
40 The lovely **Liberace.**
41 War torn **Vera Lynn.**
42 Man from UNCLE **David McCallum.**
43 Eve Of Destruction and latter day religious guru **Barry McGuire.**
44 Kilt-wearing madman **Kenneth McKellar.**
45 Often dancing **Chris Montez.**
46 Greek babe **Nana Mouskouri.**
47 Country jailbird **Willie Nelson.**
48 Chicken In A Basket soul man **Lou Rawls.**
49 Aussie folk chirpies **The Seekers.**
50 Some bloke called **Frank Sinatra.**

Plus soulsters The Temptations, lush-alive Ray Conniff, the barber shopped Cornell Glee Club, Percy Faith, Gary Farr, Ferrante And Teicher, Bobby Goldsboro, the unrelated Andy Williams and Roger Williams, jazz man Wes Montgomery, Alma Cogan, opera singer Kiri Te Kanewa, guitar virtuoso Placido Domingo, bible bashing Tennessee Ernie Ford, ugly bug Burl Ives, Jack Jones, the bubblegum popsters Kassenatz-Katz and the subtle steel guitar of former Flying Burrito Brothers man Sneaky Pete Kleinow.

Dizzy Miss Lizzy
Written by Williams

Rubber Soul

Parlophone PMC 1267; PCS 3075.
Recorded: October 12-November 11, 1965.
Released December, 1965.
Number one in the UK and USA.

Singles released

Yesterday (Released US September 1965, number one)

Nowhere Man (Released: February 1966 US only, reached number three)

It's all change. Inspired by meeting Bob Dylan, turned on to the weirder side of the world, everything about Rubber Soul is about a group of people midway through a rites of passage experience. They're heading off to pastures new after experiences old. Ballads meet fuzzy noise, orchestras meander, melodies are brought way up front and lyrics reach deeper and deeper.

What the sleeve says: Nothing other than that the picture is as distorted as their world view.

What Q said: Rubber Soul is almost always gorgeous, and all the more intriguing in the way that its pop simplicity is turning weird around the edges.

What John Lennon said: "Rubber Soul was Paul's title. It was like Yer Blues, I suppose meaning English soul."

What Brian Wilson said: "When I heard Rubber Soul I said, I have to top that."

What George Martin said: "Previously we'd made albums as just as a collection of singles. With Rubber Soul we were making something that was a bit of art in its own right."

The Best Of The Covers

Drive My Car

Famous bits: Bobby McFerrin's a capella treatment of contemporary music eventually led him to The Beatles and he rhythmically ran through Drive My Car on his 1988 album Simple Pleasures.

Inevitable happenings: It's Tony Treschka on his banjo.

And the rest: The Gary Thomas Empire, The Bo Street Runners, The McCoys and Gina X.

Norwegian Wood (This Bird Has Flown)

Slap that snare: The Buddy Rich Big Band version is awesome. Shrieking brass and Buddy paradiddling into oblivion.

Semi-famous people lost in the forest: Brian Hyland, Vikki Carr, The Kingston Trio, Hugh Masakela, The Hour Glass, Mahogany Rush and Jan And Dean.

We love these: Gone rap soul-like with PM Dawn, psychedelic with Bangor Flying Circus, raga with Cornershop, power popped by The Radio Stars, cha cha cha's by Sergio Mendes, or funked out with Herbie Hancock.

But we're not sure about these: Gary Burton, Charlie Byrd, Electric Love Muffin, Johnny Keating and a whole lot more.

You Won't See Me

Two invisible efforts: Bryan Ferry and The Bee Gees did it some justice. Not together mind you, that would be just too much.

And some more: Playboy mod Ian Whitcomb, country mother Anne Murray and AOR giants Reo Speedwagon.

Nowhere Man

Infamous offspring and various other people: A wide selection including the rat pack descendents Dino, Desi And Billy, folk troubadours The Settlers, Beatles' fans World Party and Placido Domingo pay homage among others.

Think For Yourself

Slim pickings for this George Harrison-penned tune with only Fabrice and The Music Company nodding in time.

The Word

Ditto this Lennon and McCartney number with The Music Company this time joined by Don Sebesky.

Michelle

No such problems here, though.

The romantic kings and queens: The Four Tops full of Motown soul and the mellow groove of The Sandpipers.

There's always room for the strange: Doug E Fresh And The Get Fresh Crew - when rap was young and hip hop was unexplained, Doug E took the Beatles' chorus and inserted it in his hit 45 The Show. Not to mention what the USAF Strolling Strings did with it. And David McCallum.

And the same old same olds: Ray Anthony, Count Basie, Stanley Black, Boston Pops, Andre Kostelanetz, Enoch Light And The Brigades, Paul Mauriat, Billy May, Midnight String Quartet, The Music Company, Boots Randolph, Sarah Vaughan.

And the rest: Ed Ames, The Bachelors, Willie Bobo, Booker T & The MGs, Ace Cannon, Perry Como, David And Jonathan, Ferrante And Teicher, The Four Freshmen, Free Design, Tommy Garrett, Bobby Goldsboro, The Iguanas, Harry James, Jan And Dean, Jack Jones, Stan Kenton, King Curtis, Yusef Lateef, The Lettermen, Gordon MacRae, Peter Nero, The Overlanders, Bud Shank, Rudy Vallee, Billy Vaughn, Bobby Vinton and Andy Williams.

And some more: Wayne King, Maurice Larcange, Rufus Lumley, Johnny Mathis, Buddy Merrill, Mexicali Singers, Oliver Nelson, Wayne Newton, George Shearing, Singers Unlimited and Paul Mauriat.

What Goes On

Not so many here though. Only the countrified Charles River Valley Boys and Orphan.

Girl

Celtic variations: In France, there was Johnny Hallyday. He is The Beatles and Elvis all rolled into one.

Tulip frenzy: Tiny Tim. How much more infamous can you be?

The one to cherish: Well, my personal favourite is the resonating guitars and wholesome joy of Jeremy's Secret, an independent release that sneaked out unceremoniously in the early '80s. But what do I know?

And the others: Brothers Four, Charlie Byrd.

And Petula Clark: Yes. Really.

I'm Looking Through You

Good stuff from over the pond: Roots time with Steve Earle and Rock Salt And Nails all giving it and Americana view.

Meanwhile, elsewhere: Megon McDonough and Danielle Denin sound almost related. But they're not.

In My Life

The classics: Both Judy Collins and Jose Feliciano delivered the song with their own eerie grace. Then there was Rod Stewart, Bette Midler and Stephen Stills.

The what-have-you: Keith Moon's 1975 album Two Sides Of The Moon included the song sung almost lovingly.

And the esoteric: Stephan Grappelli, Lena Horne and Astrud Gilberto to name but three studied this autobiographical story in depth..

Wait

The famous one (with shades): Roy Orbison covered the song as the flipside to Breaking Up Is Hard To Do back in 1966.

If I Needed Someone

A motley crew of pretenders in order of obscurity: The Hollies (groovy pop stars), The Kingsmen (they did Louie Louie), The Cryin' Shames (Pop from the '60s), Hugh Masekela (African trumpeter), Livingston Taylor (brother of James), The Wall (late '70s punks), Stained Glass (dunno), Bit A Sweet (don't care).

Run For Your Life

She knows Frank: Nancy Sinatra in a walking boots way.

They don't: Poppily by Gary Lewis And The Playboys, twangily by Johnny Rivers and jazzily by Al Hirt.

Revolver

Parlophone PMC 7009; PCS 7009.
Recorded: April 6 - June 21, 1966
Released: August, 1966.
Number one in the UK and USA.

Singles released

Yellow Submarine (number one in the UK, number 2 in the USA.

Put simply, Revolver re-evaluated music as it stood in 1966. The staid and very normal British way of life erupted in mild rounds of applause when England won the World Cup little knowing that this monstrous vision of a different planet had been festering as Banks and co began the qualifying groups. Revolver changed everything. From whimsical humour to drug references, poignant life-effacing ballads through to futuristic visions, it was much much more than just a bunch of songs and its repercussions are still being unravelled. Witness: Elliot Smith on his album XO still extolls the virtues of the album on the glorious song Baby Britain, where he intones "Revolver's been turned over, and now it's ready once again…" It's that type of album. Playable and replayable.

What the sleeve says: Nothing much other than who sang what and that the sleeve was designed by Klaus Voormann.

What Q said: Revolver liberated pop from the limitations of commercial beat music; at the same time it inspired a deluge of indulgent tripe and bad poetry that rock has never recovered from.

What Mojo said: The discovery of drugs, eastern mysticism and fraternisation with freakier peers (Dylan, Stones, The Byrds, Brian Wilson) has traditionally taken the rap for the swift metamorphosis the Fab Four underwent in 1966. Yet one shouldn't underestimate the disorienting effects of pop mega-stardom without precedent and the heady mixture of fear and creative power that comes with it.

What engineer Geoff Emerick said: "Revolver became the album where the Beatles would say, OK, that sounds great, now let's play it backwards."

The Best Of The Covers

Taxman

The good song: Stevie Ray Vaughan's interpretation, spiced with his Texan soul.
The back home take: Black Oak Arkansas, from their confines of their own village and lake resort in darkest America, decided to cover the song in the mid-'70s for the album Ain't Life Grand.
The jangle-friendly tunesmiths: The Music Machine's proto-psyche punk garage on their Turn On The Music Machine album from '66 and the Deighton Family's modern country roots folk from their 1990 album Mama Was Right.
And the rest: Talismen, Rockwell and Rootjuice. What a combination.

Eleanor Rigby

Celebrity specials: Tony Bennett, Ray Charles, John Denver, Aretha Franklin, The Four Tops, Bobbie Gentry, Johnny Mathis, Oscar Peterson, Diana Ross And The Supremes and Frankie Valli to name but a few.
Infamous perps: Rick Wakeman gone all classical with it. Doodles Weaver getting the words mixed up on a comedy spoof.
The ones to cherish: Richie Havens getting all emotional on his album Mixed Bag from 1967, Booker T & The MGs give it some Memphis funk, and Teegarden And Van Winkle roll out their hippie psychedelic psychosis.
Evereyone's here: The Boston Pops, Dick Hyman, Paul Mauriat, Tony Treschka on banjo as you might expect.
And the list goes on forever: Joan Baez, Blonde On Blonde, Bloodrock, Gene Chandler, Stanley Jordan, Levellers 5, Rare Earth, Realm, Lonnie Smith, Wes Montgomery, The Mystic Moods Orchestra, Junior Reed, The Standells, Vanilla Fudge, Young-Holt Unlimited.
And the weird ones came too: Walter Carlos, The Esperanto Rock Orchestra, Godhead, One Blood and The Pure Food And Drug Act.
And then there was: The Violet Burning, The Tim Ware Group and The Wing And A Prayer Fife And Drum Band.
Not forgetting: Vincent Bell, Sonny Criss, The Eliminators and Martin Gould.

I'm Only Sleeping

Groovy versions: Suggs, from Madness, had a hit single in 1996, dusting of his career and re-introducing the Lennon legacy to a new generation.
The best of the groove: Roseanne Cash beat Suggs by a year with a similarly heartaching version.

Love You To

No takers?

Here, There and Everywhere

Division one people doing it: Emmylou Harris (on Elite Hotel), Jose Feliciano (guitar and shades), The Fourmost (single, 1966), Episode Six (ditto), Jay And The Americans and Hugh Masakela (on trumpet).
Division two: Jennifer Warnes (before she was better known), Kenny Loggins (blue-eyed soul), George Benson, Bobbie Gentry, Johnny Mathis and Matt Monro (from Blackpool).
Northern Premier League: Sonny Curtis, Perry Como, Tony Trischka, Liberace.
Sunday morning football: Vince Hill, Andy Williams, The Baja Marimba Band and Petula Clark.
Footballer of the year: Claudine Longet and her paper thin vocal.
Reserve team: Dick Smothers, Libby Titus and Billy Ed Wheeler.

Yellow Submarine

It's for the kids: The Happy Time Children's Chorus And Orchestra, Pinky And Perky, The Pickwick Children's Choir and Spike Milligan.
It's too deep to really be for the kids: The California Poppy Picker and The Thought Police.
Let's take the words off: Ferrante And Teicher, The Baroque Inevitable and Enoch Light.
Hi, I'm French: Maurice Chevalier.

She Said, She Said

Love it to death: Matthew Sweet's poppily pert version.
The Ones to look for: Feelies on the 1987 album Slipping Into Something. The Walking Seeds indie-pop version and similar from Overwhelming Colourfast and Yeah Yeah Noh.

Good Day Sunshine

Back in 1967 you could have the waspish wife of Andy Williams doing Good Day Sunshine - that's Claudine Longet - or you could have those crazy guys The Tremeloes. I don't know, it's your choice.

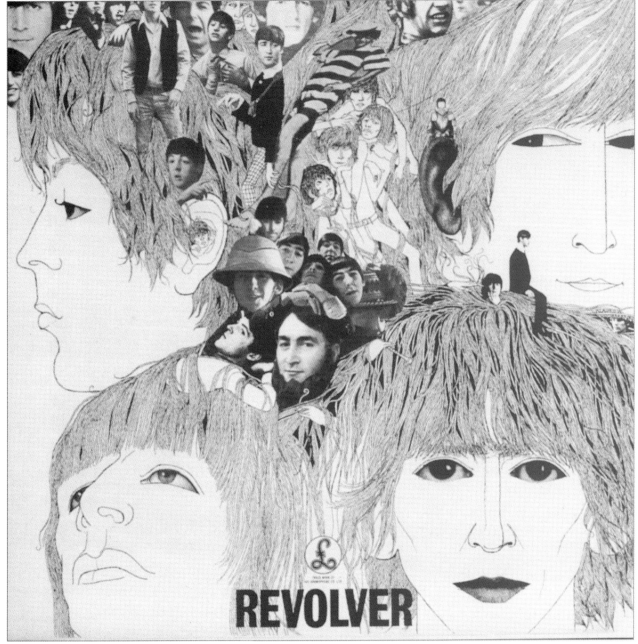

REVOLVER

Dr Robert

None found believe it or not.

I Want To Tell You

Ted Nugent, his former band The Amboy Dukes and The Grateful Dead. What a long strange trip it's been.

Got To Get You Into My Life

This swinging opus is well known for its Earth, Wind And Fire version. Brass-stung and rollicking, it was previously covered by original brass rock out-fit Blood, Sweat And Tears and has also been given a royal send off by Cliff Bennett And The Rebel Rousers, French icon Johnny Halliday, The Four Tops, Sonny And Cher and Ella Fitzgerald among others.

Tomorrow Never Knows

Done weirdly by: Former Roxy Music man Phil Manzanera with his band 801.
Drummed out by: Phil Collins.
With eastern promise by: Monsoon.
Indie-poppingly by: The Chameleons, Bongwater, Jad Fair And Daniel Johnston and A Witness.
Psychedelically by: The Marshmallow Overcoat and Jimi Hendrix.
New ageingly by: Yukihiro Takahashi
And Gothicly by: The Mission, Our Lady Peace and Danielle Dax.

And Your Bird Can Sing

Ones we have loved: Talking power poppy and with a touch of mod glamour, how about The Jam, The Flamin' Groovies and Australian band Guadalcanal Diary. Then there's new Australian power poppers Even and indie nonsense from The Sex Clark Five.

For No One

Beautiful temptresses: Emmylou Harris and Cilla Black.
Similarly attractive versionaries: Caetano Veloso, Maura O'Connell, Maureen McGovern and Janis Siegel.
And a bloke: Theo Bikel.

Sgt. Pepper's Lonely Hearts Club Band

Parlophone PMC 7027. PCS 7027.
Recorded: December 6, 1966 - April 21, 1967.
Released: June, 1967. Reached number one in the UK and USA.

Singles released:

None

After Revolver, there was six months at the end of 1966 where the Beatles were virtually quiet. They'd been omnipresent since bursting onto the music scene in 1962. They'd conquered America. Done two films and made news wherever they went. The word was that they'd dried up... how wrong could that have been.

George Martin had set about extracting the ideas that the quartet had been working on. Lennon and Harrison were experimenting heavily with drugs and the ideas were getting larger and larger.

George Martin: "Lennon was the least articulate of the three writers. I would have to dig deep into his brain to find out what he wanted to do."

The result was formidable. And its repercussions and influences have lasted for several decades. It was made into a film, done as an orchestral album by The Royal Academy of Music Symphony Orchestra and covered in full for an NME charity album in the '90s.

What Q said: "A rich tapestry of texture, melody and panache, Sgt pepper is today restored to its rightful place in 20th century culture."

What Mojo said: "Sgt Pepper reeks of confidence and the desire to set new standards. McCartney was especially daring challenging Lennon to come up with the sparkle to match."

The Best Of The Covers

Sgt. Pepper's Lonely Hearts Club Band

The anthemic crawl was covered by Jimi Hendrix, who dallied with its psychedelia on stages, by Psychic TV, in usual irreverent pastiche mode and Bill Cosby of all people.

With A Little Help From My Friends

Without a doubt, Joe Cocker made this song his own with his emotional gurning at Woodstock in 1969, but it was also covered ably by fellow Woodstockians Santana on 1968's Soul Sacrifice album and Richie Havens.

Elsewhere, creditable performances ensued from Ike And Tina Turner, The Beach Boys and Steve Cropper.

Less likely seekers of help included Bon Jovi, Sham 69, Herb Alpert, Sergio Mendes, Booker T guitarist Steve Cropper, Joe Brown, Wet Wet Wet and Barbara Dickson.

Lucy In The Sky With Diamonds

The most memorable: Elton John's single with John Lennon in the background and William Shatner in all his madcap thespian glory, from his album The Transformed Man.

The most forgettable: The Hooters, Bill Murray from the soundtrack of Where The Buffalo Roams, Noel Harrison and Natalie Cole.

And the rest: Hugh Montenegro and The Alan Lorber Orchestra.

Getting Better

Apart from the whole album being covered, which accounts for the inclusion of Peter Frampton, Status Quo, The Bee Gees and The Wedding Present, people who've taken on Getting Better include erstwhile prog rocker Steve Hillage and The Rubber Band.

Fixing A Hole

Again it's George Burns from the film of Pepper and Hue And Cry from the NME album, plus The Royal Academy of Music Symphony Orchestra and Big Daddy.

She's Leaving Home

Top ten suitcase in hall affiliates include:
1 **Billy Bragg** in aid of Cambodia.
2 **The Royal Philharmonic Orchestra.**
3 **Ofra Harnoy** and her cello.
4 David And Jonathan's 1967 single.
5 **Nilsson** from the album Pandemonium Shadow Show.
6 **Bryan Ferry** formerly of Roxy Music.
7 Super slick soul man **Al Jarreau.**
8 Easy listening staples **The Baja Marimba Band.**
9 All strumming **Richie Havens.**
10 Joe Fagin.

Being For The Benefit Of Mr Kite

It's Frank Sidebottom and The Royal Academy of Music Symphony Orchestra. But not together in Timperley.

Within You, Without You

A couple of gorgeous efforts from the new agey Angels Of Venice and the late Arizona-based guitarist Rainer Ptacek. Oh, and Sonic Youth too.

When I'm Sixty Four

Famous virtual pensioners: Noel Harrison, Claudine Longet, Bernard Cribbins, Courtney Pine, Kenny Ball And His Jazzmen and Gerogie Fame.

Three who didn't make it: John Denver, Keith Moon and Frankie Howerd.

And those USTV sit-com stars: Archie and Edith Bunker.

Lovely Rita

From the covers albums there's Roy Wood, Michelle Shocked and the inevitable Royal Academy of Music Symphony Orchestra. Plus Fats Domino who released the song as a single in 1968.

Good Morning, Good Morning

Just George Pehlivanian apart from the album concept team.

Sgt. Pepper's Lonely Hearts Club Band (Reprise)

No takers for the second coming.

A Day In The Life

Hardly the easiest of songs to interpret in your own unique style but there have been attempts. Notably from jazz guitarist Wes Montgomery, Eric Burdon And War and the groovy Brian Auger And Trinity. Perhaps less notable, there's Lighthouse, Sting and Shirley Bassey.

The Magical Mystery Tour

CDP 7 48062. Released as an album in 1976.

Originally released as an EP (The Magical Mystery Tour; Your Mother Should Know; Flying; Fool On The Hill; Blue Jay Way; I Am The Walrus) in December 1967. Reached number two in the UK.

The subsequent album added:
Hello Goodbye (which was released as a single with I Am The Walrus in November 1967. Number one in the US and UK)
Strawberry Fields Forever/Penny Lane (which was released as a double A side in February 1967, reaching number two in the UK and number one in the USA)
And All You Need Is Love/Baby, You're A Rich Man (which was released as a single in July 1967 and reached number one in the UK and USA).

The Magical Mystery Tour album was captured from a number of sources during one of The Beatles' most fertile periods. During 1967 they were producing epic after epic with incredible ease.
The original EP was centred on the film they produced as an antidote to the formula features of A Hard Day's Night and Help!. It was rambling and went nowhere. In fact it was shot without a script but any film that featurs mindless singing and Ivor Cutler can't be all bad.

Neil Aspinall, Beatles aide: "We went out to make a film, and nobody had the vaguest idea of what it was about."

What the sleeve says: "Away in the sky, beyond the clouds, live four or five magicians. By casting wonderful spells they turn the Most Ordinary Coach Trip into a magical mystery tour."

What Q said: The TV film was not the happiest of Beatles ventures but it yielded a double-EP soundtrack of great merit, which was later repackaged in the States with some A and B-sides of the period.
   The songs are definite Sgt Pepper's era types: George being weird and Eastern, Paul melancholy and John out of his tree.

The album is glorious though. A moment captured in time. Something that Bud Shank tried to do also by covering the whole shebang. But it just didn't quite come off.

The Best Of The Covers

The Magical Mystery Tour
The usual weird collectives, The Hollyridge Strings and Dr Fink And the Mystery Band, plus pop metal crew Cheap Trick and crazed guitar thrashers Das Damen.

The Fool On The Hill
A Beatle staple that attracted a host on stars.
The good fools: Bjork, Shirley Bassey, Stone The Crows, Bobbie Gentry, Santo And Johnny, Sergio Mendes And Brazil 66 and Sharon Tandy.
The forgotten fools: The King's Singers, former Monkee Mickey Dolenz, Petula Clark, Ray Stevens, The Boston Pops, Mulgrew Miller and Libby Titus.

Flying
This one attracted the strange battalion, including Eugene Chadbourne's Shockabilly, four blokes with papier mache eyeballs for heads: The Residents. And another bloke who'd just got a papier mache head for a Frank Sidebottom.

Blue Jay Way
The honours go to former Wire man Colin Newman. But not to The Bentmen, Buddah Pest or The Poets.

Your Mother Should Know
Don't mention The Hollyridge Strings. Please, oh please.

I Am The Walrus
Only mad people should apply here. They include: Lol Coxhill, Oasis, industrial hobgoblins Foetus and legendary guitar-sliging beardwearer Frank Zappa.
None mad people who've grappled the walrus: Sassafras, Gray Matter, Hash, metal mothers Love/Hate, Spooky Tooth (although they did it pretty well) and Men Without Hats.

Hello, Goodbye
Not much to write home about here, although there is Milton Nascimento from his 1993 album Angelus.

Strawberry Fields Forever
The ten best version are... in no particular order...
1 **The King's Singers** deranged barbershop on Tempus Fugit
2 **Candy Flip**'s crazy house version
3 **Noel Harrison**'s short-lived pop career collision
4 **Don Williams'** country swerve ball
5 **The Ventures'** instrumental twang on Super Psychedelics
6 **Tomorrow**'s awesome psychedelic brew
7 **Plastic Penny** pert pop
8 **Richie Havens'** emotive groan
9 **Todd Rundgren**'s glorious version from his album Faithful
10 **The Beatles**, of course.

Penny Lane
Impossible to sing without thinking of fish and finger pie and pronouncing the word "customer" exactly as John Lennon did, let's take a look at a few who've tried.
Orchestrally: Paul Mauriat.
Instrumentally: Klaus Wunderlich and Kai Winding.
Poppily: The World Party.
Thespianly: David McCallum.

Baby You're A Rich Man
The odd trio of coverees includes Australian industrial techno outfit Severed Heads, rap large fellahs The Fat Boys from the soundtrack of Disorderlies and under rated Beatles-inspired songwriter Martin Newell. They have all wrestled with the song's play on words.

All You Need Is Love
Real lovers who said what they meant: Echo And The Bunnymen, Tom Jones and The Fifth Dimension.
Some people who said it without words: Ferrante And Teicher.
And just some people: Anita Kerr, New Musik, Tony Osborne and Anything Box.

The Beatles

(aka The White Album)

Apple PMC 7067-8. PCS 7067-8
Recorded: May 30 - October 14, 1968.
Released: November 22, 1968
Reached number one in the UK and USA.

Singles released

None, although Revolution turned up on the B side to Hey Jude in 1968.

Their wildest venture yet with Revolution 9 confusing everyone who might have thought they'd got a handle on the group. Every genre is tackled on the album, from out and out rock 'n' roll to flamboyant experimentalism, ragtime nostalgia and twee top pop. The Beatles were physically drifting as the album was being made. Arguments erupted, new alliances were formed, new avenues were being explored.

Paul McCartney: "It was the tension album. There was a lot of friction."

What Mojo said: "Whatever the traumas, The White Album became simply breathtaking in its diversity - lush ballads, heavy metal, country, reggae, whimsy, avant garde collage and throwaway pop tunes all find a comfortable home - and most of it is wonderful."

What Q said: "Falling apart, they still made music that eclipsed most other groups."

The Best Of The Covers

Back In The USSR

Famous interpretations: Elton John's live hammering of the tune when he actually played in Russia went down in folkloric history but on vinyl there's not a lot of contenders.
OK. Who did a reasonable facsimilie: One man band Don Fardon, twist master general Chubby Checker and be-shaded mods John Fred And The Playboys.
Meanwhile, there was also: Cliff Bennett And The Rebel Rousers, The California Poppy Pickers and Billy Joel who also did the live Elton thing.

Dear Prudence

Exquisitely: The Five Stairsteps
Heavily: The Leslie West Band.
Gothically: Siouxie And The Banshees.
Canadianly: Martha And The Muffins.
Acoustically: The Jerry Garcia Band and, in part, Victoria Williams on This Moment Live in Toronto.
Clap handedly: The Jackson Five.

Glass Onion

Arif Mardin, come on down.

Ob-La-Di, Ob-La-Da

The big hit: Marmalade.
The big hitters: Arthur Conley and Johnny Mathis.
The people who do it without words: Peter Nero, The Boston Pops, Herb Alpert, Floyd Cramer and Waldo De Los Rios.
And with a doobedoobedoop: The King's Singers.

Wild Honey Pie

Who ate all the pies? No-one. Well, no-one's owning up anyway.

The Continuing Story Of Bungalow Bill

Eccentric German Klaus Beyer is one of the few who put his hand up for this one.

While My Guitar Gently Weeps

Orchestrally by George Pehlivanian and The Riga Recording Studio Orchestra and electrically by blind guitarist Jeff Healey.

Happiness Is A Warm Gun

What a live bill this would be: U2, The Breeders, World Party and The Strangulated Beatoffs all playing with their artillery.

Martha My Dear

Black country legends, Slade actually covered this one in their early skinhead days.

I'm So Tired

Not many takers here. In fact, just the one. The Plums. Whoever they may be.

Blackbird

Famous interpretations: Crosby, Still And Nash and Billy Preston.
Pop Gods: Harpers Bizarre and The Waterboys
Experimental a capella bloke: Bobby McFerrin.
Ex-members of The Monkees: Mickey Dolenz.
Respectable folkies: The Chieftains.
Annoying blokes: The King's Singers.
Former Flying Burrito Brothers: Sneaky Pete Kleinow.
And the rest: Terri Lynn Carrington, Tony Williams, Catherine McKinnon, Kenny Rankin, Moose Jones, Jaco Pastorius, Dionne Farris and Beachfront Property.

Piggies

Danbert Nobacon of Chumbawamba and folklorist Theo Bikel.

Rocky Racoon

Only the brave should apply here and they include fearless Richie Havens, jazzed-out old-timer Benny Goodman, those Australian guys Crowded House and former Amen Corner man Andy Fairweather-Low.

Don't Pass Me By

An triumvirate of terror with German techno industrials Freiwillige Selbstkontr, American roots rockers The Georgia Satellites and classical player George Pehlivanian all involved.

Why Don't We Do It In The Road?

The sweeter pop of The Velvet Monkeys and the extreme nonsense of Botulisme are two of the few takers here.

I Will

An early '60s single from The Vogues, a track on an album by Rocky Horror man Tim Curry and versions by Maureen McGovern and Maura O'Connell all exist.

Julia

Gloriously delivered by Bongwater and Ramsey Lewis. Tepidly jazzOR'ed by Charlie Byrd and LA Express.

Birthday

Underground Sunshine and Freiwillige Selbstkontr are the only two.

N⁰ 0271606

Helter Skelter

Apart from Charles Manson scrawling it on the wall of his Family's murder victims, the song was also covered "heavily" by Siouxsie And The Banshees, Pat Benatar, Gillan, U2, Aerosmith, Motley Crue, Husker Du and Soundgarden.

Long, Long, Long

Only Terry Scott Taylor has so far been traced.

Revolution 1

People have tended to cover the single flipside version of Hey Jude. (See singles section in this chapter.)

Honey Pie

Das Damen and The Pixies with irony high on their separate agendas and as it comes by John Arpin who has released an album called Ragtime Beatles featuring various Fabs classics in the ragtime style.

Savoy Truffle

Big star voice: Ella Fitzgerald.

Cry Baby Cry

By an act that isn't Throwing Muses: Del Shannon
By someone that isn't Del Shannon: Throwing Muses

Yer Blues

The Jeff Healey Band from the album Cover To Cover.

Mother Nature's Son

It's Ramsey Lewis again, this time joined by bespectacled country-styled crooner John Denver and pal of John Lennon Harry Nilsson.

Everybody's Got Something To Hide Except Me And My Monkey

Done as a pert preppy pop thing by The Feelies and soulfully by Barry Cowsill.

Sexy Sadie

Ramsey Lewis is this time joined by Paul Weller.

Revolution 9

Surprisingly no cover versions of this abstract gem.

Good Night

Merrily performed at face value by former Monkee Mickey Dolenz, those cabaret trifles Manhattan Transfer, soul outfit The Flirtations and The Cyril Stapleton Orchestra.

Yellow Submarine

Apple PMC 7070. PCS 7070 (CDP 46445 2)
Released: January 1969
Reached number four in the UK, number two in the USA.

Singles released

Yellow Submarine (Released August 1966, reached number one in the UK, number two USA)

The music from the film, featuring a number of George Martin Orchestra originals, Ringo's title track which had originally appeared on Revolver, complete with the epic All You Need Is Love which was prepared by the group for the first global satellite TV broadcast.

Paul McCartney: "All You Need Is Love is basically the message of the Yellow Submarine movie. I think that is still what people need."

The Best Of The Covers

Yellow Submarine

It's for the kids: The Happy Time Children's Chorus And Orchestra, Pinky And Perky, The Pickwick Children's Choir and Spike Milligan.
It's too deep to be for the kids: The California Poppy Picker and The Thought Police.
Let's take the words off: Ferrante And Teicher, The Baroque Inevitable and Enoch Light.
Hi, I'm still French: Maurice Chevalier.

Only A Northern Song

Not too many here. In fact none.

All Together Now

The strangest collection of coverers so far includes James Last, The Muppets, The Original Marauders and One Groovy Coconut.

Hey Bulldog

Again, there's obviously a certain degree of craziness involved with Yellow Submarine. The people who've taken up the bulldog gauntlet include pop psyche outfit The Godz, female metal act Fanny, male metal acts Skin Yard and Boxer, latter day US pop icons Toad The Wet Sprocket and Rolf Harris.

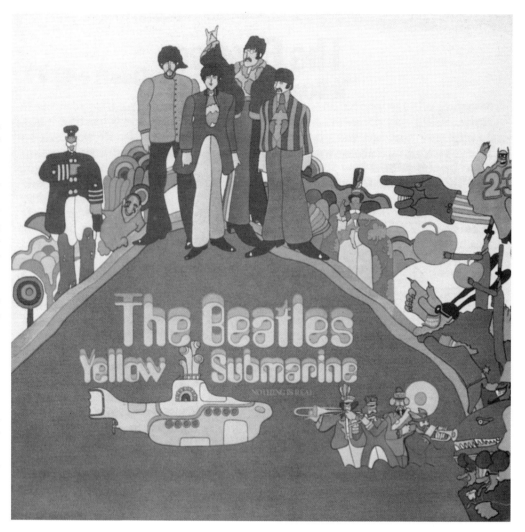

It's All Too Much

A trend is emerging. These loons include prog rock meanie Steve Hillage, MOR giants Journey, the strangely forgotten Senator Flux and Australian goth pop outfit The Church.

All You Need Is Love

The ones who really meant it, man: Tom Jones (released it as a single), Echo And The Bunnymen included it in their live show and The Fifth Dimension (they were from the age of Aquarius anyway).
And the rest: Ferrante And Teicher and their mad pianos, Anita Kerr, dodgy new romantics New Musik and The Anything Box.

The second side was made up of continuous incidental music by George Martin and Orchestra as played in the film.
The album was issued as The Yellow Submarine Songtrack in 1999 and included 15 newly remixed Beatles' tracks from the original film. The new songs included were: Eleanor Rigby, Love You To, Lucy In The Sky With Diamonds, Think For Yourself, Sgt Pepper's Lonely Hearts Club Band, With A Little Help From My Friends, Baby, You're A Rich Man, Only A Northern Song, When I'm Sixty Four and Nowhere Man. The Martin tracks were left for the original soundtrack.

Abbey Road

Apple PCS 7088.
Recorded: February 22-August 25, 1969.
Released: September 1969. Number one in
the UK and US.

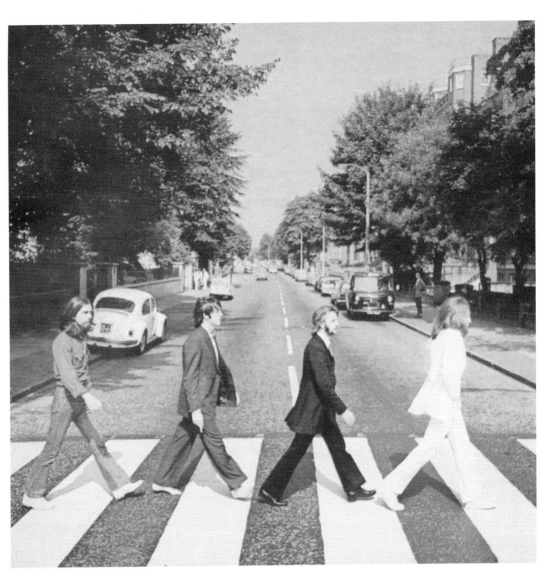

Singles released:

Something (Released October 1969, number four UK, number three US. Re-issued 1989 US, reached number one)

Abbey Road sounded the death knell for The Beatles. Ringo was threatening to leave, Allan Klein was pulling the purse strings - Paul's You Never Give Me Your Money was born in the midst of numerous legal wrangles - and tension was in the air. The second side comprised of half-ideas and part works thrown into a hypnotic, moving stew. It was still highly impressive but all was not well.

The album's global arrival signalled universal gasps of amazement. Another huge step (etc). It also produced outlandish behaviour in some. George Benson and Booker T And The MGs followed virtually the whole plot and Mike Westbrook and his jazzily-appointed band were commissioned by Commune di Reggio Emilia, from Italy to do the whole album in the same order. Although they did miss out Her Majesty.

What the sleeve says: Paul is dead.

What Q said: Abbey Road could well be the group's best effort since Revolver, and is actually a more rounded work than Sgt Pepper's.

What Mojo said: Like The White Album, Abbey Road is a collection of individual efforts, but there's a greater semblance of harmony among the grooves.

The Best Of The Covers

Come Together

The ones you've heard for all these years: Diana Ross, coming together since 1970 and Ike And Tina Turner ditto.

Those orchestral types: Only James Last this time around.

And some oddities: Claude Denjean on his Moog synthesiser and no doubt Howard Jones on his new synthesiser.

Soulfully: Michael Jackson, The Brothers Johnson, The Meters, The Neville Brothers, Shalamar and Dionne Warwick.

And groovily: Paul Weller from the charity Help! Album.

Metally: Aerosmith did a single in 1978, but they can't quite remember it. And Soundgarden grunged it much later. Not to mention Texan tormentors The Butthole Surfers and Meatloaf.

And there's plenty more: Blues Traveler, The Ice Man's Band, Buddy Miles, Sink Manhattan and Whipped Cream 69.

Something

What Frank Sinatra said: "Something is the greatest love song of the last 50 years."

The roll call is enormous. Even if Frank Sinatra famously introduced the song as the best Lennon and McCartney song, ever.

This George Harrison gem stands up even when sung in the shower by any one of the following: Bloodstone, James Brown, Joe Cocker, Peggy Lee, Bill Medley, Lou Rawls, Johnny

Rodriguez, Frank Sinatra, Sonny And Cher, Dionne Warwick

Or when instrumentally done by: Booker T. & The MGs, Duane Eddy, Percy Faith, Ferrante & Teicher, Bert Kaempfert, Liberace, Hugo Montenegro, Peter Nero, Waldo de los Rios and Junior Walker And The All Stars.

But perhaps not so by these funky grandparents: Tony Bennett, Perry Como, Lena Horne, Engelbert Humperdink, Jack Jones, Howard Keel, The Lettermen, Johnny Mathis, Jim Nabors, Ray Stevens, Telly Savalas, Sarah Vaughan, Bobby Vinton, Andy Williams

Maxwell's Silver Hammer

Only strange people could consider covering this pre-American Psycho tale of woeful murder. Beckon in then The Good Ship Lollipop, Brown Hill's Stamp Duty and "comedian" Steve Martin.

Oh! Darling

And there's not much call for Oh! Darling either. Just from Bela Fleck And The Flektones from their 1993 album Planet Bluegrass.

Octopus's Garden

It's Ringo's tune and suitably be-jewelled copyists include Reparata And The Delrons and Joanie Bartels from the late '80s album Bathtime Magic.

I Want You (She's So Heavy)

It's grunge, John, but not as we know it. Of course, crazy George Benson will do it but did black metal stalwarts Coroner really have to?

Here Comes The Sun

Easy going. Easy pickings from a variety of friendly and accessible performers (no sign of Coroner anywhere). But lovingly crafted versions exist from Richie Havens, Steve Harley and Cockney Rebel and soulful extrovert Nina Simone all strike a chord here.
Perhaps not so convincing though are: The King's Singers choral meandering and the version by Hugo Montenegro.

Because

Warning: More King's Singers.
Also look out for: The New Christy Minstrels, Percy Faith, Nylon and The Nashville Mandolin Ensemble.

But cherish: Elliot Smith's a capella version from the closing brouhaha of the excellent movie American Beauty.

You Never Give Me Your Money

Flutes ahoy: Herbie Mann.
Look out stage show: Paul Nicholas.
Lay the funk down, if you please: Booker T And The MGs.

Sun King

Version not by Booker T: The Bee Gees.
And the other one: Booker T And The MGs.

Mean Mr. Mustard

Comedy moment: Frankie Howerd.
Booker T: Booker T And The MGs.

Polythene Pam

A fine collection to invite to dinner, along with Pam herself, would have to include the avant-nebulous Dr Fink And the Mystery Band, former Move and Wizzard man Roy Wood, The Bee Gees and, of course, Booker T And The MGs.

She Came In Through The Bathroom Window

The legendary take: Joe Cocker
Well, they've done the rest of the "medley": The Bee Gees.
And they are called Booker T And The MGs: Booker T And The MGs.

Golden Slumbers

Strangely this tune draws together Neil Diamond, Jackson Browne and Jennifer Warnes (duetting together), Billy Joel and The Orange Bicycle. Plus Phil Collins. And the rest.

Carry That Weight

The usual suspects: The Bee Gees and Booker T And The MGs.

The End

Andmoreagain: Booker T And The MGs, George Benson, Phil Collins and Richie Havens, plus cellist Ofra Harnoy And the Armin Electric Strings and lurking in the background The London Symphony Orchestra.

Her Majesty

The wonderfully-named: D-Cups
The plummily spoken: Brian Sewell

Let It Be

Apple PXS 1.
Released: May, 1970
Number one in the UK and USA.

Singles released

Let It Be
(Released March 1970.
Number one in the USA, number two in the UK)
The Long And Winding Road (Released US May 1970. Reached number one)

So the story goes, the group decided to have one last go. The hugely successful Abbey Road had seen stress explosions but they were game (ish). Rumours were rife; not least that Paul was dead. John returned his MBE and was offered the lead role in Jesus Christ Superstar all in the space of a week and flippancy was king. Lennon is remembered for enthusing about the idea of producing a crap album so that people could see the band with their "trousers down". The whole shebang was caught in one of the first fly-on-the-wall movies which underlined the nervous jostling that was taking place. George Martin was in attendance but legendary producer Phil Spector was brought on board to overlap the bits and make it whole.

It 's a strange record and when Yugoslav band Laibach decided to cover the whole set - with the exception of the title track - the underlying menace of some of the songs was more than evident.
What the sleeve says: All four can't decide on one picture where they all look right. Facial hair is in except with Lennon.

What Q said: Although released a year after Abbey Road in 1970, Let It Be predates that album, composed for the most part of live studio knockabouts done at the time they were filming the Let It Be movie.

The Best Of The Covers

Two Of Us

No takers here. Except for Laibach of course.

Dig A Pony

Same again.

Across The Universe

Thin white duke shows interest: David Bowie

covered the song on his breaking Stateside sub-funk album Young Americans from 1975.

Other people too: The track was also covered by Beatles fans 10cc, '80s indie band The Family Cat and former Pink Floyd man Roger Waters. Elsewhere the song turned up on the soundtrack to Pleasantville in 1998, sung by Fiona Apple.

I Me Mine
Only Frank Pourcel has unwound his silky strings on this one.

Dig It
Not even Frank.

Let It Be
As one of the great classics, McCartney's Let It Be had a multitude of takers.

Great soul singers: Aretha Franklin, Bobby Hatfield, Gladys Knight And The Pips, The Persuasions and Ike And Tina Turner.

Other legends: Bill Medley from The Righteous Brothers, Dion without his Belmonts, Joan Baez, Joe Cocker and The Everly Brothers to name but a few.

Crazy instrumentalists: Floyd Cramer, Ferrante And Teicher and Klaus Wunderlich and his Hammond organ.

Just plain crazy: Chevy Chase, Tennessee Ernie Ford, John Denver and Meatloaf.

Let It Be was also used to raise money following the Zeebrugge disaster on a single by Ferry Aid.

Maggie Mae
It's a trad arr.

I've Got A Feeling
Only George Pehlivanian the old symphonic terror and Pearl Jam, the Seattle post-grungesters have headed for this one.

One After 909
Strangely enough two Americana-rooted post punk outfits, The Silos and The Smithereens.

The Long And Winding Road
The top ten versions run as follows...
1   **Diana Ross** from the 1970 album Everything Is Everything.

LET IT BE

2   **Andy Mackay** from Roxy Music from his solo sax-powered album.
3   The moody **Sandpipers** from Come Saturday Morning.
4   Soul man **Billy Ocean.**
5   That guy from the Righteous Brothers again, **Mr Bill Medley.**
6   Prince Charles' favourite opera singer **Kiri Te Kanawa.**
7   John Travolta's main squeeze **Olivia Newton-John.**
8   Soul diva **Cissy Houston.**
9   Spiritual torch singer **Aretha Franklin.**
10   **Cher,** from the album Half Breed.

For You Blue
No-one's on for this one.

Get Back
Hero of the soundwaves: Elvis Presley.
String-driven things: Ted Heath and Paul Mauriat.
Soul people: Al Green, Doris Troy and Ike And Tina Turner.
Strange people: Area Code 615 and The Wallace Collection.
Household names: The Amen Corner, Elton John and Mongo Santamaria.

The single's not on the album...

So prolific were The Beatles that a number of their songs didn't even make it to the albums in the UK. Well not until there was a Greatest Hits or another territory to introduce to their majesty. During their life time a number of tracks were only released as singles or as their flipsides and they're listed here along with the army of people who decided to cover them.

Not listed are the tracks that were scooped up to make the Magical Mystery Tour EP into an album. They were Hello Goodbye (which was released as a single with I Am The Walrus in November 1967), Strawberry Fields Forever and Penny Lane (which were released as a double A side in February 1967) and the pairing of All You Need Is Love and Baby, You're A Rich Man (which were released as a single in July 1967).

Let's take a look at those singles and their covers in full.

From Me To You
Single A side released April 1963 on Parlophone Records.
Reached number one in the UK.

Other hit makers: Del Shannon grazed the charts in 1963.
Classic covers: Bobby McFerrin's vocal gymnastics from the album Spontaneous Inventions.
Strange but true: Mae West covered the song, she can be tracked down on the Rhino Golden Throats series. And Emi Bonilla's bizarre reading can be heard in the Beatles Exotica series.
And the rest: Mournfully by The Johnny Mann Singers, gingerly by Beatles' compadre Dick James and trumpetingly by Hugh Masekela.

Thank You Girl
Single B side of From Me To You.

Covered by John Hiatt and as part of the Baroque Beatles Songbook by Joshua Rifkin.

She Loves You
Single A side released August 1963.
Reached number one in the UK.

Single versions: The Applejacks, The Haircuts, Peter Sellers and Roger Webb.
Preposterous parts of prog rock medley: Vanilla Fudge.
The scourge of modern pop music: Take That.
Some strange names to laugh at: The Beatle Buddies, Bubonic Bassoon Quartet and Dickheads.
Famous people doing it: Count Basie, Neil Sedaka and Bobby Vee.
Some people who shouldn't: Russ Conway, Homer And Jethro, Pinky And Perky and Noel Harrison.

I'll Get You
Single B side of She Loves You

International terrorists: Emi Bonilla and Fernando Concho.

I Want To Hold Your Hand
Single A side released December 1963.
Reached number one in the UK.

Good covers: Al Green and Sparks.
Nice covers: The Boston Pops Orchestra, Duke Ellington, Vanilla Fudge, The New Christy Minstrels and Enoch Light.
Daft covers: Beatle Buddies.
MOR covers: Petula Clark, Dollar, Take That, Lakeside, Pat Boone, Freddy Cannon, Keith Beckingham, The Crickets, The Merseybeats and Nelson Riddle.
Indiepop covers: The Moving Sidewalks and Game Theory.

This Boy
Single B side of I Want To Hold Your Hand

Lots of people who never really went on to do very much at all, really: The Nylons, Shirley Abicair, Deuces Wild and Dan Peek.

I Feel Fine
Single A side released in November 1964.
Reached number one in the UK and USA.

Happy clappers: Floyd Cramer, The Ventures and Alma Cogan.
Enjoying the finer things in life: Sweethearts Of The Rodeo and Nancy Ames.
Unhappy copyists: Vanilla Fudge, Wet Wet Wet and Tony Trischka.

She's A Woman
Single B side of I Feel Fine

Outspoken male opinion formers: Jeff Beck.
Sex symbols: Johnny Hallyday.
An occasionally groovy guy and his mate: Jose Feliciano and Noel Harrison.
And a ragamuffin style super duo: Scritti Politti with Shabba Ranks.
And an old soul crooner: Walter Jackson.

Yes It Is
Single B side of Ticket To Ride

Celebrated by Peter Sellers on A Celebration of Sellers and by former Shoes man Scott McCarl on Play On.

I'm Down
Single B side of Help!

Covered by Canadian Beatles fans Heart and also rap icons The Beastie Boys for their album Licensed To Ill. However, The Beatles' publishers Northern Songs denied permission for it to be included.

We Can Work It Out
Single Double A side with Day Tripper, released December 1965. Reached number one in the UK and number five in the USA.

Covered rockily: By Deep Purple on The Book Of Taliesyn, Mike Harrison, Tesla and Exile.
Psychedelically: By Fever Tree.
Pop orchestrally: By The Aranbee Pop Symphony Orchestra.
Soulfully: By Chaka Khan, Dionne Warwick, Valerie Simpson, Leslie Uggams and Stevie Wonder.
In a mod way: By Chris Farlowe.
In a bluegrass backporch picking kinda way: The Dillards.
With a high voice and a smile: Frankie Valli.
With a high voice and a rain hat: Petula Clark.
In an indie way: By Dislocation Dance.

Day Tripper
Single Double A side with We Can Work It Out, released December 1965.

Kept in the family by: Julian Lennon and The Electric Light Orchestra.
Sent up for laughs by: Mae West.
Given a heavy metal drubbing by: Whitesnake and Bad Brains.
Covered with a northern soul vibe by: JJ Barnes.
Given glorious treatment by: Otis Redding, Cheap Trick and James Taylor.
And just finger snapped all over the place by:

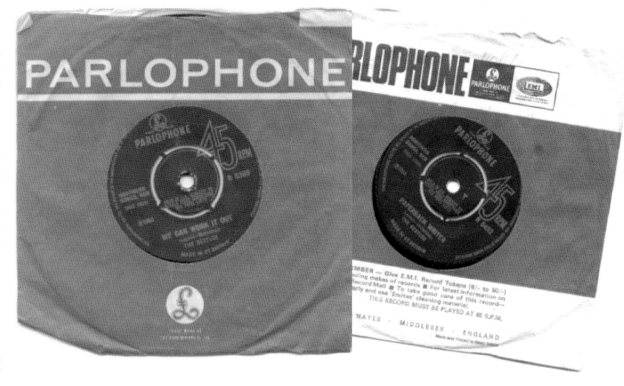

Ramsey Lewis (piano), Nancy Sinatra (boots), Yellow Magic Orchestra (synth and quiffs), Shockabilly (discordant guitars), Daniel Ash (gaunt expression), Jimi Hendrix (playing behind his head), 10cc (with rubber bullets), Ocean Colour Scene (waving to Noel), The Steve Gibbons Band (nice mullet, mate), Sergio Mendes (in a samba style), Lulu (Scottish), Vanilla Fudge (pomp), Fever Tree (psyche), Don Fardon (On acoustic guitar and bass drum), Sandy Nelson (just a drum) and Anne Murray (with or without her Snowbird).

Paperback Writer
Single A side, released June 1966.
Reached number one in the UK and USA.

The motley crew of would-be-Fabs includes thrash metallers Tempest, R&B soulsters The Cowsills, the quite famous Bee Gees and 10cc.

Rain
Single B side of Paperback Writer

In the style of some mad people with the radio on: Bongwater.
In the style of a woman who can't reach the notes: Petula Clark.
In the style of a hermit from mink hollow: Todd Rundgren.
In the style of a sunshine pop rock act from the '60s: The Sunshine Company.
In the style of a mad bloke with the guitars too loud: Beatle Hans.
In the style of a radio-friendly guy: Dan Fogelberg.
In the style of a southern bluesman: Gregg Allman.
In the style of three poorly rehearsed Japanese girls with mini skirts on: Shonen Knife.
In the style of garage rock: The Gants.

Lady Madonna
Single A side, released March 1968.
Reached number one in the UK and number four in the USA.

Delivered by legends: Fats Domino and Elvis Presley have both wooed Madonna.
The usual cast of reliables: Also on hand were Booker T And The MGs, Ramsey Lewis, Jose Feliciano, James Last, Richie Havens and Klaus Wunderlich.
Also available in multi-harmony: The Four Freshmen.
And pop: Gary Puckett And The Union Gap.
Not to mention: Kingmaker and Area Code 615.

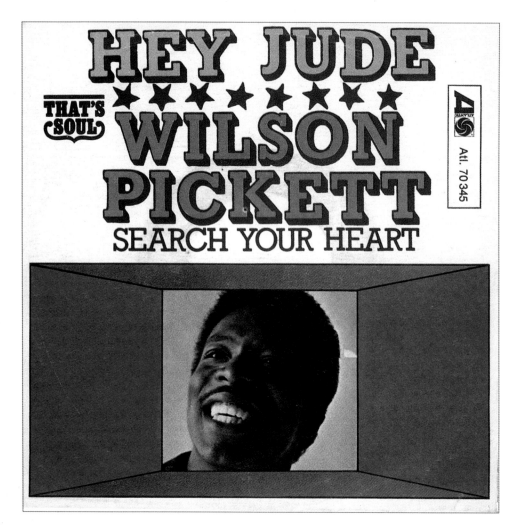

banjo-plucking John Hartford, the close harmony Ray Charles Singers, the a capella Unfinished Version and someone called Frank Sinatra. There are also various intrumentalists involved, including The Sound Symposium, Moog Groove, The Little Big Horns and Ambrose... not to mention a brace of people who've disappeared deep into the woodwork, like Don Ellis, Daniel Godfrey, John Klemmer, Pat Williams, Bill Deal and Gene Bertoncini. Information leading to the apprehension of any of these named acts will not go unrewarded.

Revolution
Single B side of Hey Jude

Done wholesomely: By country rock outfit Mother Earth and the psychedelically-primed Head Shop.
Poppily: By The Thompson Twins and Mike And The Mechanics.
Angrily: By Billy Bragg
Chockfull of Hawaiian guitar: By Santo And Johnny.

Don't Let Me Down
Single B side of get Back, released April 1969.
Reached number one in the UK and USA.

High quality covers from a short shortlist abound. They include gratifying performances from Paul Weller (on the Revolution Number Nine album) and Dillard And Clark (that's Gene Clark the former Byrd) on their excellent album Through The Morning, Through The Night. Not to mention Ben E King from the 1972 album Rough Edge, as well as fine versions from Phoebe Snow and Annie Lennox.

The Ballad Of John And Yoko
Single A Side, released May 1969.
Reached number one in the UK, number eight in the USA.

Shakily covered by Scottish pop anarchists Teenage Fan Club and worried over by Hootie And The Blowfish too. At least it wasn't Counting Crows. Yet...

You Know My Name (Look Up The Number)
Single B side of The Ballad Of John And Yoko
Sung in German under the title You Know Mein Kampf by The Sex Clark Five. What for? We'll probably never know.

The Inner Light
Single B side of Lady Madonna

Covered only by The Soulful Strings.

Hey Jude
Single A side, released August 1968
Reached number one

The covering pack included stars such as: The legendary soul icon, Mr Wilson Pickett. Another legendary soul icon, Mr Smokey Robinson with his group The Miracles. Er, yet another soul icon Mr Junior Walker And his group the All Stars. Yet more soul icons in the guise of the be-suited Temptations. Oh, and the son of Hickory Holler's Tramp, Mr OC Smith.
Away from the soul groove, Hey Jude also found a home with a strange cross section of people who redesigned it in their own sweet way. For example, there were The Residents (who fed it through a tube), Petula Clark (who attempted to become hip with it), Bing Crosby (who lost interest half way through singing it), Tiny Tim and Brave Combo (who just messed around with it in an unseemly way) and Lawrence Welk (who just did a Lawrence Welk on it).
Other famous and semi-famous people obviously threw in their ten cents. They included Jose Feliciano, The Royal Teens, Bill Medley, Sonny And Cher, Elvis Presley, Maynard Ferguson, Tom Jones, The Tams, Stan Kenton, The Jazz Crusaders, Ray Stevens, Peter Nero, The New Christy Minstrels, Area Code 615 and a whole lot more.
Less well know interpretations came from the

Orchestras,
skiffle groups,
country cousins,
Baroque
gentlepeople
and Yugoslav
dissidents...

WHOLE ALBUMS OF FAB

Not content to cover one song from the Beatles' remarkable back pages, the trend of copying a whole album's worth of tunes began early in the Beatles' life. Perhaps it was an attempt at passing off. Maybe it was an urge for the Lennon And McCartney magic dust to sprinkled over flagging careers. Whatever, beat groups, orchestras, banjo bands, country outfits and Yougoslav dissidents all pinned their hopes to the Fabs. And the practice still continues today.

Back in the early '60s Elektra Records boss Jac Holzman travelled to London and pitched his idea of a classical take on The Beatles' music to Brian Epstein, the resultant album, The Baroque Beatles Songbook, utilised the melodies of The Beatles but sank the deep into the musical myriad of Baroque austerity. A trend had begun.

Within a year Holzman also encouraged bluegrass outfit The Charles River Valley Boys to plunder the Beatles' catalogue for Beatle Country. The sound was wild and effusive and within months Elektra act The Dillards had seized the idea and the birth of cosmic country was just around the corner. Elsewhere Chet Atkins tackled a whole set of Beatles' songs, Beatles producer George Martin and a host of lush strings instigated a flood of easy listening derivatives and the likes of Santo And Johnny, Count Basie and The Big Ben Banjo Band all "did" Beatles. And it didn't stop there. Hot on their heels were The Hollyridge Strings, The Band Of The Irish Guards, Booker T, Stephane Grapelli and Laibach all trying their hand.

This section is dedicated to those people who wholeheartedly had to get The Beatles into their lives. It studies their musical interpretations. It examines the sleeve artwork they used as a homage to the Fabs and it also reprints some of the bizarre sleevenote commentary that accompanied their wares. Read on...

Abbey Road '78

Music From the Movie Sgt Pepper's Hearts Club Band
SPRINGBOARD SPB-4111.Released: 1978.

Medley: Sgt Pepper's Lonely Hearts Club Band/With A Little Help From My Friends; Here Comes The Sun; Getting Better; Lucy In The Sky With Diamonds; Got To Get You Into My Life; Strawberry Fields Forever; Come Together; The Long And Winding Road; Get Back.

The music: Surely the obvious thing is, don't try a song that's too hard for you. Don't attempt the theme from Titanic in Am Dram. It won't work. If you could do it, you'd be famous already. Similarly, don't attempt to recreate the entire soundtrack of Sgt Pepper's (The Movie) on a budget of ten pence and a bag of crisps. It's not big. And it's not clever.

Too late though, Abbey Road '78 have beaten you to it. The ill-advised inadequacy of their efforts come to a peak early on Here Comes The Sun when the tinniest of keyboards plays the melody. Ow! How much worse can it get? Quite a bit actually.

The sleeve: Crap art.
The sleevenotes: None. Surprisingly. How could you put this into words?
Classic Beatles cut: I really wanted it to be Strawberry Fields but it passes by without real offence. However, Come Together is a glorious mess, a growly piece of nonsense that sounds like Status Quo are playing the rhythm. And, indeed, the guitar solo is so bad it's superb.

Chet Atkins

Picks On the Beatles
RCA LPM 3531. Released: 1966.
RCA Starcall NL 12002. Re-issued 1977.

I Feel Fine; Yesterday; If I Fell; Can't Buy Me Love; I'll Cry Instead; Things We Said Today; A Hard Day's Night; I'll Follow The Sun; She's

A Woman; And I Love Her; Michelle; She Loves You.

The music: Chet plays his usual ringing Gretsch guitar and adds harmonica, piano and light percussion. For the most part, though, this is him going through the fretboard in the style that inspired a fledgling George Harrison. There's the trademark high lonesome sound on If I Fell, the country shuffle on Can't Buy Me Love and

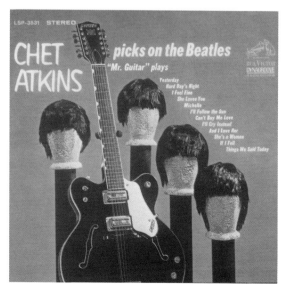

plenty of moody resonance on Yesterday.

The sleeve: Excellent graphics with Chet's guitar and four hairdresser's heads with wigs. The flipside even features the sensibly-coiffeured guitarist with a mop top toupee. Phew! The Starcall re-issue, however, is nothing short of tatty.

The sleevenotes: "I have appreciated Chet Atkins as a musician since long before the tracks on this album were written: in fact since I was at the ripe young age of 17. Since then I have lost count of the number of Chet's albums I have acquired, but I have not been disappointed with any of them.

"For me the best thing is that he is capable of playing almost every type of music but the conviction in the way he does it. While listening to this album I got the feeling that these songs had been written specifically with Chet in mind. The fact that they were not proves his eminence as an artist." George Harrison

Classic Beatles cut: Things We Said Today is great. It lifts the offbeat melody line and adds some great tremolo, a truly inspirational version.

The Band Of The Irish Guards

Marching With The Beatles
STUDIO 2 RECORDS/EMI TWO 125. Released: 1966

She Loves You; Yesterday; I'll Keep You Satisfied; From Me To You; A Hard Day's Night; All My Loving; Can't Buy Me Love; Things We Said Today; Michelle; It's For You; I Want To Hold Your Hand; Help!

The music: The Band Of The Irish Guards thrump along with tinkling xylophones and all the pomp and circumstance that they can muster. Conducted by Major CH Jaeger, the recordings here are slightly less formal than you might at first imagine. But of course they shake a lot of the life out of them anyway. No way did they don Kaftans and loosen up. Instead they extend the

middle-eight and subdue some of the rasping brass.

The sleeve: Perhaps in a precursor to Sgt Pepper's very own band, the Irish Guards are pictured marching along the Mall in London full bearskin regalia. Maybe The Beatles got the idea from them... we'll never know.

The sleevenotes: "The idea of setting the fabulous tunes of John Lennon and Paul McCartney to march tempo was the brainchild of Beatles' publisher Dick James. The decision to have the Irish Guards under the guidance of their ebullient Director Of Music, Major CH Jaeger, was the choice of EMI Records Classical recording manager, who felt that they were the most suitable military band to do full justice to these novel scores."

Classic Beatles cut: Things We Said Today reverberates around a sub-melody that simply confuses the main theme. For that it stands out as even stranger than the rest.

The Band Of The Royal Military Academy, Sandhurst

Plays Lennon And McCartney
PICKWICK SHM 758. Released: 1972.

Yellow Submarine; Day Tripper; Penny Lane; The Fool On The Hill; A Hard Day's Night; Eleanor Rigby; Yesterday; Ob-La-Di, Ob-La-Da; All My loving; Can't Buy Me Love; Help! I'll Keep You Satisfied.

The music: Downbeat brass band arrangements conducted by Derek Taylor (no relation to The Beatles' PR of many years) which are either jaggedly chirpy or wantonly longing. As with all brass band music the separation of instruments is hardly discernible and the band meld into one almost synthetic noise from time to time.

Ob-La-Di, Ob-La-Da is particularly painful, as the driving rhythm doesn't fit the melodic structures but, for the most part, the band just plough on through, seemingly regardless of what's occurring in the outside world.

The sleeve: Featuring a classic shot of Major DV Fanshawe on a horse, Thor, climbing some steps. Hey, very Beatlesy.

The sleevenotes: Sadly it's all about the other Derek Taylor without a hint of what they think of The Beatles, their songs, horses or anything.

Classic Beatles cut: All My Loving is just bizarre as it charges through each line getting more aggressive as it does. In fact the sporadic use of cymbal makes it sound like a frightening accompaniment to someone who's hitting small animals over the head with a hammer. Or maybe that's just me.

Count Basie And His Orchestra

Basie's Beatle Bag
MUSIC FOR PLEASURE MFP 1393.
Released 1966.

Help; Can't Buy Me Love; Michelle; I Wanna Be Your Man; Do You Want To Know A Secret; All My Loving; Yesterday; And I Love Her; Hold Me Tight; She Loves You; Kansas City.

The music: With all the trademark swing of a Basie session, this mid-'60s recording utilises the standard Big Band format and adds a subdued hipness to these Lennon and McCartney standards. Basie also throws in the Beatles' cover Kansas City, by Leiber and Stoller, and a slick, almost unrecognisable Hold Me Tight.

The sleeve: It's Count Basie, with a bag! And it's festooned with stickers listing his Beatles' covers. The best bit of all is the severe mid-'60s psychedelia of the background, which explodes like a primal-coloured nightmare all around the great man.

The sleevenotes: "This album brings together two giant musical forces, far removed in their essence but combining to create a unique and musically explosive sound. Count Basie's contribution to jazz and popular music in the last decade has shown him up as a rock towering above the undulating land of music. He is an original, as old as the hills themselves, one might say, and yet he is one of the few band leaders who have moved with the times and been continually aware of the need to experiment with the new ideas and use the talent of new writers.

"The writing talent of The Beatles hardly needs any more appraisal than it has already had. The works of Lennon/McCartney are of an intrinsic beauty and natural musical genius, which will carry them through time until they become recognised as classics in their own right.

"Here is the sum of these two great forces and the result is of an exciting, dynamic and inventive nature. The tremendous punch and superb phrasing of the Band is an ideal foundation for

the scintillating piano playing and, on some numbers, organ playing of the Count. The overall effect is of a new concept in Big Band playing and this LP will certainly surprise any that are not really acquainted with the sound of the Big Band.

"This must surely be the ultimate musical combination and, listening to such numbers as Michelle, A Hard Day's Night and All My Loving, one realises that it makes no difference whether one is a Beatle fan or a Basie fan - the result nevertheless is a splendid LP in the true sense of the word."

Classic Beatles cut: Hold Me Tight complete with muted trombone solo is exceptional as it throws the emphasis of the besat into mid-verse thus changing the overall sound completely.

The Big Ben Banjo Band

Banjos Go Beatles
EMI RECORDS SX 6073. Released: 1966

Do You Want To Know A Secret; Ask Me Why; Bad To Me; I Should Have Known Better; I'm A Loser; It Won't Be

Long; Tell Me Why; The Word; I'll Be Back; From Me To You; I Saw Her Standing There; Please, Please Me; Paperback Writer; Eight Days A Week; I'll Get You; Don't Bother Me; No Reply; Little Child; I Want To Hold Your Hand; I Call Your Name; I'll Keep You Satisfied; A Hard Day's Night; I Feel Fine; Can't Buy Me Love; Norwegian Wood; Rain; Nowhere Man; Michelle; This Boy; Yesterday; All My Loving; She's A Woman; You Can't Do That; Drive My Car; There's A Place; Help!.*

The music: An irreverent mixture of tinny Winifred Atwell piano, Keystone Kops brass and jangling banjos works its way through 12 medleys of Beatles' songs. Three songs are crammed into each piece as comedy trombones; washboards and all manner of strummed things carry the bar-room tempo. It's music, Jim, but not as we know it.

The sleeve: A classic illustration with four upturned banjos all given mop top haircuts. Ludicrously excellent.

The sleevenotes: "There's something very lively, happy-go-lucky and effervescent about the sound of the banjo. And Norrie Paramor and the musicians of The Big Ben Banjo Band exploit this to their fullest advantage in all their performances."

Classic Beatles cut: Somehow Help! which closes the final medley seems almost natural.

George Benson

The Other Side Of Abbey Road

A&M RECORDS. Released: 1970.

Golden Slumbers/You Never Give Me Your Money; Because/Come Together; Oh! Darling; Here Comes The Sun/I Want You (She's So Heavy); Something/Octopus's Garden/The End.

The music: Before he became super-slick, chart topping and be-suited, Benson was always pretty darn muso. A guitar whizz with a line in scat vocals, he would go on to chart high with Nature Boy and become an easy listening staple for the after hours jazz funk generation. On The Other Side Of Abbey Road he brings in a hefty team, including Herbie Hancock and Bob James on keyboards and Ray Barreto on percussion. The groove is in the house and brass and strings are augmented by Benson's breezy riffs. He picks mildly and allows some stuttering sax to lead in places but mostly it's the strings that corral the choral into a religiously soulful sound.

The sleeve: It's George crossing a road but there's not a zebra crossing in sight.

The sleevenotes: None included apart from a mega line up of players and the information that there's a Ringo tune aboard.

Classic Beatles cut: The medley of Something, Octopus's Garden and The End clocks in at nearly six and a half minutes and is well worth it.

Acker Bilk, His Clarinet And Strings

Acker Bilk Plays Lennon And McCartney

GNP CRESCENDO GNPD 2191. Released: 1987.

Norwegian Wood; With A Little Luck; Imagine; Michelle; Woman; World Without Love; Mull Of Kintyre; Fool On The Hill; Ebony And Ivory; Nowhere Man; Yesterday; She's Leaving Home; Here, There And Everywhere; Pipes Of Peace.

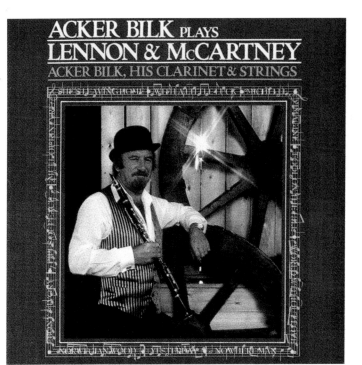

The music: Acker is the clarinettist from the West Country who charted all over the globe with Strangers On The Shore. His goatee beard is back in style and his cool blowing remains undaunted by years of musical change and a virtual technological revolution.

And, so to the '80s and, in need of a theme for a new album he, along with accomplice Terry Brown, decided to plunder the works of Lennon and McCartney both in The Beatles and afterwards to produce a new direction. A new angle. And a highly bizarre grouping of songs.

What you get is Acker playing his clarinet in a subdued and occasionally soulful manner, an orchestra whittling away the melody in the background and the occasional synth for width. It's not startling stuff and it even gets a bit turgid on the likes of Michelle and Lennon's Woman but what can you expect?

In a way you'd almost like it all to work once you hear the distant Lennon and McCartneyisms treated with sub-harmonies and the odd lounge trick, but for the most part this is very hard work indeed.

The sleeve: Acker in bowler hat, holding a clarinet. Something tells me he's used that idea before.

The sleevenotes: "Since Acker and I have been making records together we must have recorded well over 250 titles so we really had to put our thinking caps on to come up with a theme for this new album and as he and I are both huge Lennon and McCartney fans we thought - why not - let's pick out 14 of our favourites and go for it. We started working out the best songs for clarinet and after a couple of days we had enough to fill a four CD box set. We then had to prune it down to 14 - which was harder than the recording.

"Acker's interpretation of Lennon and McCartney songs is perfect for me, he's added his great jazz feel to give these familiar songs a completely new approach which I don't think the early Beatles fans would have expected."

Classic Beatles cut: Well, it's certainly not the album closer Pipes Of Peace.

The Brothers Four

Sing John Lennon/Paul McCartney
COLUMBIA CS9302. Released: 1965.

Norwegian Wood; Yesterday; All My loving; Nowhere Man; I'll Follow The Sun; And I Love Her; If I Fell; Help!; Michelle; We Can Work It Out; Girl.

The music: The Brothers were a polished and pristine quartet who cut their teeth on preppy versions of folk songs. Everything from Tie My Kangaroo Down Sport through to Walk Right In and If I Had A Hammer were fair game and their plush four-part harmonies assured that nothing ever sounded revolutionary or dangerous.

With The Beatles they applied the same theory and ensured that any spark of originality and indeed inventiveness was given a good watering down. Amid this environment little of note survives - although, listening to the album, by side two they seem to either lose their grip or succeed in making the listener think, 'hey, this ain't so bad after all'. If I Fell seems loveable enough and We Can Work It Out with its out-of-time harmonica is chirpy too. The orchestra is on call throughout but they're toned down so far in the mix that it's only on the opening of the closer Girl that they seem to awaken from the deepest, darkest siesta. The track is also punctuated by an acoustic lead holding the melody, which almost seems scarily avant-garde. In fact, the track's quite good until the Bro's arrive half way through for their customary drive-by harmonising.

Booker T And The MGs

McLemore Avenue
STAX CDSXE 016. Released 1970.

Medley: Golden Slumbers; Carry That Weight; The End; Here Comes The Sun; Come Together. Something; Medley: Because; You Never Give Me Your Money. Medley: Sun King; Mean Mr. Mustard; Polythene Pam; She Came In Through The Bathroom Window; I Want You (She's So Heavy).

The music: It's Abbey Road, but recorded at McLemore Avenue, with some of the tracks missing (ie: Maxwell's Silver Hammer; Oh! Darling; Octopus's Garden; Her Majesty) by the classic Booker T line-up - Booker T, Steve Cropper, Donald "Duck" Dunn and Al Jackson. And, it's

a strange one.

The proceedings sound like they took place late at night. Imbibed perchance. The contained mix is a loose groove through The Beatles' album that wanders, strays, gets lost and finally rallies. Cropper riffs and solos and Booker T parps the organ. Nothing much else happens. But, it's actually quite an infectious listen, even if it's incredibly unassuming at times.

The sleeve: The quartet cross the road. No zebra crossing. No-one with bare feet.
The sleevenotes: None.
Classic Beatles cut: The medley that closes the set, 10.40 of Sun King et al, is great because the musical parameters are so wide and Booker T's organ is allowed to fill. It's just a shame they didn't do Maxwell's Silver Hammer.

The sleeve: Four clean cut ivy league lookers sit atop step ladders. Skinny ties, nice haircuts. Gerooovey!

The sleevenotes: Very few. In fact none, other than the information that the album was produced by Ted Macero and that the brothers aren't actually brothers at all, they're Dick Foley, Bob Flick, John Paine and Mike Kirkland. You can't trust anyone, can you?

Classic Beatles cut: If I Fell seems to succeed best. The Brothers simply can't handle its pace and decide to let it win in the end. However, if there were any justice a remix of Girl would let them sing just one chorus instead of the verse and chorus they tack onto what's quite a tasteful instrumental rendition.

Frank Chacksfield And His Orchestra

Chacksfield Plays The Beatles' Songbook
DECCA PFS 4191. Released 1970.

Get Back; Michelle; Got To Get You Into My Life; Yesterday; Something; Hey Jude; A Hard Day's Night; Norwegian Wood; Ticket To Ride; The Fool On The Hill; Come Together; Ob-La-Di, Ob-La-Da.

The music: By the first chorus of Get Back there's a hint that this beautifully-psychedelesised package (well, the sleeve anyway) is going to swing like an outrageous vibey groove of '60s pop culture. Sadly that image soon diminishes as Chacksfield and co. return to their light programme roots and simply oodle on the MOR

qualities. Get Back, in all its glory has a wayward guitar and a well-placed chime that give it a kind of Motowny feel but the strings win hands down by the end and it's just a touch too turgid.

The sleeve: As part of the Decca Phase 4 series concentrating on the very stereoness of the proceedings, the actual "love and peace" graphics are silhouetted in a figure four with a sort of over-hip reading of the Yellow Submarine set featured in the backdrop. Various couples look contented and animals flitter by in a lovey dovey everything's just great kind of way.

The sleevenotes: There are none! The scant information only reveals that the fab sleeve is by Farmlett, Barsanti and Associates and that the arrangements were concocted by John Keating.

Classic Beatles cut: It's Get Back for all its unfulfilled promise.

The Charles River Valley Boys

Beatle Country
ELEKTRA RECORDS EKL 4006. Released 1967.

I've Just Seen A Face; Baby's In Black; I Feel Fine; Yellow Submarine; Ticket To Ride; And Your Bird Can Sing; What Goes On; Norwegian Wood; Paperback Writer; She's A Woman; I Saw Her Standing There; Help!.

The music: Revolutionary in its own way, this second stab at The Beatles' catalogue by the Elektra label - their first being the Baroque Beatles package at the hands of Joshua Rifkin - showed that modern melody could be handled by traditional instruments and players. In its

wake the '70s saw all manner of country acts trying their hand at less traditional fare. Indeed, The Dillards version of I've Just Seen A Face followed The Charles River Valley Boys in style and let the concept spill over into their other songs, taking country music to a new commercial audience,

In its own right this album has some great moments as mandolins and banjo's face off and a three-man vocal team interpret the songs in their own high and lonesome way. The backporch bravado is kept on the agenda and the simpler melodic motifs fit the bluegrass flurry affectionately.

The sleeve: A classic of four cowboys encountering the bright lights of Piccadilly Circus and swinging London for the first time. Hardly the Muswell Hillbillies but close.

The sleevenotes: None, other than a list of players and the news that the album was recorded in Nashville and includes banjo, mandolin, fiddle and dobro guitar.

Classic Beatles cut: There's lots of wildly palatable songs here, especially I Feel Fine and Help! Which give the bluegrass outfit plenty of room to shake it down.

The Leo Chauliac Orchestra
The Best Of The Beatles
CONCERT HALL SVS2571. Released: Unconfirmed.

Penny Lane; Yes It Is; Ticket To Ride; Yesterday; Eleanor Rigby; You've Got To Hide Your Love Away; I Don't Want To Spoil The Party; She's Leaving Home; A Day In The Life; Norwegian Wood; Here, There And Everywhere; Fool On The Hill.

The music: This is a strange one. Wordless vocals appear (in a doo dah dah dah way) but this is really about the quality of the orchestrations and the arrangements, which seem to build to a full orchestral sound from a string quartet set up. The choice of songs is also quite novel making this album nothing short of intriguing. Certainly, in isolation the versions of I Don't Want To Spoil The Party, A Day in The Life, Yes It Is and You've Got To Hide Your Love Away all sound palatable, filled with emotive flurries and dark major chords.

The sleeve: Classic Englishness with four bowler hats set up on brollies on the beach and some psychedelic writing over a gloriously pink background.

The sleevenotes: "The Beatles group is one of the most remarkable phenomena for many years. John Lennon, Paul McCartney and George Harrison first played together as members of a youthful skiffle group in 1956 and for four years they played in clubs, public houses and small halls in their native Liverpool. In 1960 they were chosen to support Johnny Gentle on a tour of Scotland and later in the year they played at a Hamburg nightclub. Back in Liverpool they first appeared as The Beatles in the Town Hall of one of the City's suburbs and were received with wild enthusiasm.

"The inevitable question of what it is that distinguishes The Beatles from their rivals and imitators is not easy to answer... It is a combination of factors and different views as to their relative importance. I for one respect their skill at projecting a cheerful friendliness and offbeat humour and the cleverness with which these characteristics are exploited by Paul and John who write their songs and who have never been content to rest on their laurels.

"In their earlier songs melody is the predominant feature but in the later songs harmony assumes a much greater importance. Moreover Lennon and McCartney have acquired an almost uncanny flair for matching with their music the many moods, wit, fantasy and compassion, rollicking humour of their lyrics."

Classic Beatles cut: You've Got To Hide Your Love Away and A Day In The Life are both remarkable to say the least.

The Johnny Dunne Singers
Goodbye Beatles
STEREO PLUS 3 STR 005.
Released: 1973.

All You Need Is Love; Eleanor Rigby; Day Tripper; Yesterday; She Loves You; It's A Hard Day's Night; And I Love Her; Can't Buy Me Love; All My Lovin'; Lady Madonna; No Reply; I Saw Her Standing There; I Want To Hold Your Hand; Hey Jude; Penny Lane; With A Little Help From My Friends; Yellow Submarine; Obladee Obladaa (sic); Let It Be, Ticket To Ride; Do You Want To Know A Secret; Hello Goodbye; Get Back; Michelle; Please Please Me; The Fool On The Hill; We Can Work It Out; The Ballad Of John And Yoko.

The music: The Johnny Dunne Singers deserve a medal for ingenuity. And creativity. Their clipped versions of 28 Beatles' tunes cuts out all the fat and, because of their undoubtedly lower than low budget, Johnny and his fellow crooners sing or impersonate any of the missing instruments that they couldn't afford. The end result is undeniably strange and disconcerting, to the point of utter nonsense on Eleanor Rigby. Elsewhere the drummer goes completely apeshit, especially on the likes of She Loves You where he sets off at such a pace that the Singers turn purple trying to keep up.

The sleeve: Groovy '70s stuff with pencil drawings filled out with a dab of water colour and a compass motif that points to North Pole John, Eastern Paul, Western George and Southerly Ringo. Why? Who knows?

The sleevenotes: Sadly Johnny didn't take it upon himself to explain why he did this album in all its false finger-popping grooviness.

Classic Beatles cut: And I Love Her with its bapbadabada-baps is awesomely odd, especially the falsetto screech midway through. All You Need Is Love is simply unreal and the crazy Gospel and horn-powered choruses of Lady Madonna are just wild.

Elena Duran And Stephane Grapelli

Norwegian Wood
RCA RECORDS. Released: 1981

Yesterday; All My Loving; Eleanor Rigby; Norwegian Wood; Can't Buy Me Love; Here, There And Everywhere; Michelle, Hey Jude; The Long And Winding Road; A Hard Day's Night.

The music: With Laurie Holloway on piano and taking on the job of arranging these Beatles' songs, Norwegian Wood is a quite complex reading of Beatles' material played out by Elena Duran on flute and Stephane Grapelli on violin. The two instruments, of course, compliment each other but in Holloway's arrangements there is room for some discordant play-offs and a host of seemingly irreverent time-changes that herald the arrival of classical middle-eights, jazz rolls and all manner of left-field "riffing".

The sleeve: A Magritte styled wooden apple on a backdrop of a cloudy sky hints at the surreal nature of what might go on.

The sleevenotes: Apart from two mentions about Holloway's role as arranger, he's also credited with "A musical appreciation" of The Beatles on the cover. That said, he does introduce some interesting tangential routes for the duo to head down without ever railroading the songs.

Classic Beatles cut: The title track has an austere Brubeck-styled piano rhythm to it which makes it quite entertaining but the key elements inevitably come from Grapelli as he floats in to add some swing whenever he can.

Louis Van Dyke

Plays Lennon-McCartney
CBS RECORDS S 63946. Released: 1970

Golden Slumbers/Carry That Weight; She's Leaving Home; For No One; Eleanor Rigby; Lucy In The Sky With Diamonds; Hey Jude; Goodnight; Blackbird; Nowhere Man.

The music: It's Louis live. Well as live as you can get on a Flentop Organ in the Netherlands Reform Church at Leonen a d Vecht. Wild stuff as the stops are all pulled out for a colossal blast of Beatles mayhem. Actually, there's a lingering soulfulness in the run-filled crescendos of these songs and the brooding tones of such a huge bellowing organ gives the likes of Eleanor Rigby real power. Ah yes, the psychedelic hues of Lucy In The Sky With Diamonds reverberate with real glee - any aspiring Keith Emerson would probably have tears in their eyes.

The sleeve: Louis VD is in situ in his church of choice, flecked slub-woven mod jacket, cravat and bad haircut all in evidence. No sign of Beatlesesque paraphernalia anywhere.

The sleevenotes: "This is not just another recording of Lennon and McCartney songs - it is a project that by its very dimension and unique conception immediately fitted the enthusiasm of all concerned with the production. When John Vis approached Louis to make an album of Lennon and McCartney music played on a church organ he was completely carried away.

"When choosing the songs for this album Louis and Jon were struck by their strong relationship to classical music and old church music, in a harmonic as well as a melodic sense.

"Golden Slumbers and Carry That Weight come from The Beatles' Abbey Road LP where they are companion pieces. Louis has conceived them here with a musical unity. She's Leaving Home, one of the most moving melodies from Sgt Pepper has become a two-part cantilene, whereas For No One has been transmuted into the trio-sonata form. In his performance of Eleanor Rigby from Revolver Louis has followed the procedure of the fugue. The initial section is followed by a further exposition, which develops, into a distinct statement of the tune's second theme. The third section is an improvised cadenza winding up with a re-statement of the main theme and a radiant major chord in the coda. As you listen you will rediscover these well-known songs and admire Louis superb performance as an organist and as a creative musician.

Classic Beatles cut: The indecipherable Nowhere Man which sounds like one of those modern Methodist hymns where it's just impossible to know where the words are actually supposed to come in, not that they do.

The Percy Faith Strings

The Beatles Album
COLUMBIA RECORDS C 30097

Let It Be; Here, There And Everywhere; Norwegian Wood; Michelle; The Ballad Of John And Yoko; Something; Eleanor Rigby; Because; Lucy In The Sky With Diamonds; Yesterday; The Fool On The Hill.

The music: It's grand, it's spacious, it's layered with strings - in fact, it does exactly what it says on the sleeve. The pomposity and pace doesn't really help the songs and if the fugue style on Let It Be is disturbing then the clicketty click of Norwegian Wood is simply frightening. Mind you, Michelle with its muted trumpet break has everything a ballroom smooch could require and the pizzicato delivery of The Ballad Of John And Yoko reaches surreal territory.

The sleeve: Cool front cover artwork, with the Fabs as silhouetted blue sky with clouds set against a field of late flowering oil rape. Intriguing.

The sleevenotes: "The Percy Faith Strings born a dozen years ago in a golden and inevitable album we called Bouquet, are, indeed the essence of the Percy Faith writing. In four wedges of first and second violins, violas and cellos, 48 of the finest string players in the world spread out from the podium like four exquisite ribs in a delicate fan of sound - a Beatle ballad as familiar as a friend woven into counter melodies so precisely right that they too sound familiar. Then, the startling individuality of a flugel horn, an alto sax, a trombone or a flute appears warm and confidential, then disappears into the flowing strings. Percy Faith, the composer, arranger, conductor, distils in this orchestra the complimentary talents, from which, for him, are best expressed by the bows of a family of strings.

"The songs of The Beatles which play for strings was the criterion. The most memorable and meaningful compositions of the past decade of important music are the program. To some these performances simply reinforce what they have always known - that these songs are beautiful. To some others this new and flattering expression of the songs brings, at last, the new realisation."

Well, Percy's sleeve is nothing short of self-congratulatory. You'd think The Beatles were just a bunch of chancers until he came along. The sleevenotes also show a great command of English into Gibberish.

Classic Beatles cut: The closing sub-Latin stab at Fool On The Hill is plainly set to unnerve listeners and the glorious battle which takes place on The Ballad Of John And Yoko will send most into apoplexy.

Jose Feliciano

Sings And Plays The Beatles
RCA LC 0316. Released: 1985.

Hey Jude; Norwegian Wood; Blackbird; Yesterday; She Came In Through The Bathroom Window; Here, There And Everywhere; Help!; She's A Woman; Let It Be; Lady Madonna; In My Life; And I Love Her; A Day In The Life.

The music: You've got to hand it to Jose Felciano, the shades-wearing be-beatniked crooner with a wonderfully slovenly Flamenco style and a hammered delivery, is undoubtedly cool. His style revolves around double-taking the vocal in a soulful style that dips around the main melody and it fits The Beatles' songs perfectly.

His big hit was a version of The Doors' Light My Fire and throughout his career he's slugged on The Beatles and made their music into driving, quite personal anthems. Those songs are gathered together here and when he sings they whoop with a wild abandon that's incredibly infectious. Sadly, half of the cuts are instrumentals, though. That said, even they have a refined charm. But, when he does get around to belting out Hey Jude, Day Tripper and even A Day In The Life, it's just magic.

The sleeve: A very strange shoulder-length hair version of Jose - no shades with a bit of a flowery demeanour.

The sleevenotes: "We all owe a debt of gratitude to Paul McCartney and John Lennon. Although it's pretty commonplace nowadays to mention the name Beatles to youngsters in their early teens and get a blank look of incomprehension or rejoinders like 'What?', the two songwriting Beatles provided us with a wealth of music and lyrics which will endure down through the decades just as the forerunners such as Jerome Kern, George Gershwin and Cole Porter did long before they were born. The Lennon-McCartney song treasury has the intrinsic, durable worth of melody and meaning that invests the songs with the well-merited status of standards, recognised and appreciated in all parts of the world well over a decade after the Liverpudlian foursome which originally recorded them disbanded."

Classic Beatles cut: A Day In The Life with it's mad scene-setting changes accentuated by Jose's crazed and manic strum.

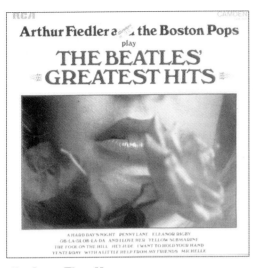

Arthur Fiedler And The Boston Pops

The Beatles Greatest Hits

CAMDEN CDS 1143. Released: 1971.
RCA INTERNATIONAL INTS 1165. Released: 1971.

Eleanor Rigby; And I Love Her; Ob-La-Di, Ob-La-Da; Hey Jude; With A Little Help From My Friends; Yellow Submarine; I Want To Hold Your Hand; Penny Lane; A Hard Day's Night; The Fool On The Hill; Yesterday; Michelle.

The music: Pomp and circumstance rule. Marching drums and intense harmonic sub-patterns surround the main melody lines here and we should all be thankful for it - well, almost. Trumpets hrumph, brass expands and tubs are thumped to propel the proceedings. Ob-La-Di, in particular, is given a real military send-off. As ever, with such a grandiose level of orchestration any solos are handled by about a dozen players and the feeling that the whole affair has been wrapped in cotton wool pervades.

The sleeves: The Camden version features pouting lips, while the RCA version has a flower power illustration of Fiedler.

The sleevenotes: "Musically, Arthur Fiedler likes to be "where it's at". In the winter of 1963 Liverpool was the place, and Mr Fiedler was there. He was conducting concerts with the Royal Philharmonic, and intrigued by the overnight popularity of the Mersey Sound, he spent some time in hearing and absorbing the local groups. As a musician he was both amazed and pleased that this music was achieving the significant goal of bringing youngsters together, causing them to participate and enjoy.

"When he returned to Boston, Mr Fiedler decided to adopt the Mersey Sound for his orchestra. He started at the top: a symphonic arrangement of I Want To Hold Your Hand the fantastically successful hit by Liverpool's most distinguished alumni: the Beatles. This became one of the most popular Boston pops encores, and their subsequent recording itself invaded the best-seller charts.

"Five years have passed, and aside from the fact that almost every male wears his hair just a little longer, it is generally accepted that The Beatles compose terrific tunes."

Classic Beatles cut: Yellow Submarine with all its drum rolls and distant xylophones is the brass band interpretation that just doesn't have enough oompah. However, there are some wandering trombones and they certainly beggar belief.

Dr Fink And The Mystery Band

Hooked On The Beatles

K-TEL ECD3227. Released: 1992.
EMPORIO EMPRCD831. Released: 1998

Please Me: Please Please Me; All My Loving; Eight Days A Week; Can't Buy Me Love. Help Me: Help!; Ticket To Ride; Day Tripper; Paperback Writer; Got To Get You Into My Life. Drive Me: Lady Madonna; Drive My Car; Nowhere Man; Taxman; Eleanor Rigby. The Tribute: Sgt Pepper's Lonely Hearts Club Band; Lucy In The Sky With Diamonds; Magical Mystery Tour; I Am The Walrus; Strawberry Fields Forever. The Window: Ob-La-Di, Ob-La-Da; Get Back; Back In The USSR; Polythene Pam; She Came In Through The Bathroom Window. The End: If I Fell; Michelle; Yesterday; Blackbird; Hey Jude; The End.

The music: Clumsily segued medleys delivered in best working men's club style from these drum-machine powered Americans. Gritty Lennonisms are well in evidence, but those pedestrian rhythms are overwhelming and proceedings are severely damp-squibbed by them. The medley entitled The Tribute, however, is madness personified, with an awful uptempo dance beat throbbing through Sgt Pepper's, which is followed by frankly worrying versions of Lucy In The Sky With Diamonds, The Magical Mystery Tour, I Am The Walrus and Strawberry Fields. It's like listening to something through a tube with a sock in your other ear. If you know what I mean.

The sleeves: The K-Tel version goes for a Sgt Pepper's-styled jacket done in computer graphics, while the Emporio version has the group in a fishing net dragged along by a yellow submarine. Crazy.

The sleevenotes: Nothing concerning The Beatles, but there is the threat of other "Hooked On" collections, including big bands, Dixie, rock 'n' roll, swing and jive. Can't wait.

Classic Beatles cut: Their version of Lucy In The Sky With Diamonds is nothing short of impressive. Well, it is actually quite a way short of impressive but you get my drift.

Guittara 3
Tributo A Los Beatles
KONGA MUSIC CSDA 216. Released: 1998.

Michelle; Penny Lane; The Long And Winding Road; When I'm 64; Get Back; Here, There And Everywhere; I Need You; Yesterday; And I Love Her; Revolution; Drive My Car; I Will; Help; Eleanor Rigby; Tomorrow; Norwegian Wood; If I Fell; From Me To You; Let It Be.

The music: Aye, caramba! Spanish guitars assault the Fabs on a heartfelt procession of their hits. Under the guidance of Pedro Javier Gonzalez fretboards rattle and aching sincerity runs rife. Probably more interesting, however, is the advance promo for the album, which features Guitarra 3 on Tribute To The Beatles Medley, a neatly-segued arrangement of Norwegian Wood, Michelle, Get Back, I Need You, Yesterday, From Me To You and Revolution just to give you a taste of what the album's about. In isolation it's just madness running amok with Spanish strumming wrapped loosely around those key tunes.
The sleeve: Great take on Abbey Road with silhouettes of The Beatles walking over the Abbey Road crossing which now takes the shape of a guitar. Spooky.
The sleevenotes: None of note.
Classic Beatle cut: The medley is great but when they begin to spar on Revolution, a Dali-esque super unreality is but a plectrum away.

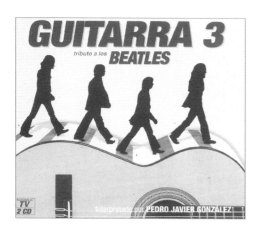

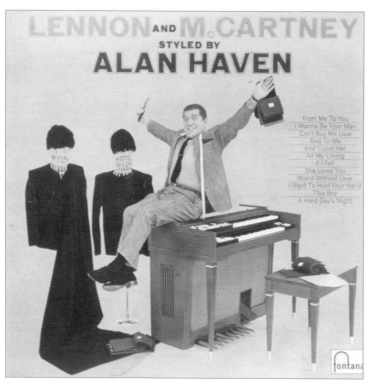

Alan Haven
Lennon And McCartney Styled By...
FONTANA TL 5232. Released: 1965.

From Me To You; I Wanna Be Your Man; Can't Buy me Love; Bad To Me; And I Love Her; All My Loving; If I Fell; She Loves You; World Without Love; I Want To Hold Your Hand; This Boy; A Hard Day's Night.

The Music: Alan Haven is probably best know for a minor hit he had with the jazz standard Image, where his swirling Lowry Heritage Organ created a formidable soundscape. And his sound remains groovy and jazzy, with flexed chords and sub-melodies scatted into every song, as he tackles The Beatles' back catalogue. A tight bass and drums pairing add power and let his fingers do the proverbial walking.

As his style, he takes The Beatles' songs on face value before straying from the main melody and switching back on it at every opportunity as octaves are changed and fills, er, fill. The sound is large and funky in a pre-funk kind of way.
The sleeve: A mad Haven sits atop his trusty organ, tailors dummies with mop top wigs on hand. He sports a pink shirt and Hush Puppies, which snazz up his be-suited appearance. Hey, cool. Daddio.
The sleevenotes: "His material for this LP lends itself well to jazz. There surely can be very few people about who do not know that John Lennon and Paul McCartney are the songwriting members of a certain quartet calling themselves The Beatles. There can surely be very few people about who insist that the songs they write are beat group ditties with no enduring qualities or balladic value. You only have to glance at the growing list of impressive star artists who are recording Lennon and McCartney songs to realise that this pair of songwriters are rapidly becoming the Rodgers and Hart of the brash and beat-laden Sixties.
Classic Beatles cut: It's got to be the multi-octaved World Without Love, which even has a drum salvo in it for good measure. Good effort Al!

The Hiltonaires
Dance To Beatles Hits
In The Glenn Miller Sound
STEREO GOLD AWARD mer 336. Released: 1971.

Moonlight Serenade; Something; I Want To Hold Your Hand; Michelle; Bird Cage Walk; Londonderry Air; Hey Jude; Let It Be; Yesterday; Diamond Rock; A Hard Day's Night.

The music: It's The Beatles on a mid-air collision with Glenn. Transmogrified through the "big band beat" of The Hiltonaires, the Beatles' catalogue is polished up and infiltrated by blasts of Moonlight Serenade and likewise. Trumpets are muted, swing is in the air and the Beatles' tunes fit snugly with the classic sound of wartime Americana. It all seems to make sense but it's damn odd though.
The sleeve: An unbelievable quartet of "hip" young ladies hold banners aloft with the complex titled spelt out. Fashion-friendly catalogue clothes are on hand. Trouser suits optional.
The sleevenotes: "Here's a dance party with two

Leaving Home; Yellow Submarine; Yesterday; Can't Buy Me Love; And I Love Her; All You Need Is Love; Eleanor Rigby; All My Loving.

The music: The Hollyridge Strings play the worst kind of easy listening, with many layers of Vaseline added to the proceedings to reduce anything they might touch to the kind of "calming" liquid sound that pre-empts dental appointments. Their take on the Beatles' songbook is spineless and almost sinister.

The sleeve: It features a speeding car going across the moors. It's probably driven by Mr Hollyridge, Stu Philips, who's being chased by The Beatles (just out of shot).

The sleevenotes: "Stu Philips and The Hollyridge Strings did the first Beatles' album ever. There have been others since, but none have come close to recreating the big Beatles' hits in instrumental versions, like the Hollyridge Strings.

"Why, you might ask, when it's a record album, is it called a songbook? That's often done when the songs are all by the same composer or songwriting team; and every song here is by John Lennon and Paul McCartney. And they were all first performed and made into tremendous hits by John, Paul, George and Ringo."

Classic Beatles cut: The flat piccolo that sounds like feedback in the middle of a particularly lacklustre Yellow Submarine almost seems exciting.

favourite ingredients - the great, nostalgic sounds of Glenn Miller and hit songs by The Beatles.

"These sweet and swinging arrangements were written by Bill Holcombe (an old Tommy Dorsey sideman), who has taken these British-bred hits and written the inimitable Glenn Miller style around them.

"The Hiltonaires under the baton of Stan Reynolds are joined by the vocal stylings (a la Modernaires) of Tony Mansell and his group.

"Here's the big band beat at its best with familiar hit songs."

Classic Beatles cut: As Moonlight Serenade melds into Something, you click right away what the Hiltonaires bag is. But the flow of tuneful-

ness sounds more and more like the background you'd encounter while waiting at the pearly gates, before the light finally dims and oblivion beckons. Maybe I'm reading too much into this but there's an eerie none-earthliness about the Glenn Miller sound even when it's riddled with Beatles' irony.

The Hollyridge Strings

Exciting Instrumentals
From The Beatles Songbook
MUSIC FOR PLEASURE MFP 5247. Released: 1968.

I Want To Hold Your Hand; Michelle; A Hard Day's Night; Norwegian Wood; She's

The Hollyridge Strings

The Beatles Music Best 12

MUSIC JOY CDW 10006. Released: Unknown.

Let It Be; Hey Jude; The Long And Winding Road; Yesterday; Sergeant pepper's Lonely Hearts Club Band; Michelle; I Want To Hold Your Hand; Please Please Me; She Loves You; All My Loving; Can't Buy Me Love; Yellow Submarine.

The Music: It's The Hollyridge Strings again. They need no introduction for their silkily orchestrated versions of Beatles' songs. However, this Japanese issue explains a lot about how Japanese pop has returned to the west in the intervening years since its release. The sound is a strange mixture of musical styles, with a filmic edge and cascading violins that sound like they're, in places, direct from some kung fu epic, especially on Please Please Me. If this is the only way that people in Japan could access The Beatles' music then no wonder their indigenous pop music is so strange.

The Sleeve: A naff play in the Apple motif.

The sleevenotes: In Japanese. Crikey.

Classic Beatles cut: Please Please Me takes some beating for its sharp as a knife string slashes.

Just no-one claiming this?

Salute The Beatles

HALLMARK 302982. Released: 1995

She Loves You; Eleanor Rigby; Eight Days A Week; Michelle; I Feel Fine; When I'm 64; Lady Madonna;

The Ballad Of John And Yoko; A Hard Day's Night; Let It Be; Help!; Do You Want To Know A Secret; From Me To You; Can't Buy Me Love; Norwegian Wood; Twist And Shout; Love Me Do; We Can Work It Out; Yesterday; Hey Jude.

The music: Poor versions of Beatles songs from various periods, played out on synthesised strings, tinny guitars and with some piss-poor vocals. I'm sure these people are very talented (although they don't give their names and they don't attempt to prove it here), but it must be soul-destroying for anyone performing 52 minutes and 29 seconds of material by someone else and trying to mimic their style, arrangements and presentation. There again, it's pretty painful for the listener too.

The sleeve: It reveals little other than telling you that Hallmark have actually attempted simple GBH of the earhole in reggae and Wurlitzer organ styles elsewhere.

Classic Beatles cut: Oh, come on now.

The King's Singers

The Beatles Connection

EMI DIGITAL CDC 7 49556 2. Released: 1986

Penny Lane; Mother Nature's Son; Ob-La-Di, Ob-La-Da; And I Love Her; Help!; Yesterday; A Hard Day's Night; Girl; Got To Get You Into My Life; Back In The USSR; Eleanor Rigby; Blackbird; Lady Madonna; I'll Follow The Sun; Honey Pie; Can't Buy Me Love; Michelle; You've Got To Hide Your Love Away; I Want To Hold Your Hand.

THE BEATLES MUSIC BEST 12

STEREO CDW-10006

THE HOLLYRIDGE STRINGS

ARRANGED AND CONDUCTED BY STU PHILLIPS

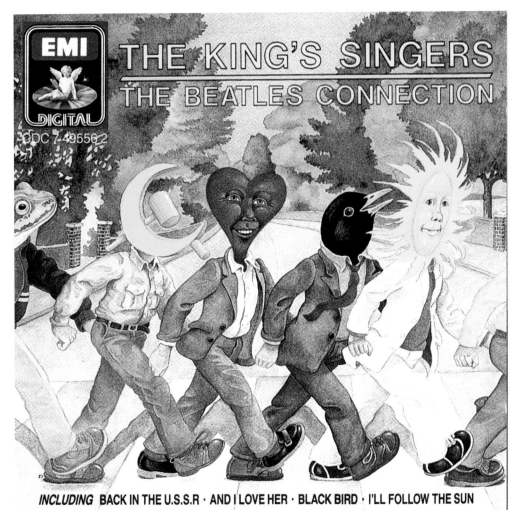

THE KING'S SINGERS — THE BEATLES CONNECTION

EMI DIGITAL CDC 7495562

INCLUDING BACK IN THE U.S.S.R · AND I LOVE HER · BLACK BIRD · I'LL FOLLOW THE SUN

The music: At a strange crossroads where choral, barber shop and the Salvation Army meet, The King's Singers rattle through a gaggle of Beatles' songs in a clean cut, precise and very intricate way. It's extremely disturbing.

The sleeve: Even moreso. It's the Abbey Road scene played out again but the cartoon figures crossing the road are a sunflower, a hammer and sickle, a heart, a frog and what might be a tadpole. It's weird. None of them have bare feet.

The sleevenotes: "It was 20 years ago today that the King's Singers were six young men, recently Oxbridge choral scholars, now at the start of their professional lives. The Beatles had become world-famous and were well on the way to breaking up. In those days the world and his dog

were recording Lennon and McCartney songs, and the King's Singers were no exception. Indeed, they went one better, their first album was produced by George Martin, who also arranged She's Leaving Home especially for them.

"The recordings here feature the King's Singers alone with no backing musicians, just some sampling and multi-tracking.

Classic Beatles cut: The sleeve also blows a trumpet for Back In The USSR where Robert Chilcott turns in a "Shouting rock 'n' roll vocal of a quality not heard since Buddy Holly". It's a strange one. Set to a backdrop of Georgia On My Mind (Georgia in the USSR-geddit), the song is delivered in best Sha Na Na style with a lead vocal that's all heart. Yuk!

The Kopykats

The Beatles Best

FONTANASFL13052-3. Released: 1968.

*You Can't Do That; Little Child; All My Lovin';
Eight Days A week; I'll Follow The Sun; Long Tall
Sally; I Feel Fine; A Hard Day's Night; The Things
We Said Today; I'm A Loser; I Saw Her Standing
There; Roll Over Beethoven; Nowhere Man;
Norwegian Wood; We Can Work It Out; Yesterday;
I'm Looking Through You; Help!; You've Got To
Hide Your Love Away; Ticket To Rise; I'm Down;
Dizzy Miss Lizzy; Please Mr Postman.*

The music: 'The Beatles Best Done By The Koppykats' boasts the sleeve and, without doubt, this mid-'60s homage is in line with The Bootleg Beatles and any other fab pretender on the pub and club circuit today. The Koppykats, for their time, were a good time pick-up band who probably paraded their talents in the same clubs that The Beatles had frequented much earlier. Their presentation and delivery is adequate without ever becoming compulsive and the end result chugs along very much like The Beatles might have had they not had any spark of creativity. It's all here, Lennon's aggressive vocal, Macca's sense of melody and harmony, George's stinging guitar and Ringo's rock hard rhythm. The Koppykats are just about OK whereas The Beatles reached a point where they could enliven any song they touched. What purpose this album serves is hard to say, still the sleeve's funny.

The sleeve: A superb selection of be-tousled hairdresser heads, very Ruud Gullit.

The sleevenotes: "In pop parlance, the years preceding 1962 have the letters BB before them, denoting "before The Beatles". Eventually there will be another definition AB, giving chronological calculations of events and happenings "after The Beatles", but this latter description is most unlikely to come into use for some considerable time yet.

"Every decade seems to produce a major and widely influential factor in pop music. For instance, the 1950's saw the rise of rock 'n' roll and Elvis Presley, who is still very much around today, even though he has graduated to different things during the interim period. The Beatle era dawned in the early 1960's, and it marked the beginning of a dramatic new force in pop

Record 1 Side 1	Side 2	Record 2 Side 1	Side 2
YOU CAN'T DO THAT	I FEEL FINE	NOWHERE MAN	HELP!
LITTLE CHILD	A HARD DAY'S NIGHT	NORWEGIAN WOOD	YOU'VE GOT TO HIDE
ALL MY LOVIN'	THE THINGS WE SAID	WE CAN WORK IT OUT	YOUR LOVE AWAY
EIGHT DAYS A WEEK	TODAY	YESTERDAY	TICKET TO RIDE
I'LL FOLLOW THE SUN	I'M A LOSER	I'M LOOKING THROUGH	I'M DOWN
LONG TALL SALLY	I SAW HER STANDING	YOU	DIZZY MISS LIZZY
	THERE		PLEASE MR. POSTMAN
	ROLL OVER BEETHOVEN		

music which will never be eradicated or forgotten long after the four Liverpudlian pioneers are senior citizens, retired and resting on their laurels and royalties.

"It is not easy to pinpoint one specific reason for the world-wide success and fame that surround John, Paul, George and Ringo, and makes their every thought, word and deed headline news in 1968, six years after they burst onto the scene with Love Me Do and the number one Please Please Me. Their appearance and personalities obviously play a large and important role in their appeal. Each member of the quartet is a distinct and individual character, and yet collectively they cohere into a composite and complete entity that strikes responsive chords in the hearts and minds of millions of all age groups all over the world.

"This double album of their work features The Koppykats, and was recorded on the continent.

As their name implies, the group claims no pretensions of presenting these Beatle ballads in a novel and different way, and indeed there would be no point in futile attempts to improve on material that has already conclusively proved itself to be the best. Instead they offer a sincere tribute to John, Paul, George and Ringo with 23 performances that capture The Beatles' best in the worthiest and most worthwhile way."

Classic Beatles cut: It's got to be the cover.

Laibach

Let It Be
MUTE RECORDS CD STUMM 58. Released: 1988.

Get Back; Two Of Us; Dig A Pony; I Me Mine; Across The Universe; Dig It; I've Got A Feeling; The Long And Winding Road; One After 909; For You Blue; Maggie Mae.

The music: Yugoslav art activists Laibach had embraced gothic horror, strange instrumentation and industrial austerity before moving swiftly into opera and other suitably austere genres when they hit upon the cover version. First of all they released a mere six versions of The Rolling Stones' Sympathy For The Devil - crazy guys - then they turned their attention to The Beatles.

Having already become legendary in their homeland, they toured Occupied Europe as they called it, visiting both sides of the Iron Curtain, and toyed with enough dodgy imagery to gain a huge cult following. And The Beatles? Well, why not cover the whole of Let It Be, except for the title track? Why not indeed.

The result is a bruising, almost frightening vision of the dark underbelly of pop music. Bending and cajoling the classic Lennon and McCartney melodies into bizarre Hitchcockian experiments. The result is haunting. Exhausting. Quite staggering.

The sleeve: A political woodcut of the quartet delivered with the vaguest of nods to the Fabs' Let It Be cover. The inside contains portraits of the Four Horsemen Of The Apocalypse. Whether this is a reference to The Beatles is unknown.

The sleevenotes: None.

Classic Beatles cut: I Me Mine takes some beating, sounding like it was dragged out of an expiring corpse after too long on the Domestos.

James Last

Plays The Greatest Songs Of John Lennon, Paul McCartney, Ringo Starr and George Harrison

POLYDOR POLD 5119. Released: 1983 (Now on German CD 815 691-2 as James Last spielt die grossten Songs Von The Beatles)

Eleanor Rigby; A Hard Day's Night; Let It Be; Penny Lane; She Loves You; Michelle; Ob-La-Di, Ob-La-Da; Hey Jude; Lady Madonna; All You Need Is Love; Norwegian Wood; Yesterday

The music: Wild synth swirls and a trace of an Indian bell open an album that's packed with sincere strings and all the Teutonic precision that you'd expect from a James Last recording. Amid the rigorous rhythms are lead breaks that are handled with mountains of emotional vibrato, whether they're courtesy of James's French horn player, a woodwind honcho or a passing violinist. Last's style revolves around dramatic melodic patterns and obviously there's no shortage of those in The Beatles' repertoire. Tightly-edited sub-melodies also drive the momentum and apart from some questionable "disco" rhythms the whole songbook is handled with some degree of affection. Most of it works remarkably well, but there are moments, like on A Hard Day's Night when the music is reduced to the kind of tinny backdrop you might hear accompanying ice-skating, immediately felling Last's lofty reputation with one wave of the baton.

The sleeve: It's James in a white suit, no mop top is evident.

The sleevenotes: None.

Classic Beatles cut: Undoubtedly the expectation that the synth-powered opening at the very start of the album is going to waft the listener to Beatlesesque plains anew is short lived. Sadly Eleanor Rigby fails to ignite into an Emerson, Lake And Palmer, Donna Summer or indeed Klaus Schulze experience but, for a fleeting moment you can dream.

Syd Lawrence

McCartney - His Music And Me

PHILIPS 9109 221. Released: 1978.

My Love; You Gave Me The Answer; Let's Love; When I'm 64; Love In Song; Live And Let Die; Yesterday; Honey Pie; The Long And Winding Road; Silly Love Songs; Mull Of Kintyre; Hi Hi Hi.

The music: It's Syd's big band, in his accustomed Glenn Miller-approved style, playing his favourite McCartney-penned tunes. Melodies remain heartily intact as strings float by and brass is given every opportunity to toot at will. In Beatles' terms, side one's When I'm 64 is joined by Yesterday, Honey Pie and The Long And Winding Road which open side two, elsewhere it's Macca's solo stuff which blends better with Syd's muse but as such remains uninspiring. Of The Beatles' cuts Yesterday and The Long And Winding Road are both slow and sombre, while Honey Pie attempts to single-handedly cut a rug, only tripping at the last on an unseen curtain pole.

The sleeve: Very poor graphics with a picture of Syd in a Miller-styled bandstand typeface farrago.

The sleevenotes: "The oldest of the songs on the album is the Vaudevillian When I'm 64, initially vamped out on a piano by a 16-year-old McCartney. 'I thought it might come in useful for a musical comedy or something,' said Paul later.

"The equally amusing Honey Pie, with its shades of the Charleston chasers, hails from the Beatles' White Album and The Long And Winding Road is also a product of McCartney's stint as a member of the Mersey moptops. Last of the Fab four melodies included here is Yesterday which, like all the Beatle songs, has the credit Lennon and McCartney, though it was entirely written by Paul. 'Yeah, Paul did that one.' Lennon revealed to Record Mirror. 'And it's a good 'un.'."

Classic Beatles cut: Well, there isn't one. It's all pretty mediocre until Syd attempts to include a funky guitar and a three-piece female harmony on Silly Love Songs. The result is frightening, an engaging advert for the importance of the generation gap.

The Vic Lewis Orchestra
Plays Songs Of The Beatles
DJM RECORDS DJSL030. Released: 1973

Eleanor Rigby; Blackbird; She's Leaving Home; Julia; Fool On The Hill; I Will; Norwegian Wood; Yesterday; Goodnight; Strawberry Fields Forever.

The music: The Vic Lewis Orchestra have a kind of dramatic flair that would suit a movie score. They add real gravitas to some of the well-worn Beatles' melodies, giving the whole proceedings a suitably off-kilter bravado that perhaps some of the tunes don't fit into. That said, their arrangement of Eleanor Rigby and, indeed, Strawberry Fields have all the ingredients of a B-movie trailer. It all goes a touch downhill when the singers arrive but, for the most part, Vic has some personality which he impresses on the songs wherever physically possible.

The sleeve: With a candid black and white picture of the Liver building in stark loneliness, it's hardly an upbeat and inviting sight.

The sleevenotes: None to speak of.

Classic Beatles cut: The slower, more orchestrally-suited songs fare best here - Eleanor Rigby, Fool On The Hill and Norwegian Wood are all bowed with some drama.

The Liverpools
Beatle Mania In The USA
WYNCOTE W9001. Released: 1964.

She Love You; I Want To Hold Your Hand; I Saw Her Standing There; Please Please Me (plus six "originals")

The music: Carbon copies of four Beatles' songs from a group who struggle hap-hazardly in the harmony department plus half a dozen self-penned items. The Liverpools' own material mixes the oohs and aaahs of the Fabs, borrows a few rhythms and glues them unsatisfactorily to some rock 'n' roll leftovers.

The sleeve: Mop top illustrations on the front and some ridiculous sleevenotes on the back.

The sleevenotes: "Imitation is the sincerest form of flattery! To the question, "will flattery get us anything?" - Wyncote replies, "flattery, in this instance, will garner amusement, bangs, pun intended (and a lot of kicks).

"Four liver-uppers have pooled their talents to present a "model" album. Since a "model", in the true sense of the word, is a good imitation of the real thing, this album, then, is a perfect model. Having this objective. The Liverpools, in making this LP, restricted themselves to the songs, style and beat that already have proven successful. Nothing succeeds like success and since the English and the Americans share and enjoy like-tastes, Wyncote hopes that this model album will also share in the great success of the original.

"Rag Mop, Rag Mop, would have given a more vivid picture as to why the original group swept America as England with such a dynamic sweep. So, with a sweeping gesture on confidence, Wyncote presents The Liverpools skillfully cutting the (h)airs which have tickled so many."

Classic Beatles cut: She Love You's powerhouse harmonies and rising key completely stumps The Liverpools. They prove that their forte is more akin to the hot rod groove of their own Chuck's Monster (which adds ooh and aahs to keep it Beatlesy), or even the Monkees-phrased precursor Whenever I'm Feelin' Low.

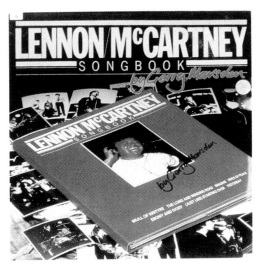

Gerry Marsden

The Lennon/McCartney Songbook
K-TEL ONE 1274. Released: 1985.

Mull Of Kintyre; The Long And Winding Road; Woman; It's For You; You've Got To Hide Your Love Away; With A little Luck; Imagine; Pipes Of Peace; Ebony And Ivory; Silly Love Songs; Let It Be; The Fool On The Hill; My Love; (Just Like) Starting Over; Love; Yesterday.

The music: It's criminal in places. OK. Gerry was Gerry and he had the Pacemakers and a nice suit. And he had hits. And he's from Liverpool, but what he does to John Lennon's Woman will have the man spinning in his grave. It's soul-less, turgid nonsense from a pick-up band that sound like they don't know the song.

In fact, the backing sounds like A Flock Of Seagulls at times. Very electronic. Totally heartless. And Gerry in turn stumbles over his words, gets thespian, loses it. There's a choir of schoolkids on You've Got To Hide Your Love Away where an already sinking ship reaches new depths of awfulness.

The sleeve: Lots of black and whites of The Beatles and a book with Gerry singing in the studio as the cover pic tossed on top of them. Pretty naff really and not a good indication of what lurks within.

The sleevenotes: "Gerry Marsden and I go back a couple of years together. Many's the time we have met while humping our equipment into the back entrance of a club, ballroom or theatre. It was no surprise to us when Gerry, his brother

Fred, and the rest of the group became so successful in the '60s. We had heard their music in places like the Cavern and we knew how Gerry could get a crowd going.

"In Liverpool his group was probably the biggest competition to The Beatles and I remember all too well sweating the outcome of our local music paper popularity poll, hoping that we could scrape together enough points to beat their band. That's how close it was!

"Anyway, that's enough chat, so sit back, get yourself comfy and listen to the luscious larynx of the lad himself. One more time Gerard!"

Classic Beatles cut: There's nothing luscious here. Even the really bad renditions are too embarrassing to be kitsch.

The George Martin Orchestra

Off The Beatle Track
PARLOPHONE PCS 3057. Released: 1964.
SEE FOR MILES CM 101. Reissued: 1982.

All My Loving; Don't Bother Me; Can't Buy Me Love; All I've Got To Do; I Saw Her Standing There; She Loves You; From Me To You; There's A Place; This Boy; Please Please Me; Little Child; I Want To Hold Your Hand.

The music: It's lo-fi and quite startling. Surely this can't be the man who guided The Beatles into the living rooms of millions. Here he delivers insipid orchestrations that lack any kind of dynamics. Released back in 1964, probably under the misapprehension that the four piece group concept would be short lived, it falls back on George Martin's arranging skills and his appeal to an older and more conservative clientele. In terms of

Beatles-lite it is undoubtedly the toppermost of the poppermost but if you do find it appealing I would consult a surgeon at your first opportunity.

The sleeve: Nice pix of him with them.

The sleevenotes, prepared by John Lennon: "George Martin is a tall man. He is also a musician with short hair. In spite of this he records rock groups such as The Beatles, Billy J Kramer, Gerry And The Pacemakers to name but four, and has earned the respect of everyone in the business (what business you might well ask).

"We all owe a great deal of our success to George, especially for his patient guidance of our enthusiasm in the right directions.

"Us Beatles are genuinely flattered that a 'real musician' as we call him should turn his talents to arranging an LP of our songs, considering that he previously worked with such great artists as Peter Sellers, Shirley Bassey, Jimmy Shand and a machine that sings Daisy Daisy.

"Tell all your friends to buy this album too, so George can be rich and famous - after all, why not?"

Classic Beatles cut: It's all pretty tawdry to be honest.

The Moonlight String Orchestra

Plays The Music Of The Beatles
MUSIC DIGITAL CD 6198. Released: 1999.

Penny Lane; I Feel Fine; Love Me Do; Here, There And Everywhere; Eleanor Rigby; A Hard Day's Night; She's Leaving Home; With A Little Help From My Friends; Can't Buy Me Love; I'll Follow The Sun; In My Life; And I Love Her; This Boy; Yellow Submarine.

The music: It's a flute frenzy on Penny Lane, before the brass salvo that infiltrates most of this album lets rip. Actually, it's all just so much synthetic bravura. Lost in the polyphonic wilderness the Moonlight people struggle to get into the right key, mixing woodwind sounds with pizzicato strings. It's a mess.
The sleeve: Simply the Beatles' instruments on a white background.
The sleevenotes: None to shake a stick at.
Classic Beatles cut: The oddest cut of all is their version of In My Life, which is delivered in the style of Hank Marvin but, reduced to a lonely synth as a climax, the result is a touch boring.

Murphy's Law

Beatles Karaoke Party
CASTLE COMMUNICATIONS MAC CD375.
Released: 1998.

Twist 'n' Shout; She Loves You; With A Little Help From My Friends; I Saw Her Standing There; Yesterday; You've Got To Hide Your Love Away;
Ob-La-Di, Ob-La-Da; If I Fell; All You Need Is Love; Yellow Submarine; Imagine; Medley: Please Please Me/I Feel Fine/ Get Back/Hey Jude.

The music: A proper karaoke selection that starts off with the first line and includes the harmony before continuing with the middle eight. It's quite funny really (but I don't get out much), it sounds like they got bored or forgot what they were supposed to sing as they keep coming back for a cameo ooooh or a half-baked aaah. The backing tries to mimic the Beatles' sound as much as it can, but the group involved have opted for a fuzz psyche pop noise and their added vibrato even resonates through on the ballad Yesterday. They're probably secretly Thee Headcoates.
The sleeve: Another silhouette shot of some people who could be fab.
The sleevenotes: None. And no lyrics to help you sing along.
Classic Beatles cut: It's got to be the medley, which closes the whole thing. Their homage to fuzz makes them sound like Generation X in rehearsal.

The Larry Page Orchestra And Chorus

John Paul George Ringo
PENNY FARTHING LARS 001. Released: 1973.
MUSIC CLUB MCCD255. Released: 1996.

Hi Hi Hi; My Love; Back Off Boogaloo; Imagine; C Moon; My Sweet Lord; We Can Work It out; Mind Games; You're 16; Mamunia; It Don't Come Easy;

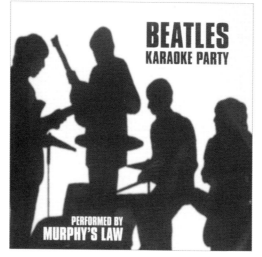

Bangla Desh; Happy Xmas War Is Over; Give Me Love; Oh My My; Instant Karma; Live And Let Die; In My Life; Bluebird; Intuition.

The music: He looks like Michael Caine circa Alfie and he has all the cheek of the man too. Larry Page is the chancer with the slacks, an expert under the covers, almost shagadelic. Here he draws together a host of solo Beatles' songs and, heralding the fact that this is the first time the quartet have been back together again on one album since they split, his James Last-styled orchestrations are rolled out. Highlighted by session vocalists who include Tony Burrows (Edison Lighthouse), Tony Rivers (Harmony Grass) and Sue and Sunny, who'd previously embellished the works of T Rex and Pink Floyd, it's a strange collection to which he adds two classic Beatles' tracks in We Can Work It Out and In My Life. The latter, he claims, is his favourite Beatles' song, but he gives it a right good seeing to, with funky keyboard, Latin percussion and a misguided arrangement which murders the melody completely.
The sleeve: It features four naff sketches of The Beatles and a staggering 33 pictures of Larry on the CD, which also has copious notes...
The original sleevenotes: "The King is dead - Long live the kings! - that surely was the cry when the Beatles disbanded. Out of the one talent have sprung four individual music sources which, to the world at large, are giving as much pleasure and to Messrs. Lennon, McCartney, Harrison and Starr, the satisfaction of doing their own thing. I have taken the opportunity of bringing the melodies of the Fabulous Four Together Again."
The CD sleevenotes: "The Beatles were, as Page still maintains, 'The best performers of their own music, without doubt. Nobody can touch what they did. What I tried to do on this record was to bring together a lot of stuff that they did as solo artists and put it on one album. I don't think that anyone else had done that at the time.'

"The selections on this tribute to The Beatles are taken from the immediate post-split era, during the early '70s, a time when the success of Ringo Starr and George Harrison all but eclipsed the solo careers of Lennon and McCartney."
Classic Beatles cut: Anyone who covers Ringo's Back Off Boogaloo is worth your attention.

THE LARRY PAGE ORCHESTRA

The LPO and Chorus Perform Imagine * We Can Work It Out * Live And Let Die
My Sweet Lord * You're Sixteen * Instant Karma * Back Off Boogaloo and many more

John
Paul
George
Ringo

MUSIC CLUB

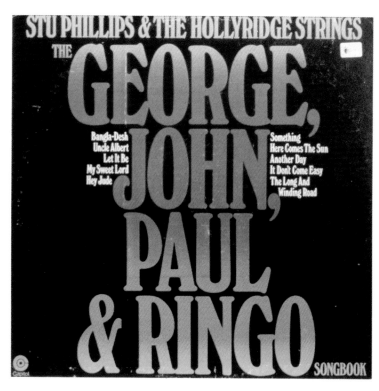

Stu Phillips And The Hollyridge Strings

The George, John, Paul And Ringo Songbook Arranged And Conducted by Stu Phillips

CAPITOL ST-839. Released: Date unknown.

Here Comes The Sun; Hey Jude; Another Day; Let It Be; The Long And Winding Road; My Sweet Lord; Uncle Albert/Admiral Halsey; Something; It Don't Come Easy; Bangla-Desh.

The music: A side of pre-split a side of post from Stu and his strings who've made a career of covering the Fabs. His strings certainly do shimmer in an uncontrollable way, like velour curtains covering up the main plot. The four diverse tracks trodden by the group when they were intact are ultimately reduced to one homogenised slush in the process. There are "interesting" bits - the interplay and strange noises on Uncle Albert/Admiral Halsey are intriguing, even it does all go awry by the second half - but for the most part it's hard work. In the end the album just stumbles on and on and even if the version of Bangla-desh is broody and a little bit "alternative", it all comes to nothing.

The sleeve: It's all type, except the flip, which features a portrait of Stu in full straggly haired mode.

The sleevenotes: "Of the many pop musicians who sprang to prominence in the Sixties, George Harrison, John Lennon, Paul McCartney and Ringo Starr (aka The Beatles)... collectively and now individually... have been the most vital, influential and durable.

"For good reason: George, John, Paul and Ringo have never stood still... They've never been predictable (and as a mark of unpredictability, Paul just recently has introduced the songwriting talents of his wife, Linda)... They've made rock something to love and respect... They've helped shape the taste of a decade... They've always been entertaining... And they've given nothing but the warmest feelings to the passing moments of an entire generation.

"Stu Phillips and his Hollyridge Strings have taken the best of G, J, P and R's recent songs - and passed on a pure, full, shimmering, unique, honest instrumental vision of the moulders of contemporary music."

Classic Beatles cut: Undoubtedly the version of Bangla-Desh.

Frank Pourcel

Meets The Beatles

STUDIO TWO TWO 371. Released: 1970

Let It Be; Help!; I Me Mine; Penny Lane; Michelle; Here, There And Everywhere; The Long And Winding Road; Eleanor Rigby; Ob-La-Di, Ob-La-Da; Don't Let Me Down; Girl; Yesterday; Goodbye.

The music: Plaintive harmonica and swirling strings add a touch of Morricone in places but perhaps the tension isn't quite what the epic soundtrack composer might have intended. But on Help! goes string crescendo bonkers with subservient organ rhythms and a turgid synth noise stretching the credulity of these arrangements to the extreme.

Amidst it all, two seldom-covered Beatles' tunes are included in I, Me, Mine and Don't Let Me Down. The former is wild. It has a Flamenco guitar solo in the middle, which appears for no apparent reason and is in a different key to the existing melody. Fantastic. The latter is a slow-paced, almost Fleetwood Mac doing Albatross-styled interpretation with a samba undertow that never really catches breath. Dreamy indeed. What were these guys on?

The sleeve: It's post-psyche Sgt Peps gone mad.

The sleevenotes: Merely listed as "orchestral stylings of Lennon-McCartney and George Harrison Songs", it also lists Frank's other efforts, including the wonderfully understated The Versatile Frank Pourcel.

Classic Beatles cut: Undoubtedly it's I, Me, Mine.

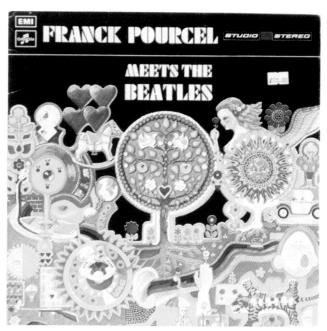

Joshua Rifkin

**The Baroque Beatles Book
Rediscovered And Edited
By Joshua Rifkin**

ELEKTRA EKS-306. Released: 1966

The Royale Beatleworks Musicke, MBE 1963 including Ouverture: I Want To Hold Your Hand; Rejouissance: I'll Cry Instead; La Paix: Things We Said Today; L'amour s'en cachant: You've Got To Hide Your Love Away; Les Plaisirs: Ticket To Ride. Epstein Variations, MBE 69A including Hold Me Tight. Last Night I Said Cantata for the Third Saturday after the Shea Stadium, MBE 58,000 including Chorus: Please Please Me; Recitative: In they came jorking; Aria: When I Was Younger, Help!; Chorale: You Know If You Break My Heart: I'll be Back. Trio Sonata: Das Kaferlein, MBE 0041/4: Grave-Allegro-Grave: Eight Days A Week; Quodlibette: She Loves You; Thank You Girl; Hard Day's Night.

The music: This is an amazing album. So the story goes, classical musicologist Joshua Rifkin was brought into the burgeoning Elektra empire in the early '60s by main man Jac Holzman. On his way to reinventing ragtime and scoring The Sting, he'd been procuring classical material for the label, when Holzman and he concocted the idea of doing Beatles songs in a classical style.

Holzman travelled to the UK, met up with the Fabs and Brian Epstein and got agreement to proceed. Rifkin then prepared a complex set of arrangements that borrowed melodies from The Beatles and compositional qualities from the varied history of classical music. The scam was set up as if it were existing found music and the album is credited to the Baroque Ensemble Of The Merseyside Kammermusikgesellschaft under conductor Joshua Rifkin.

The result is quite amazing, as classical motifs are mixed with those well known melodies to form new librettos and unique musical pieces.
The sleeve: It features three be-wigged classicists, one of whom is wearing an 'I love the Beatles' shirt.
The sleevenotes (purporting to be an original manuscript: "The Royale Beatleworks Musicke is an orchestral composition in the manner of examples by the justly famed Mr Handel and Mr Telemann. I have made use of a truly rich and full orchestra here; trumpets, drums, wind and strings (plus of course the indispensable continuo)."

The sleeve also reveals that some of the vocal libretto ideas come from Lennon's books In His Own Write and A Spaniard In The Works and the original album comes with a printed sheet featuring the conceptual lyrics for Last Night I Said, the cantata for the 3rd Saturday after Shea Stadium, MBE 58,000. Brilliant.
Classic Beatles cut: Just about all of it is great.

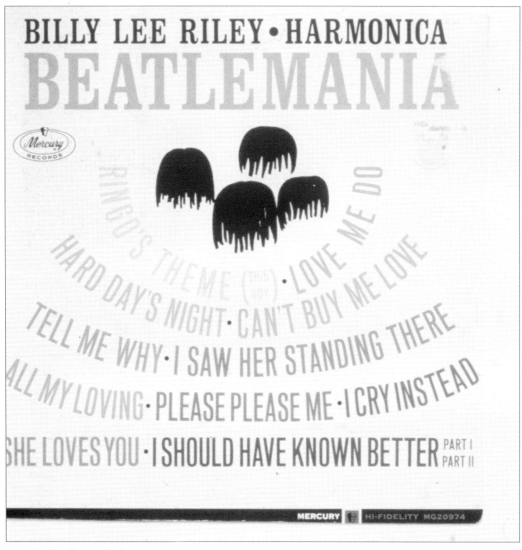

out with a tight rhythm and Tell Me Why is nothing short of, er, interesting.

The Rip Offs

Play A Golden Age Of The Beatles
STEREO GOLD AWARD MER 415. Released: 1976.

Yesterday; Hey Jude; Help!; Paperback Writer; Yellow Submarine; Get Back; Let It Be; I Want To Hold Your Hand (plus Rock Island Twist and Long Gone Woman).

The music: On the uptempo numbers, they start out like The Small Faces but seem to lose interest by the time they've reached the chorus. Then there's the two none-Lennon and McCartney songs - the turgid pub rock of Long Gone Woman and the truly dreadful Rock Island Twist which sounds like a Eurovision also ran. It's not great stuff. At all.
The sleeve: It looks cheap and tacky. And, hey, it is.
The sleevenotes: "At last on one record. A collection of the greatest hits ever recorded by the group that launched the beat explosion. Re-live the excitement of those days when Beatlemania was at its height, and the world went wild! The Rip Offs play their own musical tribute to John, Paul, George and Ringo in a way that will recreate those mad magnificent days in your home town!"
Classic Beatles cut: Without doubt, the version of Hey Jude has to be heard. It's too long, they get even more bored, they can't keep the tune. Fantastic.

Billy Lee Riley

Harmonica Beatlemania
MERCURY MG20974. Released 1964.

Love Me Do; I'll Cry Instead; Hard Day's Night; She Loves You; I Saw Her Standing There; Please Please Me; Tell Me Why; All My Loving; I Should Have Known Better Part 1; Ringo' Theme (This Boy); I Should Have Known Better Part 2.

The music: It's early Fabs when the harmonica made an appearance and a pick-up beat added spice and authenticity. Billy Lee Riley was a session guitarist on early Sun sides who had the odd hit in his own right. For this album he switched to harmonica and delivered a dozen Beatles' originals mostly in a tasteful if at times flat style. He blows his heart out and in places - on Love Me Do and I Saw Her Standing There especially. Sadly, elsewhere he seems to lose track of the backing and by the time we get to the two versions of I Should Have Known Better he's reached a plateaux of wind exertion that's obviously left him light-headed.
The sleeve: Caricature mop tops and lots of writing make this a tasteful looker. And the flipside shows Billy Lee laughing at the sheer audacity of these recordings.
The sleevenotes: Nothing but the tracklist.
Classic Beatles cut: Love Me Do actually barks

The Royal Philharmonic Orchestra

Plays Beatles Classics
DISKY DCD 5255. Released: 1992.

Yesterday; Eleanor Rigby; Sergeant Pepper's Lonely Hearts Club Band; She's Leaving Home; All You Need Is Love; I Am The Walrus; Blackbird; The Long And Winding Road; Beatlephonic Medley; Mull Of Kintyre; She Loves You; Fool On The Hill.

The music: Recorded live at the Royal Albert Hall, with appreciative audience on hand, and conducted by Louis Clark, The Royal Philharmonic "do" all the orchestral Beatles' faves (Yesterday, Eleanor Rigby, Blackbird and She's Leaving Home) and also throw in some that sit rather uncomfortably in such a straight-stringed manner. Sgt Pepper's, for instance, is delivered madly upbeat and ends up just jerkily awkward. All You Need Is Love comes with full choir, while I Am The Walrus is, as ever, menacing; the tension increased with a few Psycho-styled string slashes. And there's a Beatlephonic Medley too, a super-segueway featuring Got To Get You Into My Life, Eight Days A Week, Yellow Submarine, Get Back, Ticket To Ride and Ob-La-Di, Ob-La-Da, complete with jangling guitar. Proms-friendly indeed.
The sleeve: Another set of tacky illustrations delivered in green.
The sleevenotes: None to write home about.
Classic Beatles cut: I'm a sucker for I Am The Walrus, especially with its Anthony Perkins-styled drama.

The Royal Philharmonic Orchestra

Plays The Music Of Lennon And McCartney
AUTO PILOT/CAPITAL ROGER 46. Released: 1982

Medley; Here There And Everywhere; Norwegian Wood; Sgt Pepper's Lonely Hearts Club Band; With A Little Help From My Friends; Lucy In The Sky With Diamonds; Sgt Pepper (reprise); She's Leaving Home; All You Need Is Love; I Am The Walrus; The Long And Winding Road; Imagine; Mull Of Kintyre; War Is Over.

The music: It's orchestral as you might imagine. Neo-classical. Actually, the opening medley has this strange feel of what Beethoven might have sounded like if he'd had two record decks instead of a piano. Segued neatly into order are bowed riffs from a host of Beatles' songs, stuck together with a tinny and unconvincing rhythmic template. Fat Boy Bach indeed.
The sleeve: It's notes an stuff. And it's green.
The sleevenotes: Little information other than that they also "do" Queen.
Classic Beatles cut: Undoubtedly the string-driven flurry of I Am The Walrus.

The RSSO Symphony Orchestra

Symphony For The Stars
HORUS CD-08326. Released: 1994.
Also released as: Beatle For Strings
EMPORIO EMPRCD 694. Released: 1996.

Norwegian Wood; I Feel Fine; Something; Lady Madonna; Don't Let Me Down; Lucy In The Sky With Diamonds; Yes, It Is; She Loves You; Hello, Goodbye; While My Guitar Gently Weeps; Across The Universe; I Should Have Known Better.

The music: Melancholy sax, French horns, dramatic strings and an almost detuned, or should we say self-styled, trumpet on Lucy In The Sky With Diamonds make this a distinct oddity. Spanish in release originally, but recorded in Latvia, which isn't particularly renowned for its Beatlesness, this performance was conducted by Juris Kulakovs who sounds like an unemployed Russian general. It's wayward in the extreme, with the songs given a Vaseline sheen in the style of the old Robinson Crusoe soundtrack. Sort of lost and longing.
The sleeve: A small framed sketch of the would-be Fabs, obviously created by a distant relation of Juris's, is featured on the cover. For whatever reason Ringo is represented by just an ear (too hard to draw?), George looks like a young, concerned Kevin Keagan and John looks like Eric Burdon in the early days of The Animals. The Emporio release opts for an abstract group of instruments crossing Abbey Road.
The sleevenotes: They only reveal that RSSO, far from being the Royal Shakespearean Symphony Orchestra, stands for The Riga Recording Studio Orchestra. A lot grander as an acronym don't you think?.
Classic Beatles cut: Across The Universe is off enough to be loveable.

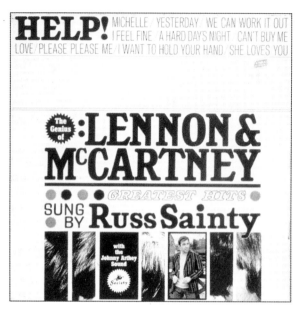

Russ Sainty With The Johnny Arthey Orchestra

The Genius Of Lennon And McCartney
ARC SOC 1035. Released: 1966

Michelle; Please Please Me; Can't Buy Me Love; I Feel Fine; A Hard Day's Night; Yesterday; We Can Work It Out; She Loves You; I Wanna Hold Your Hand; Help!

The music: Pretty darn under-produced and universally forgettable versions of The Beatles' early '60s catalogue. Lacklustre attempts to sound Beatles-esque are soon shelved as the band cha-cha through in an attempt to make it easy for the octave and excitement-challenged Sainty.
The sleeve: Black and white shots of mop toppery - in section only- and a colour snap of Russ - the man. Sadly no fan club details attached.
The sleevenotes: "There can't be an original thing to be said about the four young Liverpudlians who rocketed to fame about three years ago calling themselves The Beatles. Since that time and almost unaided, they've brought Liverpool onto the pop scene map in a big way, they've managed to break the stranglehold that American popular songs have had over use since the beginning of the rock 'n' roll era and last, but not least, they've killed stone dead the popular belief that popular songs, to be popular, must be composed of equal parts of musical rubbish and illiterate, unintelligible lyrics.

"On this disc we are proud to present Russ Sainty singing ten of their finest successes to date. Russ is a frequent performer on BBC radio, and his many appearances on such shows as Easy Beat, Saturday Club and Go, Man, Go, have shown him to be a lively, versatile singer with an easy unforced style, who is as much at home with ballads as the beatier numbers."
Classic Beatles cut: Help! Is just great. Russ sounds like he really needs it. In at the deep end with a complete lack of a talent lifejacket.

Santo And Johnny

The Beatles Greatest Hits
AMERICAN CALP 1017. Released: 1965.

A Hard Day's Night; Do You Want To Know A Secret; She Loves You; I Want To Hold Your Hand; The Beatles Blues; I Saw Her Standing There; And I Love Her; All My Loving; PS I Love You; Please Please Me; The Beatle Stomp; Can't Buy Me Love.

The music: The first of three Beatles Greatest that this duo of Hawaiian guitar and electric guitar mustered up in the late '60s. In fact, so enamoured with the Liverpool sound were these two cabaret circuit instrumentalists that they wrote a couple of their own tunes to try and cash in on the vibe. Indeed, The Beatle Blues and The Beatle Stomp have an edgy feel of their own that suggests Santo And Johnny have some form but, sadly their Beatles' covers are pretty one-dimensional allowing the lead Hawaiian guitar to carry the melody line and its ringing tone to dominate the whole album.
The sleeve: It's got Santo and indeed Johnny pictured in nice suits with The Beatles name emblazoned all over it. Good marketing guys.
The sleevenotes: "Never, absolutely never before in the history of the record business has there been anyone whose worldwide popularity compares to that of the fabulous Beatles.

"Numbered among their countless fans are Santo And Johnny! These young talented guitarists who gave you such great hits as Sleep Walk, Tear Drop and In the Still Of The Night, are noted for their distinctive sound and style. Here, accompanied by a fine orchestra under the direction of Mort Garson, they apply themselves to a task that they clearly enjoy, as they play The Beatles' greatest hits.

"The result - an exciting, downright entertaining album, which is an excellent musical salute to their fellow recording artists. Just listen to several selections and one of the secrets of The Beatles' success becomes obvious... their material is really sensational."
Classic Beatles cut: Every track sounds the same.

The Session Men

Beatle Music
WORLD RECORD CLUB T758. Released: 1967.

A Hard Day's Night; Help; When I'm 64; Baby You're A Rich Man; Yesterday; Strawberry Fields; She's Leaving Home; She Loves You; Yellow Submarine; All You Need Is Love; Ticket To Ride; Michelle; Norwegian Wood; Eleanor Rigby; Nowhere Man; Can't Buy Me Love.

The music: It's all brass-laden versions in the lowest common denominator style of post-Kenny Ball And His Jazzmen ungrooviness. That is until Baby, You're A Rich Man. The preceding When I'm 64 is a sickening muted trumpet rasp that struggles to stay on the deck, but Rich Man is something altogether different. For some reason they split the song into sections and begin with a freeform sax underneath, building the piece into a shrieking trumpet-fest, followed by trombone middle-eights and finger-clicking stabs. All along a northern soul drummer is doing his best stomping rolls, making it into a Munster-esque monster of a song. Perhaps it's not as shrieking or as stomping as it could be, but, hell, it's certainly different. Elsewhere it's muted brass all the way.
The sleeve: A groovy pic which seems to have no relevance to the Fabs.
The sleevenotes: "What is the secret of The Beatles' success? Four young men from Liverpool have conquered the entire musical world - their music is sung by other pop singers, 'standard' singers like Tony Bennett and Andy Williams. It's played by the great jazzmen - Bill Evans, Gerry Mulligan, Count Basie, Duke Ellington, and is known to be highly respected by many classical composers. Their films, Help and A Hard Day's Night are not only huge popular successes, but are considered masterpieces by august cineastes the world over.

"Throughout the Beatles' music there's a constant freshness of tune treatment. None of the abstract love songs so beloved by past generations - they write about common everyday happenings - girls leaving home, shy and lonely elderly spinsters, meter attendants, writes of paperbacks, and they write music of beauty, wit and subtlety - witness William Mann, serious music critic of The Times, who analysed and dissected their tunes, referring to diatonic clusters and such! Not only that, musical parodists have taken up The Beatles' cause with zest - thus we have the Beatlecracker Suite, Eine Kleine Beatlemusik, not to mention Beatleworks Musicke and the Beatles Concertos. I hope it isn't heresy to say so, but in one case at least, the Pas de deux of Beatlecracker, the Lennon and McCartney tune is a far finer one (All My Loving) than that which Tchaikovsky wrote."
Classic Beatles cut: Undoubtedly it's Baby You're A Rich Man.

Keely Smith

Sings The John Lennon And Paul McCartney Songbook
REPRISE R 6142. Released: 1964.

If I Fell; This Girl; Please Please Me; And I Love Him; World Without Love; She Loves You; A Hard Day's Night; Do You Want To Know A Secret? Can't Buy Me Love; All My Loving; I Want To Hold Your Hand; PS I Love You.

The music: Like label boss Frank Sinatra, Keely tries to drop off the main rhythm of these swinging arrangements to add more drama to the Lennon and McCartney basics. In places it works, elsewhere it sounds plain odd. There is, however, a finger-clicking beatnik pace to it all and the delivery for the most part is amiable enough.

Any original subtlety is of course gone in the overblown horn-laden blasts and the melancholy string backings, but that doesn't seem to particularly matter. Certainly not to Keely Smith. In fact it all goes fine until the downhome choir is added for the closing PS I Love You. That sounds just too dysfunctional on first hearing, even if it warms with subsequent plays.

And yes, for the sheer nerve of taking The Beatles' songs and working them in a completely different way, it's hats off to Ms Smith. What a crazy gal she is.
The sleeve: A typo nightmare with Smith trying to adopt a mop-top come mullet backed by a literary diatribe.
The sleevenotes: "In this startling album, Keely Smith reveals the often surprising melodic richness and beauty to be found in compositions of The Beatles' chief song writers John Lennon and Paul McCartney. Aided by imaginative arrangements by Ernie Freeman and Benny Carter, Miss Smith makes these hit songs sound as unexpected to the ears as if, say, the New York Philharmonic boomed out Little Latin Lupe Lu.

"There are still some crusty Mr Old Ears, and they still object to the music of The Beatles. Keely Smith should wipe the frowns from the old folks' furrowed foreheads. The Lennon and McCartney songs sung in sweet 'n' lovin' style by Keely, turn out right fine. For any age ears."
Classic Beatle cut: Please Please Me takes some beating for menacing sensuality.

Studio Five Orchestra Singers & Chorus perform

THE BEATLES GOLDEN SONGS

WIND★MILL

SPECTRO-STEREO DIMENSION

that looks more like Neil Morrissey of Men Behaving Badly fame.

The sleevenotes: "What can one say about The Beatles that has not been said before. For over a decade they have stamped their particular trade mark on the pop scene all over the world. Every one of their songs has been a hit and dominated the pop charts in most western countries. On this album we have selected the best known and best loved of the "Mersey-side Foursome", magnificently performed by the Studio 5 Orchestra Singers And Chorus - a salute to the genius of the most popular group of all time - THE BEATLES."

Classic Beatles cut: Help! with its superbly plodding bassline - more akin to a German oompah band - is a force to be reckoned with, it's followed by a purely schlock cabaret version of Yesterday but the closing assault on The Ballad Of John And Yoko takes some beating as a bad idea gone truly mouldy.

Sydney Thompson And His Orchestra

The Beatles Greatest Successes
SYDNEY THOMPSON RECORDS
STEREO DEST1. Released: 1970.

Yesterday; And I Love Her; Here, There And Everywhere; When I'm 64; She Loves You; Can't Buy Me Love; Ob-La-Di, Ob-La-Da; A Hard Day's Night; All My Loving; Penny Lane; Ticket To Ride; Please Please Me; Goodnight; I Want To Hold Your Hand.

The Studio Five Orchestra, Singers And Chorus

The Beatles Golden Songs
WINDMILL RECORDS WMD 130

I Feel Fine; We Can Work It Out; Day Tripper; Let It Be; Something; Lady Madonna; Hey Jude; Get Back; Hallo (sic) Goodbye; Help; Yesterday; The Ballad Of John And Yoko.

The music: Awkward and under-produced The Studio Five saunter through the hits seemingly unaware of the catcalls of neighbouring muso's.

A McCartney-esque rasp is available on occasion but the pace is so pedestrian and the sound quality so thin that there are few redeeming factors. There is some funky organ on Get Back, but it's not Billy Preston. And their version of Hello, Goodbye sounds like a nightclub soundcheck with a singer desperate to slope off for a bag of chips before his big night. Irreverent use of echo notwithstanding these guys should quickly join him.

The sleeve: Even the sleeve is a poor Letratone-heavy interpretation of the Fabs, with Paul's teeth a gleaming white next to a Harrison sketch

The music: A selection of cha cha chas, rumbas, sambas and paso doble's send The Beatles' portfolio into new dimensions. Perhaps it's to fit the rhythms, perhaps it's just because they could, but the arrangements here are just plain offbeat. Whole bars are missed from songs and parts of the sub-melody are over accentuated to get that clacking tempo just right for the ballroom dancing fraternity. It's a measured art form. So, songs are cut short and the tinkle of maracas, clipped brass and squidgey organ make this one unique vinyl experience. Indeed, it makes it hard to listen to the originals again without mentally backtracking to Sydney and his orchestra's measured massacre.

The sleeve: Three stills of ballroom dancers don't quite make up for the lack of a possibly hilarious Come Dancing-styled Mop Top illustration. But alas, that's what you get. White shirts, black ties, frilly dresses and stiletto heels - not all on one person I might add.

The sleevenotes: "The Beatles are no strangers in the ballrooms of practically every country in the world. The songs of John Lennon and Paul McCartney are being danced to and romanced to every day of every week everywhere, played by every conceivable combination under the sun, and thoroughly enjoyed by all.

"Records of the world-beating Beatles' songs abound, too, and span the entire gamut of musical expression from symphonic suites to modern jazz treatment. John and Paul invoke a unique alchemy in their songs, producing melodies of basic simplicity that are memorable and appealing in any guise, and the songs will continue to be recorded as long as popular music exists.

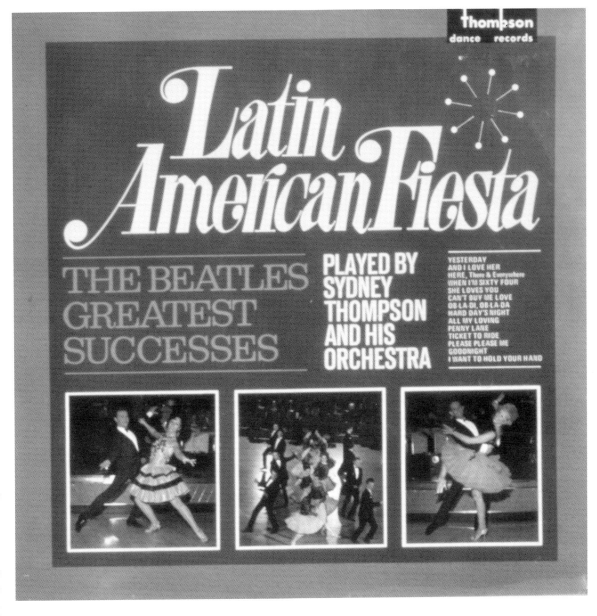

"There is a first time for everything and this album is a notable first in the annals of dance music. It is not the first album of Beatles tunes to be specifically recorded for dancing, nor the first album of Beatles tunes to be presented in Latin American rhythmic style. But it is the first album to be played in strict-tempo international Latin American style with four-bar introductions and then regular segments of 16 bars broken up into four bar movements. A such it will earn itself a permanent and popular place in the collection of all individuals and institutions dedicated to the pleasing art and recreation of ballroom dancing.

"The name Sydney Thompson is a sure guarantee of both meticulously accurate tempos and first-class musical quality in the ballroom world. Just as John and Paul create melodies of universal attraction, whether you are actually dancing or just listening. There is nothing contrived or mechanical about the Sydney Thompson Orchestra. It is alive and vibrant, and the tunes are allowed to speak eloquently for themselves.

"The Sydney Thompson Orchestra is made up of some of the finest musicians in the country and they play these excellent arrangements with faultless skill under Sydney's direction, and these Beatles ballads blossom all over again in strict tempo Latin American style."

Classic Beatles cut: The rumba interpretation of Please Please Me has the kind of lugubrious lack of urgency that makes you feel you've achieved partial deafness. In fact, virtually every track here has a disconcerting and unnerving sound. Beware!

The Synthesizer Rock Orchestra

Plays The Beatles Classic Trax
TRING TTMC 121A. Released: Unknown.

The Long And Winding Road; All You Need Is Love; A Hard Day's Night; Hey Jude; Lady Madonna; Let It Be; Love Me Do; Penny Lane; Strawberry Fields Forever; We Can Work It Out; When I'm 64; Yesterday; Here Comes The Sun; Eleanor Rigby.

The music: You just want it to be so much more. Maybe not as mad as Walter Carlos but just a little bit less melodic than Depeche Mode. Not as Goth as A Flock Of Seagulls but veering on the right

side of Nine Inch Nails. Instead the Rock Synthesizer Orchestra, who hail from Long Island, just play The Beatles' repertoire as clinically close to the original as they can. They don't get near and their synth "sound" doesn't make them any different either. Elsewhere they've also murdered the songs of Elton John. Not bad going, eh?

The sleeve: Almost the Beatles' typeface. Almost the Beatles in silhouette.

The sleevenotes: None.

Classic Beatles cut: Only their naffness makes this set worthy of note. All tracks are equally uninspiring but the magnitude of their minitude of effort for Strawberry Fields warrants special attention.

The Torero Band

Play Lennon And McCartney
Tijuana Sound
MUSIC FOR PLEASURE MFP 5015. Released: 1969.

Ob-La-Di, Ob-La-Da; Yesterday; From Me To You; With A Little Help From My Friends; All My Loving; Yellow Submarine; Please Please Me; Hey Jude; Can't Buy Me Love; I Want To Hold Your Hand; She Loves You; Eleanor Rigby.

The music: It's Tijuana, almost. The sanitised western version of Mexicala with secondary school percussion backing and some wantonly brass band-styled playing is as Mexican as Baked Bean Burritos. The Torero Band have probably never been to Tijuana. Cardiff, in fact, is probably the furthest west they've actually managed. Still, they can play lift music like nobody's business.

The sleeve: There's a picture of some brass and they've got the brass to include snaps of John and Paul to further their cause.

The sleevenotes: "In the same year that The Beatles were topping the British hit parade for the first time, a new sound was being heard in the American popular charts - a sound that had been borrowed from the mariachi bands of Mexico. Now both the Tijuana style of music and the hit songs of The Beatles are to be heard in every corner of the globe, and the surprising thing is that the two have been so rarely brought together; for the songs of John Lennon and Paul McCartney have the straight forward tunefulness that makes them the ideal subject for the Tijuana treatment."

Classic Beatles cut: The zany comedy of Yellow Submarine is actually mentioned on the sleeve but its true, universal power has no relation to what goes on here. Playing the track with all its mistimed percussion - even some of the percussionists are out of time with themselves - and layered brass is like listening to the effect Can were after when the four members performed in different corners of the arena. Staggeringly unhinged.

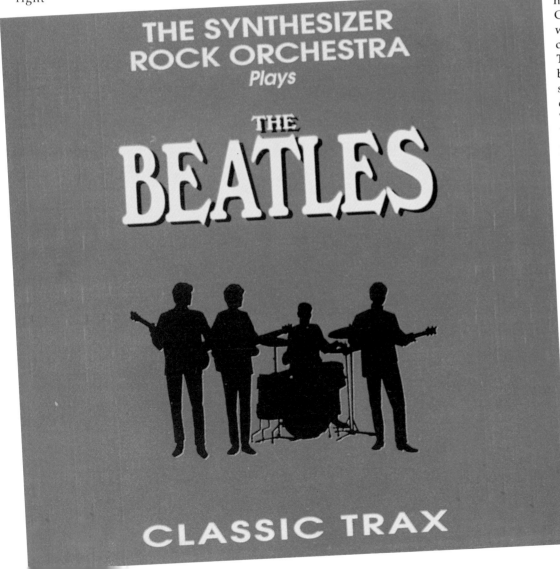

THE SYNTHESIZER ROCK ORCHESTRA *Plays* THE BEATLES

CLASSIC TRAX

The Spirit Of Lennon And McCartney
SKYLINE 492960 2. Released: 1996

Strawberry Fields Forever; Fool On The Hill; Here, There And Everywhere; Dear Prudence; Let It Be; Because; Nowhere Man; Yesterday; In My Life; She's Leaving Home; If I Fell; For No-One; This Boy; Michelle; Across The Universe; And I Love Her; Julia; Mother Nature's Son.

The music: An acoustic guitar picks out the melodies, on occasion a bird twitters in the background. All is indeed echoey. Stormclouds seem imminent and the songs just keep on coming as if they're played by a blindfolded guitarist totally oblivious to the collapse of modern civilisation under his very feet. Or something like that.
The sleeve: It's all a bit new age.
The sleevenotes: "To many of us growing up in the '60s popular music has provided the soundtrack to our lives, often evoking a memory so vivid, so magical you feel you can reach out and touch. This is illustrated none more so than the wonderful songs of John Lennon and Paul McCartney which have come to symbolise a meaning far beyond just simple nostalgia. The spirit of Lennon and McCartney is a tribute both to those songs and to their meaning - we hope that you get as much out of this album as we have making it."
Classic Beatles cut: The songs carry it through here. Dear Prudence with its echoey strum and repetitive riff and Across The Universe are great. But elsewhere doom remains on the agenda.

Sarah Vaughan

Songs Of The Beatles
ATLANTIC JAZZ. Released: 1981

Get Back; And I Love Her; Eleanor Rigby; Fool On The Hill; You Never Give Me Your Money; Come Together; I Want You (She's So Heavy); Blackbird; Something; Here, There And Everywhere; The Long And Winding Road; Yesterday; Hey Jude.

The music: Revered jazz crooner washed away by current musical trends? Common knowledge has dismissed this album as a collection of tawdry disco interpretations of Beatles' songs by a former jazz great. In part this is true - there are numerous dodgy Parliament/Funkadelic swirls and some discouraging rhythms - but there's more. In places it gets worse - I Want You (She's So Heavy) being a prime example of bad cabaret circuit disco. There are some silver linings, some jazzier interludes and the occasional moment when Sarah's best weapon, her voice, are given some space for development. But mostly this album runs true to its detractors.
The sleeve: It reveals that some seasoned players are involved. Names linked to Foreigner are rife and that blue-eyed soul feel is cemented by the guitar of Lee Ritenour.
The sleevenotes: There's not even anything about Sarah, nevermind the Fabs.
Classic Beatles cut: The samba version of Something is kitsch if nothing else.

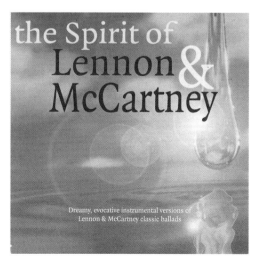

Tributes &
Compilations,
from psyche to soul,
reggae to new age
(grinding guitars
optional)

YOU LIKE ME TOO MUCH!

With the success of Beatles-related garb and the sheer number of covers available it wasn't long before whole albums were being compiled featuring a wide cross section of acts who'd all been summoned to the altar of Fab. Indeed, a veritable cavalcade of stars turned their hearts, minds and careers over to doing a Beatles' cover and quite a few of them saw their careers turn as a result of that move.

This section gathers together the exhaustively compiled collections that include not only the household names of Cocker, Ike And Tina, Cilla and Bernard Cribbins but also a few minor celebs and lesser known Artists who've added to the Beatles' bank balance. We also travel abroad, to tropical climes where Tito Puente lurks, to the Caribbean, which boasts a plethora of rock steady versions, to Spain, Latvia, America, Sweden and then back home to hear new age ambience cluttered by post-psychedelic feedback.

Witness Berry Grody's Motown roster singing the songs of The Beatles (and including their originals that The Beatles played), sample the delights of Bach and our heroes fused into one symphonic blur before reclining to the easy listening alternative of Peter Nero and Percy Faith. If only the whole world could be soundtracked from The Beatles' canon...

All You Need Is Covers

SEQUEL RECORDS NEECD 309. Released: 1999.

Tu Perds Ton Temps by **Petula Clark**
There's A Place by **The Kestrels**
Tip Of My Tongue by **Tommy Quickly**
All My Loving by **The Trends**
Don't Bother Me by **Gregory Philips**
Little Child by **Jackie Lynton**
This Girl by **Shirley Abicair**
A Hard Day's Night by **Max Bygraves**
And I Love Her by **Mark Wynter**
Tell Me Why by **Me And Them**
Baby's In Black by **The Hi-Fi's**
I'll Follow The Sun by **Glyn Johns**
I Don't Want To Spoil The Party by **The Savoys**
Help! By **Isaac Scott**
Yesterday by **PP Arnold**
We Can Work It Out by **Sacha Distel**
Norwegian Wood by **Paraffin Jack Flash Ltd**
Nowhere Man by **The Settlers**
Michelle by **The Overlanders**
Girl by **The Truth**
Paperback Writer by **Tempest**
Rain by **Petula Clark**
Eleanor Rigby by **Blonde On Blonde**
Here, There And Everywhere by **Episode Six**
Good Day Sunshine by **Jimmy James**
For No One by **Bobby Eaglesham**
I Want To Tell You by **The Lambrettas**
Got To Get You Into My Life by **Jackie Trent**
Strawberry Fields Forever by **Todd Rundgren**
With A Little Help From My Friends by **Joe Brown**
Your Mother Should Know by **Kenny Ball**
Fool On The Hill by **Dennis Lopez**
Hey Bulldog by **Bill Deal And The Rondells**
Step Inside Love by **Nina Baden-Semper**
Back In The USSR by **John Schroeder Orchestra**
Ob-La-Di, Ob-La-Da by **The 1970 England World Cup Squad**
Bungalow Bill by **Young Blood**
Blackbird by **Justin Hayward with Mike Batt**
I Will by **Real McCoy**
Birthday by **Hair Rave Up**
Mother Nature's Son by **Gryphon**

Honey Pie by **Nicky Scott**
Goodnight by **Cyril Stapleton And His Orchestra**
Two Of Us by **Penny Arcade**
The Long And Winding Road by **Vic Lewis**
Get Back by **Amen Corner**
Something by **Phillis Dillon**
Octopus's Garden by **Anita Harris**
Here Comes The Sun by **Prelude**
Because by **London Pops**

The music: As with every Sequel album, the research and cross-referencing is in depth and the ability to winkle out the most obscure of tracks seems an everyday pursuit. Collected together on All You Need Is Covers are the sublime, the ridiculous and a whole host of would-be mop tops just hoping for their big break. From Beatles-contemporary early '60s 45s from Jackie Lynton and Mark Wynter through to prog rock (Gryphon), bubblegum (Pennny Arcade), mod revival (The Lambrettas), metal (Tempest), folk (The Overlanders) and a whole host of instrumental interpretations all bases are covered here. Highlights and oddities rub shoulders, while psychedelic silliness and beat group homages co-exist remarkably comfortably.It's easy to get totally subsumed by this double CD collection as everything you hear is at least one person removed from the originals you know so well. There's some less than spectacular offerings but there are more than enough great versions to make up for The 1970 England World Cup Squad and actress Nina Baden-Semper.

The sleeve: A pop art pot pourri with silk-screened Warhol-styled sketches of The Beatles and numerous accoutrements collaged in for good measure.

The sleevenotes: "Years of listening to these toopermost of the poppermost songs on the Triumph Herald eight-track can't dim this shining musical beacon
in an otherwise greying world – nor can the legion of decaying solo records… With this in mind Sequel have assembled an alternative history of The Beatles, as heard by those around them… and those who didn't know them very well… and those who wouldn't know a Beatles record if it was stuffed up their please, please me's."

Classic Beatles cut: You've got to have a soft spot for Strawberry Fields by Todd Rundgren.

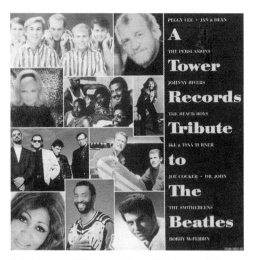

A Tower Records Tribute To The Beatles

EMI-CAPITOL 72438-19257-20. Released: 1996.

One After 909 by The Smithereens
With A Little Help From My friends by Joe Cocker
Can't Buy Me Love by Johnny Rivers
You've Got To Hide Your Love Away by The Beach Boys
Get Back by Ike And Tina Turner
Drive My Car by Bobby McFerrin
Norwegian Wood by Jan And Dean
Something by Peggy Lee
Let It Be by The Persuasions
Yesterday by Doctor John

The music: A store-bought low price collection of Beatles' covers culled from the EMI catalogue put together by the Tower Records chain. The album throws in old standards like Ike And Tina Turner and Joe Cocker, with less widely available covers like Jan And Dean's Spector-esque reading of Norwegian Wood, The Replacements' rough and ready One After 909 and Doctor John's gritty Yesterday.
The sleeve: Lots of photos of the players.
The sleevenotes: None.
Classic Beatles cut: The Bobby McFerrin cut is well known for his unique lack of instrumentation – it's all music made by mouth – and is always a "How does he do that?" experience, but Dr John's Yesterday, as rolling and tumbling as it may be, is the most repeatable track here.

Cantando A Los Beatles

PLANETA-AGOSTINI PE 03-2. Released: 1992.

Socorro! (Help!) by Los Mustang
We Can Work It Out by Massiel
Aqui Llega El Sol (Here Comes The Sun) by Miguel Rios
Baby You're A Rich Man by Los Canarios
The Long And Winding Road by Paloma San Basilio
Let It Be by Mocedades
Please, Please Me by Los Pekenikes
Hey Jude by Marisol
Back In The URSS by Orquesta Mondragon
Can't Buy Me Love by Elia Fleta
Ayer (Yesterday) by Miguel Rios
El Loco De La Colina (Fool On The Hill) by Junior
Penny Lane by Los Tonks
And I Love Him by Massiel
Blackbird by Los Angeles
L Ayuda De La Amistad (With A Little Help From My Friends) by Paloma San Basilio
Un Billete Compro (Ticket To Ride) by Francisco Heredero
Submarino Amarillo by Los Mustang

The music: This should really be in the exotica section, it's so steamy and continental. But it's also a tribute to the music of The Beatles from a host of Spanish acts who've obviously all got their own view on the importance of being Fab. Los Mustang, for example, play basic rock 'n' roll when they cover Help! Sung in their native Spanish it's almost as if Lennon and McCartney were from Barcelona. However, after such a thumping opening, Los Mus, as we like to call them, can't repeat the process when they're asked to close the set. It all goes slightly skewiff when they cover Yellow Submarine, which reaches new heights of ridiculousness. In between there's pidgin English stuttering from Massiel and Paloma Son Basilio, before the Tony Bennett-paced crooning of Miguel Rios. These, however, are all outshone by the wonder that is Marisol, with frightening sincerity, seems to pour vocal flourishes into every nook of the song like gravy left standing over the weekend.

Elsewhere, it's not all a cultural Beatles battlefield stuffed with faux pas. More appetising is the crazed theatrics and fake live sounds of the metal-esque Los Canaros and the Psycho-styled orchestration of Mocedades. They allow some form of hope for the European community, which is only dashed when the full horror of Los Pekenikes is realised. They sound like they've got the organ from Telstar and they're keen to really, really use it.

Further along, the ultimate in pub singer chic is achieved by Orquesta Mondragon who completely baffle themselves in trying to do Back In The URSS. Expect a re-ironing of the iron curtain at any moment. And, sounding like she's set to report on such an event, Elia Fleta delivers Can't Buy Me Love like a news reader who's ready to drop the bomb and reveal that, hey, those crazy Beatles guys from the Liverpool have split up. Yikes.
The sleeve: A Hard Day's Night pastiche, sort of.
The sleevenotes: "Desde la primera grabacion del cuarteto de Liverpool, la musica de los Beatles ha inspirado la obra de millares de artistas cimentaron lo mejor de su fama en algunas versiones de los Beatles."
Classic Beatles cut: Los Angeles opt for a very literal translation of Blackbird which stumbles over itself but retains a sinister charm that's almost engaging.

Cilla Black, Peter And Gordon, Bernard Cribbins, David And Jonathan, The Fourmost, Billy J Kramer, Kenny Lynch Sing Lennon And McCartney

MUSIC FOR PLEASURE MFP 5175. Released: 1968.

Bad To Me by **Billy J Kramer**
World Without Love by **Peter And Gordon**
Hello Little Girl by **The Fourmost**
When I'm 64 by **Bernard Cribbins**
I'll Be On My Way by **Billy J Kramer**
She's Leaving Home by **David And Jonathan**
Love Of The Loved by **Cilla Black**
Nobody I Know by **Peter And Gordon**
I'll Keep You Satisfied by **Billy J Kramer**
Misery by **Kenny Lynch**
I Don't Want To See You Again by **Peter And Gordon**
I'm In Love by **The Fourmost**

The music: Authentic, beat-friendly early Beatlesisms, including a few groundbreaking hits from Billy J, Peter And Gordon and The Fourmost and the tongue-in-cheek jollity of Bernard Cribbins plus the surprisingly straight-laced Kenny Lynch. Peter And Gordon's World Without Love is a glorious piece of pop music and Cilla's Love Of The Loved, her own pop single debut, is excellent. The underlying pick-up group set-up and occasional strings make the whole album ring with a really uplifting tone, making it into a surprisingly cohesive package.

The sleeve: It's a galaxy of stars with the roll of honour listed above photos of John and Paul.

The sleevenotes (delivered verbatim from the state of gibberish): "What is the magic ingredient that makes a song a hit? One may well ask, but whatever the secret, John Lennon and Paul McCartney have most certainly discovered it!

"This unique songwriting duo penned the first British recording for The Beatles, Love Me Do, the song which started the string of hits for these two writers, to say nothing of the start of the success story of The Beatles themselves. The pair was awarded ten of the hundred awards presented in the USA in 1964, and became the top songwriters that year.

"This record is – as the title suggests – stars singing Lennon/McCartney, stars who made them into smash hits."

Classic Beatles cut: Peter And Gordon's World Without Love is excellent.

The Lennon And McCartney Songbook

CONNOISSEUR RECORDS VSOP CD 150. Released: 1990.

Lucy In The Sky With Diamonds by **Elton John**
Let It Be by **Aretha Franklin**
Here There And Everywhere by **Emmylou Harris**
Anytime At All by **Nils Lofgren**
Day Tripper by **Otis Redding**
With A Little Help From My Friends by **Joe Cocker**
Hey Jude by **Wilson Pickett**
In My Life by **Judy Collins**
I Call Your Name by **The Mamas And The Papas**
Got To Get You Into My Life by **Cliff Bennett And The Rebel Rousers**
Tomorrow Never Knows by **Monsoon**
Get Back by **Ike And Tina Turner**
I Saw Him Standing There by **Tiffany**
Please Please Me by **The Flamin' Groovies**
Things We Said Today by **Cliff Richard**
Nowhere Man by **Three Good Reasons**
I've Just Seen A Face by **The Dillards**
From Me To You by **Bobby McFerrin**
She Came In Through The Bathroom Window by **Joe Cocker**
It's For You by **Three Dog Night**
Step Inside Love by **Cilla Black**
Bad To Me by **Billy J Kramer And The Dakotas**
Yesterday by **Marianne Faithfull**
You've Got To Hide Your Love Away by **The Silkie**

The music: An awesome parade of disparate talents are assembled on this rather fab album which includes several tracks which were given to artists to launch their own careers (Cilla Black's It's For You and Step Inside Love and Billy J Kramer's Bad To Me). The album also includes Emmylou Harris's gorgeous Here, There And Everywhere, which was her only UK hit, Otis Redding's raunchy Day Tripper, Wilson Pickett's Hey Jude with Duane Allman on guitar, Elton John's version of Lucy In The Sky With Diamonds (with John Lennon on backing vocals) and Monsoon's truly exotic version of Tomorrow Never Knows.

Faring less well good are Tiffany with her bubble-gummy I Saw Her Standing There and Three Dog Night's wandering It's For You but, for the most part, this is high quality stuff.

The sleeve: As minimal as you like, with Joe Cocker, Tina Turner, Cliff and Elton all pictured.

The sleevenotes: They include story snippets for each song which reveal that Three Good

LENNON & McCARTNEY
S O N G B O O K

I N C L U D E S

Lucy In The Sky With Diamonds · Let It Be · Anytime At All ·
Day Tripper · With A Little Help From My Friends · Hey Jude

Reasons, who cover Nowhere Man, were from Bradford and that the folk group The Silkie – who spent most of their time covering Dylan songs – were signed to Brian Epstein's management company.

Classic Beatles Cut: The Silkie's You've Got To Hide Your Love Away is beautiful, but there again there's sterling performances from Cocker, Monsoon, The Dillards, Wilson Pickett, the Mamas And The Papas' Mama Cass and lots more besides.

George Martin: In My Life

ECHO/UNIVERSAL UMD 80420. Released: 1998.

Come Together by **Robin Williams And Bobby McFerrin**
A Hard Day's Night by **Goldie Hawn**
A Day In The Life by **Jeff Beck**
Here, There And Everywhere by **Celine Dion**
Because by **Vanessa Mae**
I Am The Walrus by **Jim Carrey**
Here Comes The Sun by **John Williams**
Being For The Benefit Of Mr Kite by **Billy Connolly**

The Pepperland Suite by **George Martin** *(including Pepperland, March Of The Meanies, Sea Of Monsters and Pepperland reprise*
Golden Slumbers/Carry That Weight/The End by **Phil Collins**
Friends And Lovers by **George Martin**
In My Life by **Sean Connery**

The music: The fifth Beatle rallies together a group of mostly unhousebroken performers ("Friends and heroes") to record a selection of Beatles tunes as his final production job before retirement. "Why leave the last album to chance?" he quips on the sleeve, but why make this strange hotch-potch of an album with a bunch of actors who take the songs way too literally and several pop stars who seem a touch below par… and Jeff Beck.

Of the actors, few come out with credit. Robin Williams sounds like your dad trying to be modern on his collaboration with Bobby McFerrin, Goldie Hawn comes on like a cross between Ella Fitzgerald, Mae West and Deputy Dawg, Jim Carrey massacres I Am The Walrus like a demented Peter Sellers and Sean Connery hams his way through the title track. Elsewhere, Billy Connolly proves his buffoon cred is in no doubt with a wretched version of For The

Benefit Of Mr Kite.

Of the singers, Celine Dion is unspectacular, leaving Phil Collins with the only ounce of passion. Instrumentally John Williams, Vanessa Mae and a new agey Jeff Beck interpret a selection of tunes while Martin himself produces the only really innovative highlight with his Pepperland Suite from the soundtrack of Yellow Submarine.

The sleeve: It actually includes some great pictures of Martin in situ with the group, plus various postcards they sent him over the years.

The sleevenotes: Apart from reportage on each track, Martin reveals that the concept followed "the record I made with Peter Sellers performing A Hard Day's Night, when I persuaded him to use his Laurence Olivier voice in a great Richard III send-up. There are many great people I have often wanted to capture on disc, and this was definitely the time. It has been a happy task, and we have all had an enormous amount of fun. Just a shame I could not reach Django, Miles, Hendrix or Gary Cooper, Cary Grant or Rita Hayworth."

Classic Beatles cut: Undoubtedly, it's Martin's Pepperland Suite, but the competition is slim.

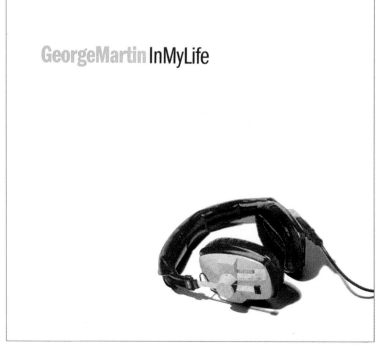

GeorgeMartin InMyLife

Motown Sings The Beatles

TAMLA MOTOWN WL 72348. Released 1984.
CONNOISSEUR COLLECTION NSP LP 500.
Re-issued: 1991.

A Hard Day's Night by **Diana Ross And The Supremes**

Eleanor Rigby by **The Four Tops**

We Can Work It Out by **Stevie Wonder**

Hey Jude by **The Temptations**

Yesterday by **Marvin Gaye**

The Long And Winding Road by **Diana Ross**

Come Together by **The Supremes**

She's Leaving Home By **Syreeta**

You Can't Do That by **Diana Ross And The Supremes**

The Fool On The Hill by **The Four Tops**

You've Really Got A Hold On Me by **Smokey Robinson And The Miracles**

Please Mr Postman by **The Marvelettes**

Michelle By **The Four Tops**

And I Love Her by **Smokey Robinson And The Miracles**

Something by **Martha Reeves And The Vandellas**

Let It Be by **Gladys Knight And The Pips**

Imagine by **Diana Ross**

My Love by **Junior Walker**

My Sweet Lord by **Edwin Starr**

Money by **Barrett Strong**

The music: Featuring straight covers of Beatles' material, a couple of things from their solo escapades and three songs from The Beatles' repertoire that they took from the Motown stable, this is an expressive collection that resonates with Stevie Wonder's harmonica, the testifying soul of The Four Tops and some typically engaging Smokey Robinson vocals. The original Motown cuts sound wholesomely grand in this ideal setting, with The Marvelettes' Please Mr Postman, Smokey's version of his own You've Really Got A Hold On Me and Barrett Strong's Money all adding to the soulful ambience.

Marvin Gaye's Yesterday is truly moving and The Temptations' Hey Jude is stripped down to its bluesy roots. Of the latter material Edwin Starr's My Sweet Lord is an inspirationally triumphant swirl and the side one closer, The Fool On The Hill by the Four Tops is a tour de force.

The sleeve: The Motown sleeve is pretty forgettable, while the Connoisseur re-issue is tasteful but not particularly exciting considering what's actually in the grooves.

The sleevenotes: there's nothing on the Motown release, but the re-issue offers: "The two most important sources of pop music in the 1960's were undoubtedly the Tamla Motown stable of artists and writers and The Beatles. Here on this unique album you get to hear the best of both of these as the great Motown acts sing some of The Beatles' best songs and also perform the original versions of some of the songs that the Beatles covered."

Classic Beatle cut: The Four Tops' Eleanor Rigby is truly moving and Smokey's version of And I Love Her is a brooding gem.

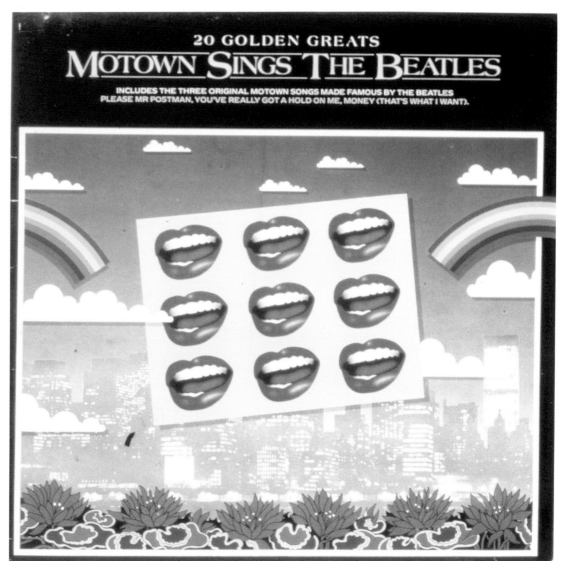

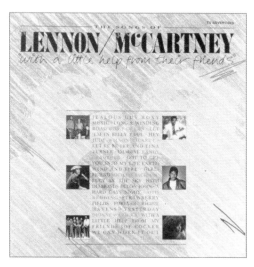

The Songs Of John Lennon And Paul McCartney

"With A Little Help From Their Friends"
K-TEL NE 1317. Released: 1985.

Got To Get You Into My Life by Earth Wind And Fire

Jealous Guy by Roxy Music

The Long And Winding Road by Billy Ocean

Girlfriend by Michael Jackson

Hey Jude by Wilson Pickett

Let It Be by Ike And Tina Turner

Imagine by Randy Crawford

We Can Work It Out by Chaka Khan

Let 'Em In by Billy Paul

Lucy in The Sky With Diamonds by Elton John

A Hard Day's Night

Strawberry Fields Forever by Richie Havens

Yesterday by Dionne Warwick

With A Little Help From My Friends by Joe Cocker

The music: This licensed-in collection follows no particular brief, other than reflecting the fact that Beatles' tunes make for quality entertainment. I'd say that anyone can shine with a Beatles song as their material but having waded through several thousand in putting this book together, I know that's not entirely true. So, these guys are pretty talented too. By decade we have Joe Cocker, Richie Havens, Wilson Pickett and Otis Redding representing the Woodstock / Monterey axis. And that soulful vibe is continued into the '70s by Ike And Tina, Dionne Warwick, Billy Paul, Earth, Wind And Fire and Michael Jackson, while the '80s display extends the MOR aspects with readings from Chaka Khan, Randy Crawford and Billy Ocean. In between Elton John and Roxy Music put in their ten penneth completing an impressive list of pop icons paying homage to The Beatles' legacy.

The sleeve: Lennon and McCartney linger in the

background in cross-etched hues while the performers are picked out with colour snaps.

The sleevenotes: None.

Classic Beatles cut: Undoubtedly the Roxy Music version of John Lennon's Jealous Guy will always hold a place in people's hearts. After Lennon's assassination the Roxy release topped the chart and kept candles burning the world over. I'm sure no-one wanted Lennon's death to be exploited but there seemed something about the disc from Ferry and co that summed up the sadness from that shot heard around the world.

The Songs Lennon And McCartney Gave Away

EMI NUT 18. Released: 1979.

*I'm The Greatest by **Ringo Starr***

*One And One Is Two by **The Strangers With Mike Shannon***

*From A Window by **Billy J Kramer And The Dakotas***

*Nobody I Know by **Peter And Gordon***

*Like Dreamers Do by **The Applejacks***

*I'll Keep You Satisfied by **Billy J Kramer And The Dakotas***

*Love Of The Loved by **Cilla Black***

*Woman by **Peter And Gordon***

*Tip Of My Tongue by **Tommy Quickly***

*I'm In Love by **The Fourmost***

*Hello Little Girl by **The Fourmost***

*That Means A Lot by **PJ Proby***

*It's For You by **Cilla Black***

*World Without Love by **Peter And Gordon***

*Bad To Me by **Billy J Kramer And The Dakotas***

*I Don't Want To See You Again by **Peter And Gordon***

*I'll Be On My Way by **Billy J Kramer And The Dakotas***

*Cat Call by **The Chris Barber Band***

The music: For the most part this 20 track collection is made up of Beatles tunes from the early part of their writing career, the stuff that didn't make the Beatles' grade but did just fine for others. Also included are a few specially-written commissions for the Brian Epstein talent agency, a gift for Ringo and a smattering of obscurities that were just tossed off so to speak. In total it's a highly interesting collection with a couple real obscurities that deserve dusting off. For instance, so the story goes, Penina by Carlos Mendes was something that Paul gave away to someone he met while on holiday in Portugal – we can only assume it was Carlos. And the perfectly-crafted Step Inside Love, which was commissioned by Epstein for the launch of Cilla Black's Saturday night TV series was the kind of thing that Lennon and McCartney specialised in, a highly hummable hook that was as infectious as they came.

Overall, the album itself has the feel of an early '60s jukebox and through the various interpretations of the songs, you begin to realise the far reaching effect that this songwriting partnership obviously had. It's timeless stuff.

The sleeve: Sketches of the performers in front of black and white line drawings of Paul and John.

The sleevenotes: "The Songs That Lennon And McCartney Gave Away concerns itself with material written by John and Paul quite early in their career. In the majority of these cases the tracks were written as potential songs for The Beatles. John and Paul wrote very few numbers for other people to specifically perform – they just picked out something that they thought would be suitable when requests arrived.

"The requests they found hard to refuse were from Brian Epstein himself. Brian would ask them to tailor something sturdy to launch many of his acts. In this way he provided Lennon/McCartney material for the initial recordings made by Billy J Kramer, Tommy Quickly, the Fourmost and Cilla Black.

"On the other hand the stuff that they gave away to Peter And Gordon and, much later, Cilla Black (Step Inside Love) was made to measure with the artists concerned in mind from the outset.

"The year 1963 was unique in the history of the UK pop charts. Never before had a single songwriting team held the number one spot for so long. A soon as The Beatles left the top with From Me To You in June, in came Billy J Kramer with a Lennon/McCartney ballad called Do You Want To Know A Secret. Another six songs were released in the second half of 1963."

Classic Beatles cut: Ringo's biographical story on I'm The Greatest, written for him

by John Lennon, is absolutely "fab". Penina by Carlos Mendes is truly an unsung gem from the McCartney back catalogue and the closing McCartney tune Cat Call has all the elegance of an out-take from the soundtrack of The Aristocats.

The Soul Of Lennon And McCartney

DINO ENTERTAINMENT DIN112. Released: 1995

Let It Be by **Aretha Franklin**
Hey Jude by **Wilson Pickett**
The Long And Winding Road by **Cissy Houston**
Come Together by **Ike And Tina Turner**
In My Life by **Richie Havens**
Yesterday by **PP Arnold**
I Want You (She's So Heavy) by **Sarah Vaughan**

Can't Buy Me Love by **Ella Fitzgerald**
Ticket To Ride by **Gwen Guthrie**
Day Tripper by **Otis Redding**
Got To Get You Into My Life by **Earth, Wind And Fire**
We Can Work It Out by **Maxine Brown**
And I Love Her by **The Detroit Emeralds**
Lady Madonna by **Booker T And The MGs**
Dear Prudence by **The Five Stairsteps**
A Hard Day's Night by **Dionne Warwick**
Fool On The Hill by **The Impressions**
Get Back by **Al Green**

The music: The soul fraternity identified with the Beatles from day one. Much in the same way that The Beatles had created their sound from their imported rock 'n' roll and R&B influences, Lennon and McCartney's songs travelled back across the Atlantic and inspired a host of joyous interpretations. This made-for-TV compilation was created before such things really existed and in its creation, several rarely heard Beatles' covers were unearthed. Sure enough, there are a bundle of classics – from Aretha, Pickett, Ike And Tina, Otis and Dionne Warwick – but it's not very often that tracks like The Detroit Emeralds' moody version of And I Love Her, Cissy Houston's bellowing Long And Winding Road, The Impressions' Fool On The Hill or The Five Stairsteps' strange mellow funk on Dear Prudence are heard. Those handful alone make this a pretty special set. The sleeve: Two soul brothers in Beatles garb shot from the neck down to the bottom of their rather recognisable guitars.

The sleevenotes: "Today Lennon and McCartney are firmly established as the greatest composers of their time. Not surprisingly, their songs have been interpreted in almost every musical form. Recorded by established solo artists on one hand, and by respected classical orchestras on the other.

"Here, their familiar melodies and lyrics are given new poignancy and power by some of America's finest soul artists."

Classic Beatles cut: Curtis Mayfield intoning Fool On The Hill as The Impressions take the tempo down and add an orchestra to achieve maximum emotion.

Tropical Tribute
To The Beatles

RMM 8 37944 2. Released: 1996.

Hey Jude by **Tony Vega**

Let It Be by **Tito Nieves**

Can't Buy Me Love (No Puedes Comprarme) by **Guianko**

A Hard Day's Night by **Johnny Rivera**

Obladi, Oblada by **Celia Cruz**

Fool On The Hill by **Ray Sepulveda**

I Want To Hold Your Hand (Dame Tu Mano Ven) by **Manny Manuel**

Day Tripper by **Domingo Quinones**

Lady Madonna by **Oscar D'Leon**

With A Little Help From My Friends by **Jesus Enriquez And Miles Pena**

Yesterday by **Cheo Feliciano**

And I Love Her (Mi Gran Amor Le Di) by **Jose Alberto "El Canario"**

Come Together (Vamos Juntos) by All Artists

The music: More exotic stuff? Sure enough, as the Latin masses take to The Beatles with ruler-twanging, maraca-shaking fervour. Included are a host of Latino stars doing it decidedly their way. From the very beginning, given but half a chance, there's whoops and hollers and come halfway through Hey Jude, once Tony Vega has found his groove, it's an explosion of fevered gyrations and twitching ankles. He's followed by Tito Nieves who brings in the legendary Tito Puente on vibes. The result is something rather slower than you might think the twin turbo-powered Tito's might muster, but, not to worry, there's bongos aplenty from Johnny Riviera following, even if his combo lose track of him midway through his word-perfect delivery.

The Beatles are lavished with Latin lurve throughout and Celia Cruz's translation of Ob-La-Di is spectacular if a little unwieldy, while Manny Manuel takes things to the farthest extremes with his macho West Side Story shenanigans on I Want To Hold Your Hand.

Cowbells and vibraslaps are on-hand when Domingo Quinones takes on Day Tripper and his attention to the pace of the song makes it one of the best listening experiences here. The rest of the album consists of slightly less palatable stuff, with electronic dalliances and Charles Aznavour-styled crooning surfacing. The album's closing all-star jamboree on Come Together is wickedly showbiz though. After all that glissando, is it any good? It's hard to say. The concept is undoubtedly flawed because the Beatles' writing style is so different from the Latin soul experience but, that said, there's a certain charm which emanates from the cast's enthusiasm.

The sleeve: A big band variation on Sgt Pepper's with the whole cast gathered around the tub-thumping Tito Puente.

The sleevenotes: "My vision of presenting the Beatles' music with a danceable, tropical rhythm began over 30 years ago," exclaims the exec producer Ralph Mercado. "Living in the Latin heart-land of New York City, I was surrounded by the sounds of my roots and its influence moulded my career. By the mid 1960's all across America the top radio stations were playing hit records coming from England by a new group called The Beatles. Impressed by their sound, unique look and tremendous success, I found myself beginning to change the way that I listened to music. But because my heart beat to the rhythm of my native tongue, I would often think that I heard the brilliant rhythms of legendary Latin musicians integrated into the compositions of the Fabulous Four."

Classic Beatles cut: Jose Alberto's version of And I Love Her has all the rasping lip curl of Elvis at his most sultry.

Beatle Classic Hitss

CONCERT GOLD CG 3654. Released: MCMXCIV

Sergeant Pepper's Lonely Hearts Club Band by **Louis Clark, the Royal Philharmonic Orchestra And Royal Choral Society**

With A Little Help From My Friends by **John Bayless**

Yesterday by **Newton Wayland And Rochetser Pops**

She Loves You by **Louis Clark And The Royal Philharmonic Orchestra**

Eleanor Rigby by **Newton Wayland And Rochetser Pops**

Fool On The Hill by **Louis Clark And The Royal Philharmonic Orchestra**

Strawberry Fields Forever by **John Bayless**

Yellow Submarine by **Newton Wayland And Rochester Pops**

All You Need Is Love by **Louis Clark, the Royal Philharmonic Orchestra And Royal Choral Society**

Please Please Me by **Newton Wayland And Rochetser Pops**

The Long And Winding Road by **Louis Clark, the Royal Philharmonic Orchestra And The Royal Choral Society**

Penny Lane by **John Bayless**

Got To Get You Into My Life by **Newton Wayland And Rochetser Pops**

She's Leaving Home by **Louis Clark, the Royal Philharmonic Orchestra And The Royal Choral Society**

Good Day Sunshine by **John Bayless**

And I Love Her by **Newton Wayland And Rochetser Pops**

Here There And Everywhere by **Newton Wayland And Rochetser Pops**

I Want To Hold Your Hand by **John Bayless**

Michelle by **Newton Wayland And Rochetser Pops**

I Am The Walrus by **Louis Clark And The Royal Philharmonic Orchestra**

A Day In The Life by **John Bayless**

The music: Three sets of neo-classicists come together on this double CD of Beatles' covers. The Royal Philharmonic do everything quite straight, with plodding drums added to gain some "teen appeal" and momentum. The

Rochester Pops add a more swinging veneer but it's John Bayless who really stars with his extrovert soldering of the writing styles of Lennon and McCartney and Johann Sebastian Bach.

The history: The Royal Philharmonic Orchestra originally released Classically Beatles in 1982. The album was re-issued in 1992 as Plays Beatles Classics, with the same track listing (*Yesterday, Eleanor Rigby, Sergeant Peppers Lonely Hearts Club Band, With A Little Help From My Friends, Lucy In The Sky With Diamonds, Sergeant Peppers Lonely*

Hearts Club Band (reprise), She's Leaving Home, All You Need Is Love, I Am The Walrus, Blackbird, The Long And Winding Road and The Beatlephonic Medley: Got To Get You Into My Life/Eight Days A Week/Penny Lane/Yellow Submarine/Get Back/Daytripper/Ticket to Ride/Ob-la-di Ob-la-da, Mull of Kintyre, She Loves You, Fool On The Hill). They also followed it up with The Royal Philharmonic Orchestra Plays The Music Of Lennon And McCartney (*Medley; Here There And Everywhere; Norwegian Wood; Sgt Pepper's Lonely Hearts Club Band; With A Little Help From My Friends; Lucy In The Sky With Diamonds; Sgt Pepper (reprise); She's Leaving Home; All You Need Is Love; I Am The Walrus; The Long And Winding Road; Imagine; Mull Of Kintyre; War Is Over.*) Meanwhile, John Bayless had also been plundering the Beatles' catalogue through the '80s. In 1984 he released Bach Meets The Beatles (*A*

Hard Day's Night, Here Comes The Sun, Good Day Sunshine / Day Tripper Maxwell's Silver Hammer – variations, With a Little Help from My Friends, If I Fell, Lucy in the Sky with Diamonds, She Loves You / Help, I Want To Hold Your Hand, Can't Buy Me Love, I Will, Lady Madonna, Strawberry Fields, Eleanor Rigby, In My Life, Good Night, A Day In The Life), closely followed in the same year by Bach On Abbey Road. In 1985 he took a namecheck too with Bach, Bayless, Beatles. Then, in 1989 he teamed up with Newton Wayland And Rochetser Pops for Beatles' Greatest Hits (*Sergeant Pepper's Lonely Hearts Club Band, With A Little Help From My Friends, Sgt. Pepper's (Reprise), Michelle, Here Comes The Sun, Eleanor Rigby, Something, Live And Let Die, And I Love Her, Let It Be, When I'm 64, Got To Get You into My Life, Yesterday, The Long And Winding Road, Penny Lane, Yellow Submarine, Here, There And Everywhere, Please Please Me/A Hard Day's Night*).

Confused? Thought so. Well better than wade through it all again, this double set gives you the best of all the above.

The sleeve: Very disappointing, just text.

The sleevenotes: "Here we've gathered together some of the world's greatest pops stars to salute the fab four. Featured are Louis Clark and the Royal Philharmonic Orchestra, Newton Wayland (the former pianist with Arthur Fielder's Boston Pops) and the Rochester Pops and celebrated pianist John Bayless. The result is a musical history tour of 22 of The Beatles' greatest hits.

"Undoubtedly the apex of The Beatles' classical efforts was 1967's Sgt Pepper's Lonely Hearts Club Band. Complete with electronic effects, sitars, blaring horns and swirling strings, this lurid menagerie forever altered the course of rock. Suddenly, The Beatles seemed sophisticated, and their music attracted a completely different audience of eager, middle-aged intellectuals. Even the industry's most respected scholars like Aaron Copland, John Cage and Ned Rorem (who compared The Beatles creativity to that of Mozart) lavished the boys with extravagant praise."

Classic Beatles cut: All of the Bayless cuts, with their ingenious melding of Bach's compositional skills and The Beatles pop sense are entertaining.

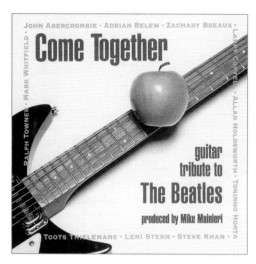

Come Together: Guitar Tribute To The Beatles

NYC RECORDS NYC 6004 2. Released : 1993.

Come Together featuring **Mark Whitfield**

She's Leaving Home featuring **Toninho Horta**

Here, There And Everywhere featuring **Ralph Towner**

Within You/Without You, Blue Jay Way featuring **Steve Khan**

Eleanor Rigby featuring **Zachary Breaux**

Blackbird featuring **Adrian Belew**

And I Love Her featuring **John Abercrombie**

Michelle featuring **Allan Holdsworth**

Norwegian Wood featuring **Leni Stern**

Something featuring **Larry Coryell**

Yesterday featuring **Toots Thielemans**

The music: It lilts, it meanders, it wanders, from the upbeat and jazzy through to the quiet and decidedly mellow. Vibes, piano and the occasional strings join the guitars but the mood, for the most part, is relaxation leading to deep pontification.On occasion the spell is broken, like on Steve Khan's medley of Within You, Without You and Blue Jay Way which sounds like the theme to a Mexican heist movie, or on Allan Holdsworth's worryingly acidic version of Michelle where his synthetic colouring dampens the mood like so much paint stripper.Amazingly for something that's supposed to be so soothing, Come Together is a lot of hard work.

The sleeve: It's subtle. An apple on a fretboard. Geddit?

The sleevenotes: The man with the plan is Mike Mainieri. He enthuses: "I invited 11 guitarists to perform and interpret their favourite Beatles' song. The response was overwhelming and the enthusiasm with which each artist approached the project made me believe that guitarists are a special breed.

"For their part the guitarists opined on the songs as follows: John Abbercrombie: "The pop music of the '60s wasn't very interesting until I heard The Beatles. Their music restored my love of the popular song and songwriting in general."

Toninho Horta: "When I first heard I Want To Hold Your Hand I thought that The Beatles were not good musicians. They broke the compass and the timing of that song. Years later I listened to the album Revolver and many songs from that album killed my heart."

Ralph Towner: "The Beatles held a special place among the musicians in New York in the early '70s. Their approach to writing and recording was refreshing to all of us who were seeking to expand the boundaries of jazz at that time."

Classic Beatles cut: Steve Khan's medley of Within You, Without You and Blue Jay Way is the most enjoyable part of this set, although Toots Thielemans' Yesterday has all the charm of a wee small hours tune played out in a smoky cellar on piano and guitar.

Here, There And Everywhere

WINDHAM HILL 01934 11251 2. Released: 1999.

You Won't See Me by **Snuffy Walden**

I Will by **Tuck And Patti**

Eleanor Rigby by **Wayne Johnson**

Here, There And Everywhere by **Liz Story**

If I Needed Someone by **Michael Hedges**

Martha My Dear by **George Winston**

Girl by **Doyle Dykes**

Within You Without You by **Angels Of Venice**

Blackbird by **Sean Harkness**

Here Comes The Sun by **Tracy Silverman and Thea Suits Silverman**

Lucy In The Sky With Diamonds by **Lisa Lynne**

Mother Nature's Son by **Free Klassic**

The Long And Winding Road by **Liz Story**

The music: New age discovers The Beatles and Windham Hill's thoughtful fluttery sounds are moulded around those classic melodies. The result is almost entirely delivered in slow motion, with Snuffy Walden finger picking against a string quartet and Patti Cathcart's breathy vocal filling all the spaces with Tuck And Patti's I Will. She also features on Sean Harkness's version of Blackbird. Farther along, Liz Story's Steinway B sounds like raindrops on a sad morning on both The Long And Winding Road and the title track, while cello and piano vie for position on Free Klassic's version of Mother Nature's Son.Elsewhere, there's a ragtime reading of Martha My Dear by George Winston, rampant Flamenco from Wayne Johnson on Eleanor Rigby and some gurgling Billy Preston-styled keyboards lurking behind the violin and viola interchange of Tracy Silverman and Thea Suits Silverman's Here Comes The Sun. The best tracks, however, are from Lisa Lynne, who tackles Lucy In The Sky

With Diamonds which features an exotic procession of instruments including tamboura, bouzouki, wire harp and mandolin, and Angels Of Venice, whose version of Within You, Without You builds Harrison's mantra with succinctly bowed violin, cello, flute, udu, tabla and hammered dulcimer.

The sleeve: It's got beetles on it.

The sleevenotes: Purely a procession of instrument details from piano tunings to string bass and Celtic harp listings.

Classic Beatles cut: Within You, Without You is a gorgeous song anyway, it's rarely heard as a poor copy. This is no exception. And the sheer breadth of instrumentation that Angels Of Venice adopt add new dimensions.

Strawberry Fields
BLUENOTE7243 8 53920. Released: 1996.

Come Together by **Cassandra Wilson And Dianne Reeves**
Strawberry Fields Forever by **Cassandra Wilson**
Tomorrow Never Knows by **Dianne Reeves**
I'm Only Sleeping by **Holly Cole**
Get Back by **Jahlisa/Junko Onishi**
The Fool On The Hill by **Dianne Reeves**
I've Just Seen A Face by **Holly Cole**
Hey Jude by **Jahlisa/Greg Osby**
Lady Madonna by **Penny Ford**
Let It Be by **Sylvia Shemwell**

The tracks have an Eastern feel, the mood wavers in and out of mindless tinkling sounds occasionally retorting with a slapped bass. Indeed, the first three tracks sound like they were recorded in one session late into the night. Holly Cole's I'm Only Sleeping underlines the shortcomings of this all too synthetic sound. It's too slick for songs that need a bit of grit and a lot of love and attention.

The sleeve: It's got a strawberry on it.
The sleevenotes: Lots of recording details and pictures of people pulling faces in a not very Beatlesy way.
Classic Beatles cut: When all else fails you know that I'm Only Sleeping will tug at the heartstrings but even that seems watered down before being fluffed up with cotton wool. Shame.

The music: Under the by-line "Bob Belden Presents", this Blue Note compilation doesn't draw together the best of the label's past masters and their hoary translations of Beatles' fare. Instead Belden uses the same team of contemporary players for the most part to weave a late-night groove that's highlighted by finger-picked guitars, breathy mid-tempo shirt-loosening vocals and a bit of epic new-agey ambience.

Reloader
DRESSED TO KILL DOP54. Released: 1998.

All You Need Is Love by **Koz Mick**
Strawberry Fields by **Dork**
Nowhere Man by **PW (Hel)L**
Norwegian Wood by **Trained Monkey**
Lucy In The Sky by **Sisters**
Hey Jude by **The Jesus Factory**
A Hard Day's Night by **Paper Parrot**
Help! by **Army Of Half Wits**
Come Together by **Sketches Of The Famous**
Day Tripper by **Dork**
Sgt Pepper's Lonely Hearts Club Band by **Plastik Ted**

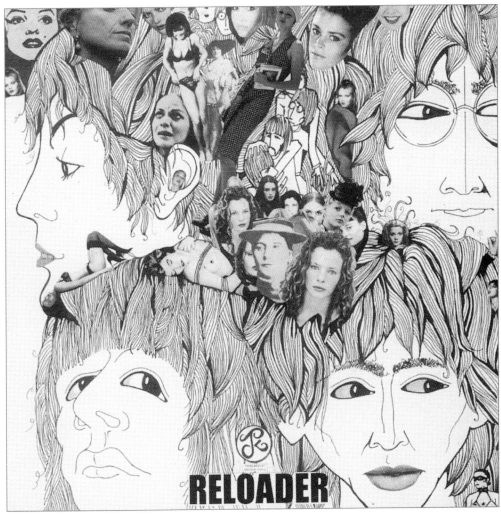

Yesterday by **Swarf Sisters**
Let It Be by **Jolly Bonce**
Here Comes The Sun by **Boxing Day Disaster**
Yellow Submarine by **Rude**
Hello Goodbye by **Koz Mick**
She Loves You by **Call The Mobile**
We Can Work It Out by **Nearly Good**
Michelle by **Trainers**
A Day In The Life by **Guru Brian**

The music: This is a strange, no-money-spent compilation featuring a bizarre selection of band names who all sound like they're the same people. Sure, a few hand-picked soloists are thrown in to add some width but the core team seems to consist of half a dozen geezers with a synth and a devout love of all things Beatles. And three of them were probably just thinking of the ridiculous names they could tag on to each of tunes. Whatever, the roll of honour includes some pretty uninspiring contributions.

For example, Koz Mick's All You Need Is Love and Hello Goodbye are two tracks that just don't sound right whichever way you squint at them. For whatever reason these two classics are reduced to flotsam by an inappropriate lack of care. They remain as just unchallenging tosh. Just a little too off-piste from their inspiration to be in any way palatable.

Then there's Dork's Strawberry Fields and Day Tripper. These two tracks sound like they've come from two completely different groups. Perhaps they split and reformed under the same name but a different ecological persuasion half way through the sessions. The end result is Strawberry Fields as a sax-led new age noodle, while Day Tripper sounds like it's fallen under the sad influence of Koz Mick, with not a sniff of sax anywhere to be heard.

PW(HEL)L turn out to be one of the better things on a poor platter, delivering an instrumental version of Nowhere Man played by a string quartet with a pulsing bass in the style of The Nice at their most strident.

Then there's Trained Monkey who achieve new levels of ridiculousness with their polka-lite version of Norwegian Wood, Sisters who add a flute and a new age sheen for Lucy In The Sky With Diamonds. But by now it's all just beggaring belief.

Jesus Factory go for a McCartney-ish slur through Hey Jude and Paper Parrott, Army Of Half Wits and Sketches Of The Famous offer A Hard Day's Night, Help! And Come Together all of which sound like they're done by exactly the same group.

Then there's Plastik Ted with big band jazz on Sgt Pepper's. The Swarf Sisters' new agey acoustic on Yesterday. Boxing Day Disaster's Here Comes The Sun on pan pipes and Rude's simply ludicrous version of Yellow Submarine, during which the singer tries to sound like Ringo which, let's face it, not even fans of Thomas The Tank Engine try to do in the privacy of their own home.

By this point the Reloaders had obviously run out of whimsical names to call themselves. And so we have Call The Mobile, who sound like a continental covers outfit trying to come to terms with the complexities of She Loves You. By contrast Guru Brian has the best name but their A Day In The Life suffers from the slings and arrows of outrageous synths. Making this a rum old listen all round.

The sleeve: Now that's good. A fine pastiche of Revolver, no less.

The sleevenotes: None existent, no-one's going to own up to this one.

Classic Beatles cut: Oh, come on.

Revolution No 9
A Tribute To the Beatles
In Aid Of Cambodia
POP GOD PAX PGLP 09. Released: 1992.

Revolution by **Billy Bragg**
True Life Hero by **The Pooh Sticks**
She She Said by **The Driscolls**
Across The Universe by **The Family Cat**
I Must Be In Love by **The Senseless Things**
Norwegian Wood by **The Moonflowers**
I Am the Walrus by **John Otway**

All Too Much by **Love's Young Nightmare**
Don't Let Me Down by **Paul Weller**
If I Needed Someone by **The Anyways**
It Won't Be Long by **Heavenly**
A Hard Day's Night by **Mega City 4**
Flying by **Frank Sidebottom**
Drive My Car by **The Brilliant Corners**
I'm Only Sleeping by **The Family**
Rain by **Beatle Hans And The Paisley Perverts**

The music: A wild selection of indie Gods and shoe gazers, most of whom went on to amount to very little. Back in the early '90s indie bands really were indie and probably paid to play at the Rock Garden, craved a Peel Session and split up before they creativity could be realised. Few reached phase two. But, with a war raging in Cambodia, Oxfam rounded up a fair few of them, topped and tailed them with Billy Bragg and Paul Weller and put this album out to raise funds for the people of the war-torn state. Why they chose to cover Beatles' songs we'll probably never know. Anyway. Billy Bragg sings at breakneck pace with feedbacking guitars and plenty of pent-up emotion and Paul Weller gives it full-scale soul on an excellent Don't Let Me Down and in between, the collected masses, even though they'd opted to do a Beatles' tribute bent the rules considerably, as you'd expect. The Pooh Sticks provided a Klaatu song and The Senseless Things went for a Rutles' cover. The wags.

There's comedy too, with John Otway's satirical I Am The Walrus and Frank Sidebottom's Flying, but most of the songs are just happy to meander in a sea of noisy guitars.

The sleeve: Arty and indie.

The sleevenotes: About Cambodia.

Classic Beatles cut: Weller is on form, Otway and Sidebottom are good fun and The Family's backwards reverb on I'm Only Sleeping is well worth it.

Sgt Pepper Knew My Father

NME/CHILDLINE NME PEPLP-100. Released: 1988.

Sgt Pepper's Lonely Hearts Club Band by **The Three Wize Men**

With A Little Help From My Friends by **Wet Wet Wet**

Lucy In The Sky With Diamonds by **The Christians**

Getting Better by **The Wedding Present with Amelia Fletcher**

Fixing A Hole by **Hue And Cry**

She's Leaving Home by **Billy Bragg**

Bring For The Benefit Of Mr Kite by **Frank Sidebottom**

When I'm 64 by **The Courtney Pine Quartet**

Lovely Rita by **Michelle-Shocked**

Good Morning Good Morning by **The Triffids**

Sgt Pepper's Lonely Hearts Club Band by **The Three Wize Men**

A Day In The Life by **The Fall**

The music: Conceived by the NME to benefit the Children In Need appeal, Sgt Pepper Knew My Father went for sartorial irreverence by teaming together UK rappers Three Wize Men, soapy popsters Wet Wet Wet and The Fall, among others to retell the Pepper story. As an artefact it works for its audacious approach and left field composition. There are winners (Wedding Present, Bragg and The Fall) and there are losers (Hue And Cry, The Christians, the Wets) but for all it's shortcomings it's always an entertaining experience.

The sleeve: A disappointingly bland out of focus shot of God knows what.

The sleevenotes: None other than those to herald the cause.

Classic Beatles cut: You almost want The Fall's version of A Day In The Life to be a monumental pastiche of The Beatles' Pepper swansong but alas it doesn't quite achieve that. It's good, but The Wedding Present's breakneck It's Getting Better All The time carries all before it and is simply wondrous.

The Beatles Tribute Anthology Volume One

TRIBUTE TR014. Released: Unknown.

Love Me Do by **The Space Cakes**

Things We Said Today by **The Ravengers**

You've Got To Hide Your Love Away by **The Inbetweendays**

Wait by **The Dilemmas**

If I Needed Someone by **Sharp Kiddie**

Taxman by **Skainsmate**

Tomorrow Never Knows by **The Persuaders**

Sgt Pepper's Lonely Hearts Club Band by **Exit**

Something By **Disgraceland**

Come Together by **Flow**

Across The Universe by **Lighthouse**

Day Tripper by **The Mourning After**

Rain by **Hipster**

The music: Made in Sweden, with the best in Spanish, Swedish and English Beatlesisms in tow, The Beatles Tribute Anthology actually throws up some of the most interesting versions of Beatles' songs in this whole book. The Space Cakes play psychedelic organ music in a Vanilla Fudge style, The Ravengers are low-key janglers and Inbetweendays sound like The Small Faces in the mood for bar-chords and feedback.

There's great harmonies and brooding psychedelic noise on Sharp Kiddie's If I Needed Someone and the '60s garage mood is maintained by The Persuaders whose backward "seagulls" guitar and harpsichord chops erupts into a Floydian middle section. It's wild! Exit do Sgt Pepper's as an instrumental with a gorgeous, almost baroque section and Flow completely dismantle Come Together, creating an industrial symphony which evolves into a mini-operatta. Absolutely fab.

The sleeve: Minimal and officious in a White Album style.

The sleevenotes: In depth write-ups and photos of the various bands.

Classic Beatles cut: Flow's Come Together, The Mourning After's strange vocal effects on Day Tripper and Lighthouse's poppy World Party-rasp are all worthy readings.

TRIBUTE CLASSIC COLLECTION

The Beatles Tribute Anthology Volume 1

Love me do • Things we said today • You've got to hide your love away
Wait • If I needed someone • Taxman • Tomorrow never knows
Sgt Peppers lonely hearts club • Something • Come together
Across the universe • Daytripper • Rain

Yesterday

TROJAN ZCTRL 294. Released: 1991.

Yesterday by **Dandy**
Hey Jude by **John Holt**
Come Together by **The Israelites**
Something by **Phyllis Dillon**
Let It Be by **Nicky Thomas**
Get Back by **Anonymously Yours**
Hey Jude by **Joe's All Stars**
My Sweet Lord by **Keith Lynn, with Byron Lee And The Dragonaires**
World Without Love by **Del Davis**
Give Peace A Chance by **The Maytals**
Lady Madonna by **The Crystalites**
Isn't It A Pity by **Nicky Thomas**
Don't Let Me Down by **The Harry J All Stars**
Blackbird Singing by **Roslyn Sweet And The Paragons**
Eleanor Rigby by **BB Seaton**
World Without Love by **The Johnny Arthey Orchestra**

The music: Billed as "16 fab Beatle Reggae Classics", Yesterday rolls around the various reggae sub-genres offering bland Bassey-esque crooning from Phyllis Dillon, rock steady from Nicky Thomas and Dandy and haunting, echoey interpretations of Liverpudlian-ness by The Israelites on Come Together. Throughout, the rhythms are obviously pretty rudimentary and few of the star cast take liberties with the Lennon and McCartney canon. Roslyn Sweet And The Paragons offer a lovers rock skank on Blackbird, Nicky Thomas's Isn't It A Pity has a soulful feel and Harry J And The Allstars' organ-fuelled instrumental of Don't Let Me Down has an alluring rough-hewn charm all of its own. BB Seaton's version of Eleanor Rigby has an unnerving off-centre rhythm, which makes it into a fantastically eerie piece, undoubtedly the standout of the set.

The sleeve: Nothing startling here at all.

The sleevenotes: "This specially compiled collection is a tribute to and a reflection of the exceptional songwriting of John Lennon, Paul McCartney and George Harrison. Collected here for the very first time are 16 Beatles tracks recorded by some of the eminent and respected artists from Jamaica. Each and every cut included is worthy of being considered a sincere interpretation of the original as, without exception, they were all committed to vinyl at least half a decade before John's death."
Classic Beatles cut: BB Seaton's Eleanor Rigby.

A Reggae Tribute To The Beatles Volume Two

EMPORIO EMPRCD 718. Released: 1997

Ob-La-Di, Ob-La-Da by **The Heptones**
All Day Night by **Sugar Minott**
Yesterday by **Tyrone Taylor**
My Love by **Ken Boothe**
You Won't See Me by **Ernie Smith**
And I Love Her by **The Mohawks**
Norwegian Wood by **Marshall Williams**
My Sweet Lord by **Fitzroy Stirling**
Don't Let Me Down by **Marcia Griffiths**
Here Comes The Sun by **Dawn Penn**
In My Life by **Jackie Robinson**
Imagine by **Susan Cadogan**
Hey Jude by **The Dynamites**
Let It Be by **The Soulettes**
Carry That Weight by **Dobby Dobson**
Happy Xmas (War Is Over) by **John Holt**

The music: Somehow these reggae rhythms, whatever sub-genre they're stuffed into, seem to fit The Beatles' sense of melody. And having stapled it to whatever beat they see fit, the result is a procession of danceable moments punctuated by some irreverent soulfulness. The Heptones, for instance, go rock steady on Ob-La-Di and Sugar Minott goes double entendre crazy on A Hard Day's Night, where he reports his full rub-a-dub antics. Tyrone Taylor heads for a dancehall vein and Ken Boothe has a shuffling rhythm to hold the attention. Harmonies collide, rhythms shuffle and bonafide rock steady pacing is dusted off.

For the most part, this is a finger-clicking selection. Sure, the guitar on Fitzroy Simmons' My Sweet Lord is powered by a resurrected cheese grater, but elsewhere there's panting vocals, lovers rock and some embracing whistleable choons. Undoubtedly The Soulettes should be apprehended and certified for their lyric-dropping Let It Be – they resort to the classic line "Jah, jah, jah, jah, jah, jah", but mostly this is fun.

The sleeve: A Rastaman sketch of The Fabs on a Jamaican holiday.

The sleevenotes: None.

Classic Beatles cut: Sugar Minott got soul.

Yesterday Part Three
TROJAN CDTRL 365. Released: 1996.

Carry That Weight by **Dobby Dobson**
More Weight by **Dobby Dobson**
Imagine by **Susan Cadogan**
My Sweet Lord by **Fitzroy Stirling**
Let It Be by **The Mohawks**
Something by **Susan Cadogan**
You Never Know (I'll Be Back) by **Errol Dunkley**
And I Love Her by **The Mohawks**
All Day Night (A Hard Day's Night)
by **Sugar Minott**
You Won't See Me by **Ernie Smith**
My Sweet Lord by **Ken Lazarus**
Here Comes The Sun by **Sharon Forrester**
Blackbird by **Desmond Dekker**
Here Comes The Sun by **Dawn Penn**
Ob-La-Di, Ob-La-Da by **The Heptones**
Hey Jude by **Rico And The Rudies**
Yesterday by **Tyrone Taylor**
Let It Be by **The Soulettes**

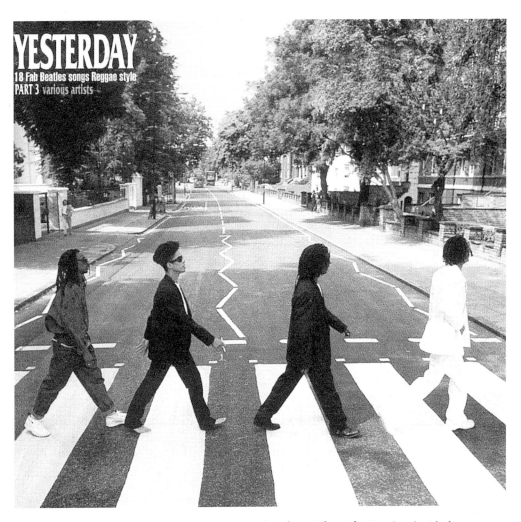

YESTERDAY
18 Fab Beatles songs Reggae style
PART 3 various artists

The music: released prior to Emperio's Volume Two, this album features some of the same tracks but, in addition, it has some key moments in the Caribeatles equation. They are quite simply Desmond Dekker's Blackbird, with its itinerant horns, and Rico And The Rudies' trombone-powered Hey Jude, which is an epic of off-the-cuff skanking, sharp, edgy and confused but fully functional on the dancefloor.

The sleeve: The Abbey Road crossing with four brothers en route.

The sleevenotes: Chris Prete reveals: "The popularity of The Beatles across the whole musical spectrum, is truly amazing. As the years go by they seem to lose none of their appeal. Perhaps one of the reasons for this is the songwriting genius of John Lennon and Paul McCartney, who were responsible for most of the group's timeless hits. When The Beatles decided to pursue solo carers, the split sent shock waves through the music industry, and it seemed as if an era had come to a close. As a group The Beatles had taken Britain by storm, going onto conquer America as well.

"Looking at the artists featured in this collection is like looking at a who's who of reggae. Susan Cadogan, Dawn Penn, Errol Dunkley and Desmond Dekker have all achieved success in the UK charts, whilst The Soulettes, Heptones, Tyrone Taylor, Sugar Minott and Dobby Dobson have made an immeasurable contribution to the advancement of Jamaican music. Their talent, added to the songs of Lennon and McCartney, produced these outstanding tracks."

Classic Beatles cut: Hey Jude by Rico And The Rudies for all its wayward spirit.

The Easy Listening Beatles Songbook

EMBASSY RECORDS EMB 31101. Released: 1973
CBS CAMEO 32664. Re-issued: 1985.

*Hey Jude by **Ray Coniff***

*Fool On The Hill by **Percy Faith***

*Yesterday by **Ray Coniff***

*Eleanor Rigby by **Johnny Mathis***

*You've Got To Hide Your Love Away by **Percy Faith***

*My Sweet Lord by **Johnny Mathis***

*Something by **Peter Nero***

*The Long And Winding Road by **Andre Kostelantez***

*Michelle by **Andre Kostelantez***

*Variation on the theme – Ob-La-Di, Ob-La-Da by **Peter Nero***

*Let It Be by **Jerry Vale***

The music: Cut-price fare from the Columbia label scooping together an unlikely collection of smooth swingers and their Beatles-lite offerings. Strings and sub-melodies dominate from Coniff, Faith and Kostelanetz with plenty of the easy-going ba-ba-ba-baddahs from an assembled group of faceless female crooners on offer. Moving on, Johnny Mathis at least has a voice to do the talking, unlike the troubled Jerry Vale, while Peter Nero's bittersweet piano allows Something an extra layer of poignancy – even when some hyena howling erupts in the middle-eight. The strangest cut of all comes with Nero's take on Ob-La-Di, Ob-La-Da which purports to follow the same route but sprinkles the proceedings with tinny xylophone and a chorus played out in hammy Beethoven minuet style. To fully confuse matters it bursts into a Latin verse before

reverting to cod-classical. Crazy.

The sleeve: A superbly ironic send-up with two old-timers wigging out in full Sixties clobber as their shocked son arrives home in preppy garb. The headphone-wearing duo are also set off by an impressive bong placed in the centre of their chintzy coffee table. The re-issue opted for a straight none-pic image. Shame.

The sleevenotes: Sadly there are none on the

original, but the sleeve pic kinda makes up for that.

On the re-issue, however, Ed Lawson lets fly: "It was back in 1964 that Ed Sullivan introduced a quartet of musical mopheads from Liverpool to a panting America. This country hasn't been the same since. Sociologists tell us that our dress, culture and other allied lifestyles have changed. More importantly, serious critics tell us that our

music has undergone a significant transformation from that fateful date. Whatever anyone says, you'll have to admit that The Beatles as entertainers, and particularly as composers, have given an extra dimension to the world of pop as we know and appreciate it today.

"Of the 11 songs on this album, nine are written by John Lennon and Paul McCartney, two by George Harrison. Maturing from their early days of rock. Paul, John and George have written what are today considered important standards, generally impressive parts of every contemporary pop artists' repertoire. "Vocally, the McCartney / Lennon songs range from the big baritone of Jerry Vale on Let It Be, to the Ray Coniff Singers, as they raise their myriad voices in two of John and Paul's most popular ballads, Hey Jude and Yesterday. And Johnny Mathis lends his own unique interpretation to the poignant Eleanor Rigby. George Harrison, not as prolific as Lennon and McCartney, has been a successful composer in his own right. His religious-flavoured My Sweet Lord, sung by Johnny Mathis; and Something, set to the music of the nimble fingers of Peter Nero complete the 11 selections here.

"So sit back listen and enjoy the songs of three relative youngsters who parlayed their many talents into millions of dollars, then went their individual ways, leaving and indelible stamp on modern music. When performed by some of today's great musical practitioners, these songs are an unforgettable listening experience."

Classic Beatles cut: Variations On The Theme 'Ob-La-Di, Ob-La-Da' by Peter Nero.

Named and
shamed:
Bongwater,
Alma Cogan,
Tom Jones,
Richie Havens,
Billy Pepper,
Liberace,
Junior Walker,
Val Doonicon and
many, many more

EVERBODY'S GOT SOMETHING TO HIDE....

After whole albums of Fab, after the tributes and the compilations, the Beatles' bug was biting hard. Everywhere I went there seemed to be Beatles' songs. And everyone seemed to have their own style of interpretation, their own reading, indeed their own reason for covering such and such a song.

Some took the whole premise of Fabdom and the use of Beatles as the theme for their whole album. It just made them groovy. Others just slotted a track in here and there amid a whole range of stuff. And some were just doing something so totally unconnected that the last thing you'd expect to crop up on their album was a Beatles' tune. But crop up it did.

It seems that The Beatles are clearly identifiable with masters of melody, soft rock legends, psychedelic buffoons, easy listening pioneers, eccentrics, electronic engineers and anyone who knows where Liverpool is on the map. Even roughly.

This section looks at those wayward spirits, checks their written credentials and far-ranging associations with Lennon, McCartney, Harrison and co. It deciphers their claims, however clouded and unconventional, and explains what, in the cold light of day, actually happened.

Everybody's got a Beatles song inside them bursting to get out. There are thousands of them, here's just a few that are notable for their audacity, charm, and on some occasions, a highly-inventive streak. Marvel, then at the works of Yes, James Last, John Williams, The Buggs, The Four Tops and many, many more...

Ronnie Aldrich

Fool On The Hill and **Lucy in The Sky With Diamonds** from Tomorrow's Yesterdays
Decca SKL 5305. Released: 1979.

What the sleeve says: Ronnie is the silver-haired daddy who wants to be Dr Who. Surrounded by antiquated keyboards and techno-phobic doppelgangers, the sleeve lets you know that this is going to be a weird one.

The sleevenotes concur: "He believes that the personality impact of Elvis Presley, The Beatles, The Moody Blues, Leo Sayer and many others must provide a commentary on the popular music of our times. So this time capsule includes many titles that he hopes will awaken happy memories not only today but tomorrow, when today is yesterday."

What really happens: Ronnie plays piano (the double 88 it's called), has brass and strings on hand but he's also fond of introducing a few effects, synthesised or otherwise, as he trawls through standards by 10CC, The Stylistics, Procul Harum and the aforementioned Elvis, Beatles and Moody Blues. It's tame stuff. Easy listening-lite, the kind of music that makes you think there's no music on.

Best thing about it: Actually, Fool On The Hill and Lucy have a quirky electronic presence. They're almost moderne, the latter breaking into a Bontempi middle section that's as camp as you like.

quered over here on what's an underproduced version. But, give her a balmy evening and a smoke filled club and George's bank balance would be bristling.

Best thing about it: Shirley's dress.

Beatle Hans

Rain from It's Beatle Hans
FIERCE RECORDS FRIGHT 043. Released: 1990.

What the sleeve says: Very little other than the fact that Beatle Hans have eclectic taste in music and Beatle Hans is actually a bloke who sings and plays tambourine.

What really happens: Beatle Hans sound like Oasis in places but with plenty more guitar feedback and a penchant for the grinding riff when duty calls. They can also cut it like The Ramones given half a chance. The album itself sounds like it was recorded in a barn (in fact it was The Milky

Laurindo Almeida

Michelle from A Man And A Woman
EMI RECORDS ST 2701. Released: 1967.

What the sleeve says: This is groovy bachelor pad music played out by this South American guitarist who admits that playing guitar is "his passion". Phew!

What really happens: An orchestra swivels around the main melody while Laurindo picks the harmony out of the song.

Best thing about it: Not that much really.

Shirley Bassey

Something from Her Favourite Songs
MUSIC FOR PLEASURE MFP 158347. Released: 1985.

What the sleeve says: Shirley likes a lot of good tunes, including Tom Rush's No Regrets and Rod Mckuen's If You Go Away.

What really happens: The Welsh belter really carries the torch for Harrison's emotive ballad

way up high. To be truthful numerous live renditions of Something by Shirley Bassey have beaten this hands down and her trademark scorching high note finish is pretty much lac-

Way in Amsterdam) and the wall of overloading instrumentation sets the perfect backdrop for Hans' detuned nasal vocal. Included are covers of Tommy James And The Shondells' Crimson And Clover, The Bangles' Eternal Flame, the Stones' Citadel and Dylan's My Back Pages, which they attack head-on. And Rain itself is given scant respect - but there again all of the songs are treated the same and end up as a reasonably monosyllabic trickle of slurry.

Best thing about it: The pure noise. (Man!)

Cilla Black

Step Inside Love from Sher-oo!
PARLOPHONE PCS 7041. Released: 1968

What the sleeve says: Cilla's hair needs some attention.

What really happens: Cilla Black was already a pop star through Beatles-written tunes from the early '60s onwards by the time she did Step Inside Love. Managed by Brian Epstein she had access to the mighty pens of Lennon and McCartney and when she premiered her BBC Saturday night TV series the duo gave her Step Inside Love as a highly-palatable, commercial and hit-sensitive theme tune.

Best thing about it: Step Inside Love fitted her blue-eyed tortured ballad style perfectly and

gave her the opportunity to belt it out when needed. But, it's some of the other songs here and the album's George Martin production that really impress. This Is The First Time and her version of Tim Hardin's Misty Roses are both really excellent.

Bongwater

Rain from Too Much Sleep and Julia from Double Bummer
Both included in the Bongwater Box set SHIMMYDISC SHHM 5555. Released: 1998.

What the sleeve says: The 'water is weird.
What really happens: Bongwater comprise of experimental former Shockabilly dude Kramer and actress Ann Magnusson. He noodles and

adds layers of unrelated noise (especially on Rain) and Magnusson sings in a hot babe way. For some reason she seems to have stepped out of the studio for Rain and the proceedings just meander into oblivion where half a dozen radios are left on and a saxophonist is tooting in the next apartment. Julia is another disjointed affair with guitars chiming and Ann singing but the general anarchy that reigns makes it sound like a rehearsal you've just snook in on.

Best thing about it: Kramer's whining guitar break and the ridiculous telephone messages that litter Double Bummer.

The Buggs

I Want To Hold Your Hand and She Loves You from The Beetle Beat
CORONET RECORDS CX-212. Released: early '60s.

What the sleeve says: On the front: "The Beetle Beat, featuring I Want To Hold Your Hand / The Buggs. The original Liverpool Sound, Recorded in England."
On the back: "England has invaded America! From the banks of the Mersey River, by Liverpool, England a new sound, a new beat, has gained tremendous popular acceptance.

"The Mersey Beat! The Liverpool Sound! Remember these names for a new trend in popular music has arrived. The year of Beetlemania. The Mersey Beat features a string guitar rhythm attack backed with a solid beat producing a driving, stomping, rock and rolling tempo.

"The Kings of Mersey Best to date are The

Walter Carlos

Eleanor Rigby and a snatch of Yellow Submarine from Walter Carlos By Request

CBS 73163. Released 1975.

What the sleeve says: "Walter Carlos by whose request? Since releasing Switched-On Bach, Tempi has been continually bombarded by repertoire suggestions from interested listeners for future Walter Carlos records."

So opens the sleeve of this mid-'70s monstrosity. Carlos had come to fame through his electronic reworkings of the classics on etudes for instruments with special rhythmic problems. Walter did 'What's New Pussycat?' as an exercise in early 1967 as his first attempt at an eight-track realisation, it was very nearly his very first Moog synthesiser piece. Popular songs continue to provide material for occasional experiments until 1967, with the completion of Eleanor Rigby."

What really happens: Amid a classical fug, Carlos attempts to redefine Eleanor Rigby and slips into the middle consciousness of atonal nether-worldliness. (Or something.) More interesting, perhaps, is his meandering Pompous Circumstance, which takes up most of a side. His homage to Elgar is played out with a nod to various contemporary sounds, including the briefest of sideways keyboard rattles that leads him to the melody of Yellow Submarine.

Best thing about it: The sleevenotes are pretty indecipherable in all their serious techno-babble, the Eleanor Rigby track is quite charming but it's the sheer madness and the seemingly uncontrollable farting noises that the synth offers that are the most memorable things here.

Beatles, followed by Billy J Kramer And The Dakotas and Gerry And The Pacemakers. In this album you will hear the original Liverpool sound recorded on location in England by The Buggs, a fast moving, well paced group that we are sure you will like."

What really happens: The Buggs are The Rutles before they were ever thought of. Their songs are made up of Beatles' melodies delivered in a different order or just simply re-worded. It's actually bizarre hearing "I want to hold your hand" reworded as "Why don't you leave that man".

Whatever, for all we know, it may have sold albums in middle America where, so the legend goes, Beatlemania didn't strike until 1981. Musically, both of their covers have a youthful energy but their own songs - written in the style of the fabulous Merseybeat era - struggle for authenticity and pizzazz. The Buggs almost look the part too. But there again there's just something that isn't quite right about the whole deal. Best thing about it: The titles of their other songs - Mersey Mercy, Soho Mash, East End, London Town Swing, Liverpool Drag, Swingin' Thames and Big Ben Hop are just great, even if the titles bear little relationship to the actual songs themselves.

the soundtrack of A Clockwork Orange and his complex life (he was later to have a sex change and become Wendy Carlos) and Teutonic attention to melody, fused with a love of primal electronics led him to a unique vision and some strange readings of contemporary music. Back then the synthesiser wasn't as well behaved as it is today and as he/she proves on What's New Pussycat?, the odd bleep and splurge noise can't help but creep in. For whatever reason.

"Popular songs offer no profundity of content to hide behind; in performance they dance or utterly die. They make splendid

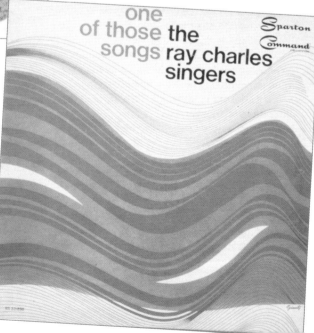

The Ray Charles Singers

Yesterday from One Of Those Songs
COMMAND RECORDS RS 33 893. Released: 1966

What the sleeve says: "There are some songs that mean something very special to every one of us. And there are others that capture the essence of a feeling or a mood or a style or a personality so well that we can identify a whole area of music by that single song.

"Yesterday is one of those Beatles songs - but a song so different from the type of song with which they first made their reputation that, as Ray Charles notes, it serves as a comment on the English group. 'They are the great musical experimenters of our time,' Charles said when he chose the song. 'They keep moving and changing, they never become stagnant.' The Ray Charles Singers, just the men this time, do the song as a glee club with Tony Mottola's reflective, gut-string guitar as their sole accompaniment."

What really happens: The Ray Charles Singers are an odd confection. Their sound is singularly gentle, friendly and unthreatening and their version of Yesterday lilts from the stereo like a piece of featherlite fluff. Inoffensive and full of harmony, it winkles out every last but of emotion and leaves it on the cutting room floor, reducing what is a beautifully brittle song to something that just lacks any real passion.

Best thing about it: It's quite short.

The Carmen Cavallaro Camp

Eleanor Rigby, Yesterday, Here, There And Everywhere and Let It Be from Plays The 3 B's (The Beatles, Bacharach And Bach)
PYE PKL 4402. Released: 1971.

What the sleeve says: "The record of the best and happiest moments of the happiest and best minds. Carmen Cavallaro, the poet of the piano, weaves a masterpiece, a harmoniously vivid painting of the souls of genius. Rhythm, melody, vision, spirit... emotions recollected in tranquility... rhyme and reason... imagery, fantasy. The elusive past - the thundering present. Gifted, skilful, ethereal, rendering of love."

What really happens: Cavallaro goes completely keyboard crazy. Sweeping time and tempo changes, flowing strings and madcap Latin rhythms augment his attacking style. Yesterday breaks into a mariachi middle eight, Eleanor Rigby chops through with classical phrasing and Here, There And Everywhere rallies like a jam-friendly jazz number with minor chords building the tension. Let It Be is tame in comparison, which is a shame.

Best thing about it: Yesterday rocks once more.

What the sleeve says: Cocker, under contract, was forced to do a coast-to-coast tour of the States following his success at Woodstock, the album is a the record of the tour.

What really happens: The assembled motley crew became a large scale soul revue who meandered through the blues, classic R&B and the best of the new peace and love sentimentality. This double album is horn-laden, filled with shrieking female-powered harmonies, all centred around Leon Russell's wandering arrangements and Cocker's diamond cut groggy soul vocal.

There is a mood to the whole piece into which She Came In Thru The Bathroom Window seems to fit perfectly. The troupe's world view of peace, love and alien travel all the more palatable for it.

Joe Cocker
With A Little Help From My Friends from the album of the same name.
A&M SP 4182. Released: 1969.

What the sleeve says: The front suggests that Joe Cocker is a possessed gurner, the back that he's assisted by the likes of Jimmy Page, Stevie Winwood and loads more. His selection of material is key too, there's Traffic's Feeling Alright, the hoary old chestnut Bye Bye Blackbird, a couple of Dylan's cast offs and a pair of self-penned tracks including the awesome Sandpaper Cadillac.

What really happens: Cocker's cracked soul vocal is colossal throughout the album and when he turns his attention to With A Little Help From My Friends he makes it his own in a howling storm of emotion. Anyone who's seen his contorted delivery at Woodstock couldn't doubt the passion that he lavishes over the song. The end result is awesome.

Best thing about it: The backing vocals of Madeleine Bell, Rosetta Hightower and Sunny Wheetman that simply rip the roof off.

Joe Cocker
She Came In Thru The Bathroom Window from Mad Dogs And Englishmen
A&M 6002. Released: 1970.

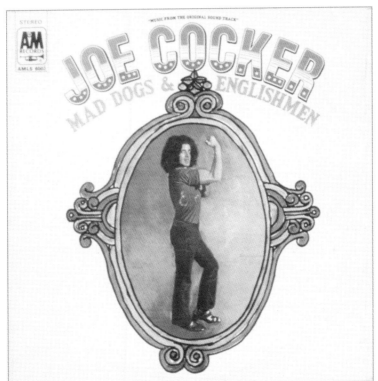

Best thing about it: The rasping horns that wallow around Cocker's lead on Bathroom Window, the woohs and aahs on Space Captain, the bedraggled reading of the Womack's Let's Go Get Stoned, the awesome version of Cry Me A River and Otis Redding's I've Been Loving You Too Long to name but a handful.

Alma Cogan
Help!, Eight Days A week and Yesterday from The Alma Cogan Collection
EMI ONE UP OU2168. Released: 1967.

What the sleeve says: "In October 1965 just 12 months before she died, Alma Cogan went into the studio to record several songs by her two close friends John Lennon and Paul McCartney. The two Beatles attended the recordings and were reportedly "knocked out" with Alma's big ballad version of Eight Days A Week."

What really happens: These three gems are tucked away at the end of this 21 track collection from Alma's past. She has a great voice and on occasions has a suitably friendly set of arrangements to let it flow over.

More Beatles-specific, the cover of Help! is rampant and she struggles to keep time as sub-melodies are introduced. Yesterday is more straightforward, echoey and Bassey-esque but it's Eight Days A Week that really flies. The tempo is slowed completely and she's allowed to sashay through the song with great charm, giving it a truly individual polish.

Best thing about it: The curling lip sensuality of Eight Days A Week.

The Congregation

Something from Softly Whispering I Love You

COLUMBIA SCXJ 6490. Released: 1972

What the sleeve says: "Congregation-a musical wall of sound consisting of massed choirs, rough vocal voice and jangular guitar."

What really happens: The Congregation brought together vocalist Brian Keith and guitarist Alan Parker who took a Cook-Greenaway song, Softly Whispering I Love You to the top of the charts in the late '60s. Their trick was to have a 20-plus choir giving the arrangements a choral resonance for Keith's gritty Joe Cocker-esque vocals to grate against. The resultant album fea

tured the tune, a Cat Stevens song, Procul Harum's A Whiter Shade Of Pale and a limp furrow of the brow on Something.

Best thing about it: Keith's vocal is more than convincing on Something but the sombre choral backing is too subdued, so you don't really get the play-off between his gravel rasp and the gentler end of the vocal spectrum.

Arthur Conley

Ob-La-Di, Ob-La-Da from More Sweet Soul

ATCO 288 019. Released: 1967.

What the sleeve says: "Arthur Conley is on top, as this album will attest. In fact, this album is a

look at what Conley is all about. He can shout soul with the best as he does on Shing-A-Ling and he can be mellow and rhythmic as he is with Ob-La-Di, Ob-La-Da. This tune is part of a new influence in music called "rock steady" that originated in Jamaica. Conley took the song and its beat added a dash of his special soul treatment and came up with the first soul steady recording."

What really happens: More Sweet Soul has some tempered Conley crooning, very restrained in a pop style for the most part, and the occasional throaty rasp that harks back to the blues and his big hit Sweet Soul Music. However, the album opener is Ob-La-Di, Ob-La-Da and you'd be forgiven for thinking that Arthur hadn't actually turned up for the session. The multi-tracked vocal is low in the mix, struggling against an unwise rock-steady swagger. The collision of styles leaves no room for any Conley bravado and any Beatles magic is pretty strained too.

Best thing about it: The classic element to Conley's version of this Beatles' genre-bender is the guitar solo which is so clumsily edited that it sounds like a Steve Cropper-esque character has been locked in a cupboard which Arthur busts open mid-bar. What's more, the psychedelic salvo jars with some grace against the reggae plod. Messy all around.

Floyd Cramer

Yesterday and You've Got To Hide Your Love Away from The Big Ones

RCA VICTOR LSP-3533. Released 1966

What the sleeve says: "Even a fellow gifted with the Midas touch likes to bet on a sure thing every now and then. And that's what Floyd has done in choosing the ingredients for his latest album."

What really happens: Under the heading "Hits That Have Been Craving The Cramer Treatment", Floyd presents a brace of contemporary tunes including The Toys' A Lovers Concerto, Tom Jones' What's New Pussycat?, Ramsey Lewis's The 'In' Crowd, Len Barry's 1-2-3 and The Beatles' Yesterday and You've Got To Hide Your Love Away. It's four in the morning stuff. Orchestras bow, a Cor Anglais does its thing on Yesterday and the country pianist rolls his hand over the melodies on a traditionally sharp-tuned piano. You've Got To Hide Your Love Away receives similar mid-paced treatment but it also resonates with a vocal of aahs that sound like a bored newsagent was on hand for the performance.

Best thing about it: At least neither song is treated to the same flat horn salvo's that 1-2-3 suffers from before the staccato (read stuttering) flute break.

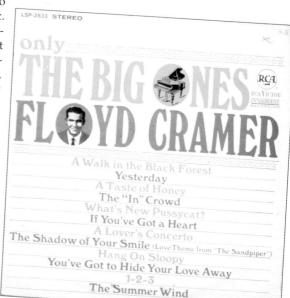

standing ovation on November 21, 1968. For a singer who made his first record in 1926, and has since sold over 2,000,000 records, this on the surface would not appear to be that extraordinary. However, this particular ovation was probably the most complimentary of his career. The people who stood and gave the salute were musicians who had just backed Mr Crosby in the recording of this album."

What really happens: Bing, obviously in career go-slow, seems to have been persuaded to get "hip" and sing some of the new tunes. He does, with a Dean Martin-styled swagger - especially on Little Green Apples - and even attempts to look like that young guy Sinatra on the back of the sleeve. The resultant music plods along in gentle mode. In fact very gentle mode.

Best thing about it: On Hey Jude the sombre orchestra and airy production do little to create a mood for Bing until some thundering drums drive the action. It's almost like there's a battle royale brewing with the orchestra desperate to uptempo but Bing staunchly pronouncing every word as it should be. The middle-eight - all girlie vocals and trouser suits a-swishing - is OK, but as soon as Bing returns from the break he staggeringly pom, pom, poms into the chantalong fade out, like the knowing professional he was, he refuses to get involved in such frippery. Whatever, the sleeve concludes that the orchestra discussion, after their standing ovation, went like this:"The older ones said, 'He still sings great.' The younger ones said, 'He's a gas' and he is, and so is Hey Jude/Hey Bing!."
Yeah, right.

Crazy Otto

Ticket To Ride, And I Love Her, Yesterday and Help! from Crazy Otto Beat
POLYDOR 249025. Released: 1971

What the sleeve says: This man is mad.
What really happens: German institution, Crazy Otto plays a funky barrelhouse piano and hums like a mad monk when trumpets, saxs and what have you take the lead melody. No words exchange hands here and each song is segued into another. The Beatles rub piano forte with the Stones, Lovin' Spoonful, The Supremes, Beach Boys, Sonny And Cher and even Bob Dylan and Barry McGuire. Whistles and annoying whoops and the sound of people impersonating chipmunks recur throughout. All in all, it's something that probably gave the songwriters in question great comfort that their art was being treated so well.
Best thing about it: In pure kitsch terms there's just so much that's truly great about this album. Certainly the Stones' Last Time is worth checking out as is the ridiculous Stop In The Name Of Love. But, yes, the classic moment is when Otto fuses together Don't Ha Ha, I'm Henry The Eighth and Help. Truly spectacular.

Bing Crosby

Hey Jude from Hey Jude/Hey Bing!
LONDON RECORDS SHU 8391

What the sleeve says: "Bing Crosby received a

Petula Clark

We Can Work It from My Love and Rain from I Couldn't live Without Your Love

SEQUEL RECORDS NEMCD 391. Released as a two pack 2000.

What the sleeve says: I'm desperately trying to look groovy.

What really happens: Petula Clark had charted high with Downtown and a repeat performance was demanded as 1966 rolled on. Two albums My Love and I Couldn't Live Without Your Love were put together with a host of Tony Hatch songs and a bunch of likely covers for good measure. Among them were a lacklustre attempt at We Can Work It Out on My Love and a truly offbeat version of Rain. Forgetting the fact that Pet can't quite hold the pace of the arrangement, which is over-enthusiastically poppy, the song teeters on the edge of disaster in an almost loveable way as the chorus looms.

Best thing about it: Rain's perverse wrangle with its own melody and an uptempo snare slap that makes the whole shebang just plain weird.

The Cyrkle

I'm Happy Just To Dance With You from Neon

COLUMBIA CL 2632. Released: 1967

What the sleeve says: These guys are serious musos with a sense of humour. Well, nearly.

What really happens: The Cyrkle are a psychedelic oddity. The quartet throw in all styles of music, from jug band to vaudeville and for The

Beatles track they change time and key throughout the song and have a sitar playing the melody. Unfortunately the sitar can't keep up with everything else and it goes from sharp to flat and back at the drop of a whatever. It's strange to say the least. But memorable. They also assault various other songwriters along the way.

Best thing about it: It's just mad. Hear it to believe it.

Ray Davies And The Button Down Brass

Fool On The Hill, Something, And I Love Her from 16 Startracks.

PHILIPS 6308 065. Released: 1968.

What the sleeve says: "The unique trumpet sound of Ray Davies - captured frequently on records, heard just as frequently on the radio: that button-down sound described as "funky"."

What really happens: Ray slices through 16 songs including Up Up And Away, Close To You, United We Stand, Melting Pot and Ain't No Mountain High Enough, plus three Beatles' tunes. Each and every one is treated to the same mid-tempo rumble with brass rasping away and session singers approximating the lyrics. Funk is in small supply, however there is a choppy guitar on Ain't No Mountain High Enough. It's the kind of stuff that would play in the background in a Tarantino movie while someone is "finished off".

The Beatles' cuts themselves are very tempered. Fool On The Hill wanders haplessly with cho-

rus-crooning and Something is solo trumpet involuntary. So it's And I Love Her that promises to be the "gem" if that's the right word. Orchestrated in true Martin Denny style with a tropical mist and sound effects backing the toot-ing trumpet and chorus, it's almost soulful. Almost. Honest!

Best thing about it: Those tropical howls. Just so Liverpool.

Dillard And Clark

Don't Let Me Down from Through The Morning Through The Night

A&M RECORDS. Re-issued on Edsel (1986) EDCD 195. First released: 1969.

What the sleeve says: These are good time country boys.

What really happens: After Doug Dillard moved on from family band The Dillards, he hooked up with departing Byrd Gene Clark. The duo became Dillard And Clark and developed a more country-slanted version of the Flying Burrito sound drafting in various Burritos to get the mood right. They lasted two albums of which this is the second and closed their partnership with a moving version of Don't let Me

Down led by Clark's emotive vocal.

Best thing about it: It's pure passion, removed from Merseyside, heading for the fields of Kentucky with Gene Clark giving it full back-porch credentials.

The Dillards

I've Just Seen A Face from Wheatstraw Suite

ELEKTRA EKS 74035. Released: 1969

What the sleeve says: Nothing about The Beatles. It just pictures of *this* Fab Four in ridiculous chirpy mode, aware that they'd probably invented country rock, unaware that The Eagles would take the jump on them and make big bucks from the genre.

What really happens: A traditional bluegrass group, The Dillards were besotted with The Beatles and when Sgt Pepper's came along they tried to move contemporary country into new areas. It's hardly psychedelia, but their mix of songs - they also do Tim Hardin's Reason To Believe, a version which in turn inspired Rod Stewart's - and their multi-harmonies make I've Just Seen A Face a rip-roaring pop opus complete with rabid mandolins and banjo.

Best thing about it: The Dillards' word-perfect rendition at breakneck speed.

The Dillards

Yesterday from Copperfields

ELEKTRA EKS 74054. Released: 1970

What the sleeve says: The Dillards aren't as cheerful as they used to be, but they've still got some strange clothes.

What really happens: In the style of trad. country, The Dillards are a touch more melancholy on this follow up to Wheatstraw Suite. Strings and woodwind have fleshed out the sound and Yesterday sits snugly within their achy canon.

Best thing about it: Rodney Dillard's down at heel take on McCartney's lyrics.

The Dillards

We Can Work It out from Decade Waltz

FLYING FISH FF082. Released: 1979

What the sleeve says: This is The Dillards back together ten years after their groundbreaking Wheatstraw Suite album.

What actually happens: It is indeed virtually most of The Dillards reformed and to emulate their Beatlesy insight, they cover We Can Work It Out in a similarly bluegrassy way. Fingers fly like billy-o!

Best thing about it: It's just darn great.

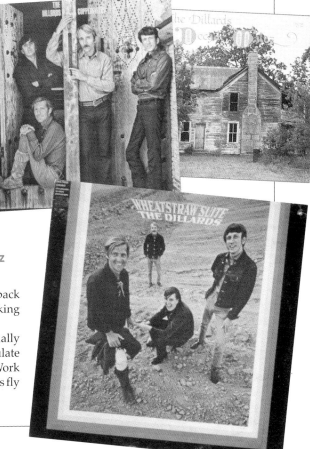

Val Doonicon

All You Need Is Love from Gentle On My Mind

CONTOUR 6870 599. Released: 1970.

What the sleeve says: It suggests that Val is a clean cut guy with a bar stool and a fine taste in songs to cover. The track list includes The Lovin' Spoonful's Daydream and Bobby Hebb's Sunny among others.

What really happens: Doonicon is Mr Mild. During the '60s and '70s he anchored his own BBC TV programme that mirrored the American Perry Como series. Each Saturday night he'd feed unsuspecting songs into his unthreatening range and deliver them all in the same tempo with the same lack of humanity. Add his Irish brogue and his latter-day trademark of an old rocking chair and you'll guess that All You Need Is Love is sadly lacking.

Best thing about it: Nothing.

Jose Feliciano

She's A Woman, Lady Madonna and Hey Jude from 10 To 23.

RCA SF 8044. Released: 1969.

What the sleeve says: Eclectic Flamenco-styled, shade-wearing post-beatnik groover picks three Beatles' songs amid soulful belters like Little Red Rooster, I've Gotta Get A Message To You and Miss Otis Regrets.

What really happens: Jose is destined for a "favourable" comeback I'll wager. He's a belter and he can whoop up a storm in a strumming Richie Havens style. Sure, some of the orchestrations lack a bit of snap but on 10 To 23, which features an archive recording when he was 10 and a batch of contemporary stuff from when he was, you guessed it, 23, he's got some finger-popping soul. And it's all powered by congas, 12-strings and all manner of coffee shop instrumentation. Cool.

Fever Tree

Day Tripper/We Can Work It Out from Fever Tree

UNI 73024. Released: 1969.

What the sleeve says: We're psychedelic and we dug Sgt Pepper's.

What really happens: It's a broody medley of Day Tripper and We Can Work It Out with a sultry harpsichord and an echoey feedback intro that bursts into an irreverent mystical eastern pattern before the main song is sub-sectioned by orchestral riffs from Norwegian Wood and Eleanor Rigby. With Dennis Keller's gritty vocal over the top, it's every bit the epic psychedelic experience the sleeve would suggest, throwing a withering glance towards Love and Buffalo Springfield along the way. Phew, excellent. (Etc, etc!)

Best thing about it: It's just great.

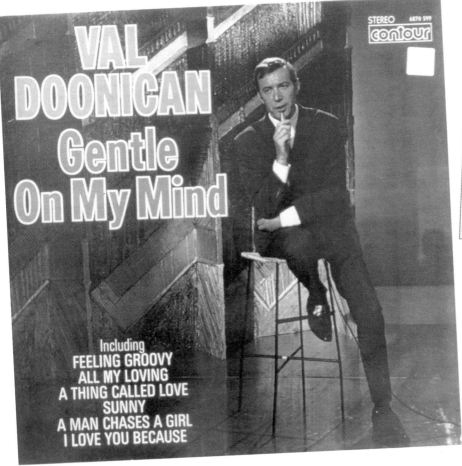

FLAMIN' GROOVIES SHAKE SOME ACTION

The Four Tops
Got To Get You Into My Life from Soul Spin
TAMLA MOTOWN STML 11138. Released: 1969

What the sleeve says: We're the Four Tops and we're doing contemporary shit too, including Light My Fire, and Californian Dreamin' too.

What really happens: By 1969, the Tops were laying it on thick in the "hepcat daddy in a commercial world" stakes. On Soul Spin the brass embellishments and vibe rhythms struggle to escape the big showtime arrangements but the group's vocals never falter from delivering an awesome performance, whatever the material.

Best thing about it: It's part of a real soul opus, filled with screeching vocals, religious deliveries and beautiful harmonies. A true gem.

Bobbie Gentry
Eleanor Rigby, The Fool On The Hill and Here, There And Everywhere from Local Gentry.
CAPITOL ST 2964. Released: 1968

What the sleeve says: "Her microcosmic reflection of the world's local gentry is simply one of the distinctive and sympathetic tenderness. (It's) the sound of lonely people... faceless beings, unheard voices and unheeded oracles... Eleanor

Rigby's and Fools On The Hill... where do they all come from?... from here, there and everywhere."

It also features an awesome picture of Bobbie.
What really happens: Bobbie Gentry, bluesy country singer is a snuggled up, close-in-your-ear storyteller. She's also a pretty impressive songwriter and her lushly-stringed delivery lends itself perfectly to the trio of Beatles' songs that are included here. All are mid-paced, evocative and sensual in their presentation and the arrangement on Eleanor Rigby is especially tasteful, but all three songs are handled with style.

Best thing about it: There's an irreverent air and an impressive build on Fool On The Hill. Subdued brass, distant strings and a rasping acoustic guitar lead Bobbie's seemingly disjointed vocal on a meandering journey through foolish middle distances punctuated by snapping drums and a throaty bit of spiritualism.

The Flamin' Groovies
Misery from Shake Some Action
PHILIPS 6370 804. Released: 1976

What the sleeve says: We wanna dress like The Beatles. We want to write our own songs. But we like Misery.

What really happens: The Flamin' Groovies returned their American interpretation of The Beatles' pop vision on the cusp of the punk revolution in the UK. Their stylish pop was hip and the title track is awesome but their verve was never realised. Their version of Misery is workable club stuff and enjoyable too.

Best thing about it: Undoubtedly it's the rest of this album that is absolutely drenched in early period Beatles' riffs, harmonies, charm and panache.

Emmylou Harris

**Here, There And Everywhere
from Elite Hotel**
REPRISE K54060. Released: 1976.

What the sleeve says: She's just a country girl with a penchant for cool songs.
What really happens: Emmylou's debut album sees her sail through covers of Buck Owens, Burritos, Don Gibson, Hank Williams and Gram Parsons material. Pretty much standard stuff, but she opens side two with Here, There And Everywhere, dropping the tempo way down and letting her latter day trademark vibrato really do the work.
Best thing about it: Her cool, throaty warmth.

Richie Havens

Here Comes The Sun; In My Life; Strawberry Fields; Imagine; My Sweet Lord; Eleanor Rigby; The Long And Winding Road; Let It Be; Working Class Hero; Rocky Racoon; With A Little Help From My Friends from Richie Havens Sings Beatles And Dylan.
RYKODISC RCD 20035. Released: 1987

What the sleeve says: "(After Woodstock) I was sitting in a photographer friend of mine's apartment and we were talking about the fact that there might never be another festival because the politicians had missed their chance to side with the "new awareness". We talked into the night and thought that we'd found the answer. We'd do a concert in a crater in Hawaii and televise it live at theatres across the country. Who could stop that?

"Eventually we settled for the idea of the group appearing holographically in the middle of your living room, life-sized. As the smoke filled the air we realised that no-one would understand what this was about except for those four hip guys from England, The Beatles. We saw a sympathetic parallel and thought they might help, so we laughingly both asked the wind three times to help.
'We want to meet the Beatles.' We repeated. And we left it at that."

"Two days later the phone rings and the photographer's ex-editor at Life magazine says she wants him to do a story on some young businessmen in the news - The Beatles! They had just opened Apple Records. Truth!

"The photographer and I couldn't decide if we should tell them the idea, but we had three days to think about it. In the meantime I saw that The Chambers Brothers were playing down the street and I decided to drop in. I spotted Jimi Hendrix in a corner in his usual dilemma and sat with him until he split.

"The guy on the door said, his brother wanted to meet up with me, so I waited around. Then his brother showed up and I recognised him as a guy who'd driven me to Palisades Park once. But tonight he was driving, you guessed it, John Lennon and Paul McCartney, and they proceeded to come right to our table. My mouth never left the floor! Well, that's how I met The Beatles. And they never did hear about our ideas."

What really happens: Richie Havens, famed for his passionate politicism, rampant acoustic and edgy soulful delivery at Woodstock had mellowed a bit by the '80s. His album of Beatles and Bob covers is easy going, emotive but hardly ever cutting edge. Between times he'd charted Stateside, in fact he went Top 20, with his version of Here Comes The Sun but his version here doesn't have that original drive.
Best thing about it: His version of Rocky Racoon is well worth a listen.

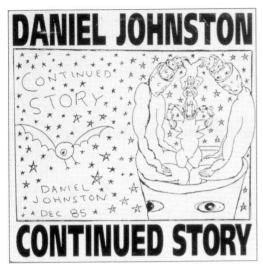

Daniel Johnston

I Saw Her Standing There from Continued Story
HOMESTEAD HMS 155-1. Released: 1991.

What the sleeve says: I'm a little bit arty.
What really happens: Indie wunderkind (the new Brian Wilson) faltered through a few self-penned albums of psychological examination and naïve innocence in the late '80s and early '90s. On Continued Story he added a George Jones song and I Saw Her Standing There which he delivers accompanied by a minimal piano. Awkward and disturbing it is.
Best thing about it: His simple left-field take on a recognised melody.

Tom Jones

Hey Jude from This Is Tom Jones
DECCA SLK 16 605-P. Released: 1969.

What the sleeve says: I'm goin' to Vegas.
What really happens: The boy from the Valleys swivels his hips and delivers blue-eyed soul on covers of Otis Redding's Dock Of The Bay, Jimmy Webb's Wichita Lineman, The Ev's Let It Be Me and The Beatles' Hey Jude. The latter closes side one and builds to a classic roll of brass as Tom goes all evangelical underneath. He's testifying, he's soul stompin'... he's actually really rather good.
Best thing about it: The yows and yelps that he just throws in. Smoothie.

James Last

All You Need Is Love from Goes Pop
POLYDOR 249 160. Released 1967

What the sleeve says: Very little other than suggesting, from its decadent bright pink hue, that James is at one with "the kids".
What really happens: James, temperamental goatee notwithstanding, strings together a host of pop choons into a seamless mass that's punctuated by party atmosphere and lots of unnamed people humming along. The only Beatles' moment comes at the start of side two and segues into The Turtles' She'd Rather Be With Me. It is truly one of the most ham-fisted, pedestrian, can't-be-bothered takes on a song ever heard.
Best thing about it: It's mercifully short and isn't quite as lacklustre and plodding as side one's closing couplet of The Beach Boys' Heroes And Villains and Traffic's Paper Sun. Wee-yud!

The James Last Band

Yesterday from Beat in Sweet
POLYDOR 249 002. Released: 1966

What the sleeve says: I've got a roll neck sweater and I'm modern.

What really happens: James Last tackles more contemporary fare with banks of strings. It's a heady brew of almost-hipness with versions of Eve Of Destruction, Mr Tambourine Man, Baby Don't Go and Like A Rolling Stone suggesting a certain level of queasy unease.

Best thing about it: For some reason a truncated version of Yesterday has been tacked on to the end of side two, where it eloquently fits in all its chorale glory. Delivered straight it's eventually spannered into the inevitable string sandwich, making its brief appearance entertaining if nothing else.

The Kestrels

Please Please Me from Smash Hits
PYE GOLDEN GUINEA GGL 0232. Released 1963

What the sleeve says: This is cheap cash-in stuff from The Kestrels, The Eagles and Jimmy Justice.

What really happens: Club circuit versions of top pop beat songs and early R&B standards from a trio of likely outfits. Actually, The Kestrels deliver Please Please Me with some panache and the would-be Shadows of the album, The Eagles, have their Hankisms off-pat too.

Best thing about it: The youthful innocence of the sleeve.

Mike Leander

Fool On The Hill, Hey Jude and Here, There And Everywhere from Migration
MCA MUPS 383. Released: 1969

What the sleeve says: "Sweep thy faint strings, musician, with thy long lead hand; downward the starry tapers burn, sinks soft the waning sand; the old hound whimpers cased in sleep, the embers smoulder low; across the walls the shadows come and go.

"Sweep softly thy strings, musician, the minutes mount to hours; frost on the windless casement weaves a labyrinth of flowers; music has called them, dreaming, home once more."

What really happens: Mike Leander who would later develop the sound of Gary Glitter and The Glitter Band made an album of flowing strings punctuated by his piano and the kind of echoey drums and tambourine that suggest he was attempting to achieve a kind of Phil Spectorish wall of sound. The end result is indeed ultra-lush but the pace is lagging. Accompanying tracks make this an oddity in itself with "grooviness" abounding on Time Is Tight, a couple of Jimmy Webb numbers and two from the soundtrack to Hair, but really there's not a lot to write home about apart from the sleeve poem.

Best thing about it: Undoubtedly it's the classical-styled Beethoven chops that punctuate Fool On The Hill. A double-take on the orchestra also means that the track is like a multi-layered morass of psychedelic classicism that eventually disappears up its own inventiveness. Well, that's almost what it's like.

beautiful and evocative Something."

What really happens: It's staccato with a smile as the orchestra swish through and Liberace goes oh-so-slightly soulful before swamping Something with grandiose keyboard-covering rolls. In an attempt to make him move with the times the selection of tracks here is nothing short of interesting but it's that chandelier shuffle and classical pomposity that still shines through, especially on the climax to his homage to George.

Best thing about it: The major chord lift at the close of Something is invigorating but not as lamentable as his troubled assault on Crosby, Stills And Nash's Suite: Judy Blue Eyes.

The London Philharmonic Orchestra

A Hard Day's Night and Something from Swinging London
STEREO GOLD AWARD MER 329. Released:

What the sleeve says: "Any mention of swinging London automatically brings to mind dolly mini-skirted girls, lively discotheques and Carnaby Street. But there's a lot more to the swinging capital than just those attractions.

"Music for a start. The kind of music that keeps the ear drums pounding in discotheques and adds weekly excitement to the nation's pop charts. The kind of music that the London Philharmonic Orchestra turn into a snappy musical picture of London.

"For these are the hits that emanate from London. From singers like Tom Jones, Englebert Humperdinck, Donovan and The Beatles."

What really happens: The London Philharmonic have an armoury of effects including filmic blurring, a strange way of reading melodies which lead them to orchestrate them like some epic David Lean feature. Or alternatively like a Hitchcock horror scene.

For the most part this album juggles the songs, with new arrangements and a smattering of "groovy" soul to little effect. However, their version of A Hard Day's Night, with its repetitive melody line and a stabbing string signature is highly memorable.

Best thing about it: The strange drama of ly A Hard Day's Night.

Liberace

Something from A Brand New Me
WARNER BROS WS 1847. Released: 1970

What the sleeve says: "This latest recorded supplement to the Liberace musical library will prove a source of unqualified delight to those who have loved and followed him since his rise to superstardom in the mid-1950's. Note the precision and perfect musical economy of his attack on such contemporary favourites as Raindrops Keep Fallin' On My Head, Na Na Hey Hey Kiss Him Goodbye, and Beatle George Harrison's

The Mamas And The Papas

I Call Your Name from If You Can Believe Your Eyes And Your Ears
RCA LSD 10076. Released: 1967.

What the sleeve says: "The bawdy Vaudeville analysis which Cass inflicts upon I Call Your Name projects the Beatle song in an entirely new light. John and Paul, one feels, would approve."

What really happens: Of course, Mama Cass's version of I Call Your Name is a marvellous noise. Truly musichall, multi-harmonised and moving, it has all the drama of the original and, within the context of the album it fits perfectly. The Mamas And The Papas' jug band roots and west coast flightiness make the song as thrillingly dysfunctional as the lyrics intended.

Best thing about it: The backwards guitar solo.

Marmalade

Ob-La-Di, Ob-La-Da (single)
Available on I See The Rain
SEQUEL RECORDS NEMCD 463. Released: 2000 (originally 1968)

What the sleeve says: "Marmalade's version of Ob-La-Di, Ob-La-Da was actually issued the same week as The Beatles' White Album, having been recorded the previous Sunday and rush-released: 'We were up in Scotland and had to charter a plane to fly down to London to record it. We got to CBS's Bond Street studios at about four in the morning, put down the backing, added the vocals then they put the brass on in the afternoon. They were playing it on the radio the next day.' Ironically their manager was against it and sent them a telegram saying that a Beatles cover at this stage of their career would be a backward step."

What really happens: Marmalade didn't do another Beatles cover after and didn't achieve that kind of international success that the songwriters had, but their output, as sampled on this CBS years set and the following Decca years collection, proved they were a spirited bunch of pop-friendly performers, far deeper than their big hit might have suggested.

Best thing about it: Ob-La-Di, Ob-La-Da is such an overplayed song by Marmalade that it's hard to take a view all these years later. And that jocular close of "And if you want some jam. Ha, ha, ha..." is pretty difficult to love after the 123rd play.

Paul Mauriat And Orchestra

Penny Lane from the album Blooming Hits
PHILIPS SBL 7837. Released: 1967

What the sleeve says: "For this album the Mauriat orchestra presents a wonderful pop pourri. The top beat composers are represented. The version is a musical distillation of the composition. The harpsichord is plainly evident, but there is an incredible horn solo complete with scat riffs."

What really happens: Alongside the likes of Puppet On A String, Somethin' Stupid and Cher's Mama, Penny Lane bends under shards of strings. The harpsichord is sadly played down in the mix and its only note-for-note take on the French horn solo that raises an eyebrow.

Best thing about it: Undoubtedly the sleeve picture of a naked woman painted with flowers and a butterfly. Now that's what we call modern.

David McCallum

Yesterday from **Music A Part Of Me**
CAPITOL T2432. Released: 1966.

What the sleeve says: "In the fall of 1965 I devised the idea of an album using the combination of instruments used here. It was born out of my past and out of my enjoyment of music today. I wanted a sound that could play the current hits and at the same time possibly project something of me - a part of me."

What really happens: David McCallum (aka Ilya Kuryakin of Man From UNCLE fame) conducts an orchestra under the guidance of currently hip arranger David Axelrod. They "take on" various tunes of the day, including the Stones' Satisfaction, The Byrds' version of Turn, Turn, Turn, Len Barry's 1-2-3, The Animals We Gotta Get Outta This Place and Yesterday. No-one gets hurt. But few have fun.

In reality, the idea might be fine but the arrangements and delivery are just a little slack. The rhythms don't stride, the instrumentation doesn't snap and sadly it all gets a touch lacklustre.

Best thing about it: Well, he did work with Napoleon Solo. Didn't he?

Kenneth McKeller

Yesterday *from* **Great Love Songs**
DECCA SKL 4817. Released:

What the sleeve says: "Drink To Me Only is the traditional English tune with the lyric by the Elizabethan playwright Ben Johnson.

mono

Music - A Part Of Me
David McCallum
Conducts Personal Impressions Of
One, Two, Three
Yesterday
Turn, Turn, Turn
A Taste of Honey
The "In" Crowd
I Can't Get No Satisfaction
Downtown
We Gotta Get Out Of This Place
...and others

It dates from several hundred years before Paul McCartney's Yesterday - but the two songs have many qualities in common."

What really happens: Omnipresent on New Year's Eve TV for what seemed like centuries, Kenneth McKellar has that kind of Sunday afternoon light programme voice that easily bends itself around a brace of hoary old chestnuts that built the generation gap. Ken's stab at Yesterday is suitably languid with all the sub-operatic character that such a treatment demands.

Best thing about it: That the song is reduced to the level of self-parody and a characterless choral at the drop of an octave is quite amazing.

Sergio Mendes And Brasil '66

Fool On The Hill from **Fool On The Hill**
A&M SP 3108. Released: 1968.

What the sleeve says: Brasil '66 are a super-real sextet, perched on a throne in either the desert or on the collaged frame of a nubile woman. Meanwhile, Sergio is featured on the reverse, bearded, smiling like a gigolo.

What really happens: Sergio and compadres have an easy samba going on. Young ladies croon, rhythms rumble and brass arrives uninvited to accentuate. They also cover Scarborough Fair and their "bababadah" vocals give both that and Fool On The Hill an off-beam ambience of their very own. For the title track the European

echoey party-styled slices as he wends his way through material by Creedence and Crosby, Stills And Nash amid virtually twice-removed strings, reverberated trumpet and good-time chanted vocal embellishments. His attempt at Something is pretty one-dimensional but Come Together sits like a very tinny death rattle between the haunting theme from Midnight Cowboy and the scat-like ramble of Pretty Belinda.

Best thing about it: The sleeve and the thought that Tony is still lurking about. Somewhere.

The Mersey Sound

She Loves You, Love Me Do, I Wanna Be Your Man, Can't Buy Me Love, from The Mersey Sound

FIDELIO ATL 4108. Released: Mid '60s.

phrasing is kept reasonably intact, while the rest of the album slips out to more eerie quarters and a host of atmospheric avenues.

Best thing about it: The tuneful weirdness of the chorus make it simply enchanting.

Tony Mimms

Come Together and Something from Tony Mimms

RCA PSL 10454. Released: 1970

What the sleeve says: Merely that this guy is strange. He chooses Marrakesh Express, Proud Mary, the theme from Midnight Cowboy and Suite: Judy Blue Eyes to let his gaggle of pals party down to and he appears emerging from a trumpet with wings on the front, while the back sleeve shows an array of

suitably-branded beer bottles.

What really happens: Tony Mimms plays a mean trumpet and the songs are arranged in

What the sleeve says: Very little. Although there's a beautiful charcoal sketch of what looks like George Harrison The Younger strumming on the banks of the Mersey.

What really happens: Some group wails through some Mersey-related fare including a whole darn batch of Beatles' songs, and a handful of their favoured covers of the time. They're trying to be incredibly Beatlesy but they lack any kind of confidence or stylistic ideas. And they really suffer on the harmonies. On the driving, more rock 'n' roll riffs they do better but they probably couldn't even get a booking at the Cavern as a support act.

Best thing about it: The cover.

Alan Moorhouse

Fool On The Hill, Something, Yesterday and With A Little Help From My Friends from Beatles, Bach And Bacharach Go Bossa

MUSIC FOR PLEASURE MFP 5206. Released: 1971

What the sleeve says: "You probably never realised that The Beatles, Bach and Bacharach wrote some marvellous bossa novas! Mind you they didn't really sound like bossa's when they were first performed.

"The four Beatles numbers are already well known to you, but they sound really fresh and inviting in their bright new Brazilian style.

"So, if your party ever looks like sagging in the middle, switch onto The Beatles, Bach And Bacharach in Bossa beat - and give the party a swinging new lease of life."

What really happens: All the B's done bossa nova? On the drawing board of conceptual musicology how on earth did they ever think of that one? Actually, the whole idea of rampant Brazilian rhythms running rife through music by the Fabs, Burt and Bach sounds exciting, the only problem is that by the time Alan Moorhouse and his crew have filtered it down it's all just a touch too MOR.

Best thing about it: There's a modicum of charm about Fool On The

Hill, but both Something and Yesterday are insignificant and With A Little Help From My Friends staggers before it falls into a crumpled heap.

The Mystic Moods Orchestra

Eleanor Rigby from Emotions

MINT MINT 5. Released: 1970.

What the sleeve says: This is about sex.
What really happens: Music to bonk by comes of age (as it were). The Mystic Moods' albums featured various sensuous readings of all manner of music with sound affects - hot, arid nights a speciality - and regulated rhythms (surprise, surprise) at the centre of their lush, repetitive readings of the tunes themselves. Their take on Eleanor Rigby falls into a typical travelogue mode that could have come from any cheap rate porn film (or is that just my imagination running away with it all?)
Best thing about it: It's just odd, strangely played and slightly left field. Great.

Oliver Nelson

Yesterday and Michelle from Michelle

HMV 3570. Released: 1966

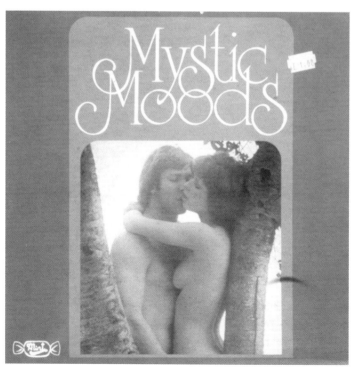

What the sleeve says: "Yesterday by John Lennon and Paul McCartney of The Beatles is a further example of the Nelson enrichment of pop songs. 'The introduction', he observes, 'is made up completely of tone clusters - and approach that sounds normal now but would have been regarded as unusual a couple of years ago.' Nelson's lithe lyricism on alto is entirely apposite to the original character of the tune.

"Michelle, another Lennon and McCartney song, led Nelson to say 'These guys do have talent because we're all winding up playing their music. And a song like Michelle inspires you once you get into it. Still, however, they don't know too much about form, so here too it was also a question of providing extra structuring'. For this listener, Nelson's wistful, poignant solo is one of the key achievements of the album as he brings to the song more disciplined, penetrating passion than it has received in previous interpretation."
What really happens: Oliver Nelson toots wildly throughout this album as it strays too close to mellow nonsense before refraining with some jazzy passion. Michelle, for all its sleeve note tomfoolery isn't delivered as a higher grade package, however his subtle sax on Yesterday leads the song into a less orthodox vein.
Best thing about it: Oliver's struggle with, and the discordant trumpets on, Flowers On The Wall. Frightening stuff.

Peter Nero

Yesterday and And I Love Her from Up Close

RCA RD-7799. Released: 1966.

What the sleeve says: "For his baroque-influenced reading of Paul McCartney's Yesterday, Peter is in concert with a traditional woodwind quartet. And Peter's arrangement of The Beatles' charming And I Love Her delineates a classical ballad in the truest sense of the word."

What actually happens: Undoubtedly Peter Nero is a seasoned pianist and his attack and sustain on some of the songs here is impressive. And I Love Her is pretty straightforward but Yesterday is spiced up by a strange scraping rhythm and the eventual arrival of some brass.

Best thing about it: Those ruler scraping rhythms.

The Original Brasso Band

Ob-La-Di, Ob-La-Da from Stereo Galaxy, A New World Of Sound

MUSIC FOR PLEASURE MFP 50004. Released: 1972.

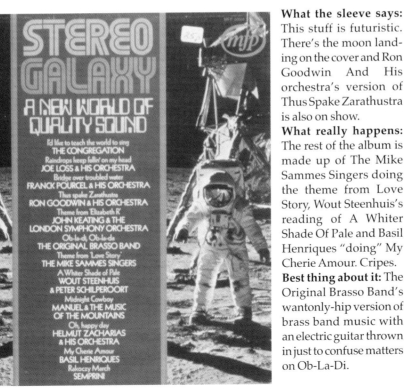

What the sleeve says: This stuff is futuristic. There's the moon landing on the cover and Ron Goodwin And His orchestra's version of Thus Spake Zarathustra is also on show.

What really happens: The rest of the album is made up of The Mike Sammes Singers doing the theme from Love Story, Wout Steenhuis's reading of A Whiter Shade Of Pale and Basil Henriques "doing" My Cherie Amour. Cripes.

Best thing about it: The Original Brasso Band's wantonly-hip version of brass band music with an electric guitar thrown in just to confuse matters on Ob-La-Di.

The Larry Page Orchestra

Imagine, My Love, My Sweet Lord, Give Me Love, Live And Let Die and C Moon from Imagine

CHEVRON CHVL 156. Released: 1979.

What the sleeve says: "The Larry Page Orchestra pay their tribute to some of the great songwriters of the last 20 years to bring you this album. Featured are six songs by ex Beatles John Lennon, George Harrison and Paul McCartney, plus one of the greatest pop classics of all time, Paul Simon's Bridge Over Troubled Water."

What really happens: Actually you also get Love Grows which was made famous by Edison Lighthouse and a couple of others too. Page's versions are mostly slow-paced bachelor pad smoochers for lights out late night action. A chorus of ladies croon the words and the mood is mellow. Except for My Sweet Lord, of course, where the guys rap, the bass throbs a bit and when the ladies add the "hallelujahs" it sounds like an absolute shambles.

Best thing about it: Strictly speaking this isn't Beatles' stuff but the grin factor of Page's struggle with Live And Let Die's uptempo break and the pure banality of C Moon is worth it.

Billy Pepper And The Pepperpots

I Want To Hold Your Hand and I Saw Her Standing There from Merseymania
PICKWICK/HURRAH HUR ALL 731. Released: 1964

What the sleeve says: "It burst on to the British music scene unannounced one day in October 1962. 'It' of course, refers to Mersey Mania.

"Emerging from Liverpool - England's second largest sea port - Mersey Mania was first brought to national prominence by four long-haired young men - The Beatles. It was not surprising then that for a city with three quarter of a million people there was plenty more talent waiting to be discovered. And it wasn't long before groups like Gerry And The Pacemakers, The Searchers and The Swinging Blue Jeans, stepped into the limelight and quickly became household names in their own rights.

"In this album you will hear aspects of Mersey Mania from the out and out rhythm and blues numbers to the more sedate ballads and you will agree that the latest Liverpool find - Billy Pepper

And The Pepperpots - certainly do justice to the Beat City on this really sensational album."

What really happens: Three part harmonies, twangy guitars and clacking drums litter this album. You can almost feel the sweaty ambience as Billy and his boys go carbon copy close on their chosen Beatlesisms but somehow those vocals lack the sexy cheek of the originals.

Best thing about it: The "oooooooohs" on I Want To Hold Your Hand.

Martha And The Vandellas

Something from Natural Resources
TAMLA MOTOWN STML 11166. Released: 1970

What the sleeve says: Martha and her Vandellas are into peace, love and good songwriters. Included are songs by Jimmy Webb, Fred Neil, Jackie De Shannon, Ashford And Simpson and, of course, George Harrison.

What really happens: Beyond their early pop hits and the steamy Motown machine from whence they came, by 1970 Martha and co had

developed a more tempered sound, concentrating on her belting soul vocal and her compadres neat chorus harmonies. Natural Resources is not a spectacular album but, in its songs, it has some commendable high points. And, even though Something limps into action, at the last minute it changes tempo to become a snappy soul mover.

Best thing about it: That last hot minute.

The Buddy Rich Big Band

Norwegian Wood from Norwegian Wood
SUNSET SLS 50174. Released:

What the sleeve says: "At the Chez in Hollywood, the older audiences gave way to the younger ones with strange hair after the first week. They dig their music - the sound, the beat, the excitement."

What really happens: It's a jazzy juxtaposition. Recorded live it isn't the classic version by Rich - it's too short - but the maestro hammers it out and his trusty brass section fills the song to bursting point. Elsewhere, the latter day swinging drummer with a penchant for big bandery continues in a be-bopering fashion.

Best thing about it: Rich's aggression, pace and enthusiasm.

Bob Rowe

Something from Bob Rowe's Music Box
DJM DJSL 029. Released: 1973

What the sleeve says: "On this, Bob's first album, are two of his own compositions."

What really happens: A gloriously complex sleeve suggests that Bob Rowe is going to adapt the classics of contemporary songwriting - it also includes songs by Gilbert O'Sullivan, Jimmy Webb, Elton John and The Sweet, as well as Harrison's Something - into a gloriously souped-up synthetic whirl. His own compositions sound like tinny versions of Joe Meek and when he actually turns his hand to Something you'd be hard-pressed to tell anything was actually synthesised as Bob goes out of his way to make it sound like "proper" instruments. A sad shadow of what the sleeve lends your imagination to believe he might do in the mangling of George's classic.

Best thing about it: The sleeve information that there exists an album by The Mike Batt Orchestra (remember, he was a Womble) called Portrait Of George Harrison, not to mention one called Portrait Of Bob Dylan. Where are these priceless artefacts?

The Sandpipers

**Things We Said Today
from Guantanamera**
A&M AMLB 1004. Released:
1970

What the sleeve says: "The Beatles' The Things We Said Today is tailor-made for The Sandpipers."

What really happens: It's actually pretty pert, an emotive melancholy version. Featuring plenty of harmony without drifting into the realm of the insipid as they do later on the album, The Sandpipers have soul.

Best thing about it: The underplayed guitar, brooding wood-windery and gentle strum. Very late '60s hippy dippy.

The Silkie

**You've Got To Hide Your Love Away
from the album of the same name**
FONTANA SRF 67548. Released:

What the sleeve says: "It all began as a routine session really. We'd no intention of making a record at the time. After working out a basic arrangement with Paul (McC), we asked John (Winston Lennon) to come up and help us prepare

the number for recording. He happened to bring George with him. At first we were not getting it at all. Too many people making suggestions at once. Then Paul started to play rhythm guitar. It's what you hear at the start of the record. John shouted: 'Yeah, let's use it'.

"Then we found that one of the recording studios was empty and we decided to hear what the tape sounded like. When George heard it he decided it needed something else and he added the tapping on the back of the guitar. Finally we put on the vocal with George playing the tambourine. Four takes and we finished the record as you hear it."

What really happens: The Silkie, moved from Hull Uni into the music biz in 1963. Their album consisted of eight Dylan covers plus a few standards and, of course, the title track. Bestowed with two excellent beards, thin ties and a big hair lady folk vocalist, they were hip beatniks and the Fabs loved them.

"The Silkie sound... very silky," enthused John Lennon. And who are we to argue.

Best thing about it: It's actually great. Their version of You've Got To Hide Your Love Away is everything that Merseyfolk wanted to be.

Sounds Like Someone

**Lady Madonna from
Sound Like Hits Number One**
FONTANA SFL 13054

What the sleeve says: "Sound like Hits is an album that expertly exemplifies the sparkle and variety that is to be found in today's hit parade. The first track is The Beatles' Lady Madonna - it's almost impossible to write about the most talented team of this generation. All the superlatives are well-worn and familiar. Suffice to say that Lady Madonna is yet another confirmation of their exceptional qualities and, of course, it was number one in the charts for weeks all over the world."
What really happens: It's workmanlike until the chorus, then a sax break and some inopportune humming takes it off down it's own timeless cul de sac.
Best thing about it: Sadly, it's a bit ordinary. But you should hear what they do to The Small Faces' Lazy Sunday, though.

Spooky Tooth

I Am The Walrus from last Puff
ISLAND RECORDS ILPS 9117. Released: 1969

What the sleeve says: We're weird. We're in league with weird things. And we play music.
What really happens: Spooky Tooth, by 1969, had surpassed any preconceptions of pop acceptance and on Last puff they headed off down the "heavy" Traffic route. Their version of I Am The Walrus becomes a prog rock anthem as keyboards congeal (as if someone has fallen asleep on them) and guitars clash in a way of truly expressing themselves. All that and a vocal that's shredded by an overzealous cheesegrater.
Best thing about it: It's just evil.

Suite Steel

Yesterday, Something and Blackbird from The Pedal Steel Guitar Album
ELEKTRA RECORDS EKS 74072. Released: 1970.

What the sleeve says: "Five of America's top pedal steel players, Buddy Emmons, Jay Dee Maness, Red Rhodes, Sneaky Pete and Rusty Young who, between them had turned out for The Byrds, Flying Burrito Brothers, Poco, Buck Owens and Michael Nesmith, were brought together to do an album of steel-powered playing."
What really happens: The mix of styles and delivery are odd enough but the material, which includes three Beatles' songs along with Fred Neil's Everybody's Talkin', Creedence's Down On The Corner, Cream's Sunshine Of Your Love and a title track which strays into the kitsch and

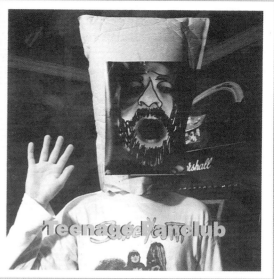

forgettable, make this an odd collection indeed. Buddy Emmons and Sneaky Pete deliver Yesterday untainted, while Red Rhodes' take on Something goes for a far too literal tack until he sings through his steel in a bizarre Peter Frampton-like moment. Meanwhile, Sneaky Pete's version of Blackbird plucks at all the right harmonious chords.
Best thing about it: Sneaky Pete's Blackbird has a late night charm. But it's his duet with Rusty Young on Cream's Sunshine Of Your Love that puts real spin on the madness of this whole concept.

Teenage Fanclub

**The Ballad Of John And Yoko from
Deep Fried Fanclub**
FIRE RECORDS FLIPCD 002. Released: 1995.

What the sleeve says: We're mad and a bit groovy. And Scottish.
What really happens: Like it says on the box - they're mad and a bit groovy. The Fannies were born on the cusp of The Beatles and Badfinger and their songs reflect this perfectly. Their cover of John And Yoko, if truth be known, is a throwaway football chant that originally came out in 1990 as a single. They're actually sharper than that. Much sharper. But, hell, they're good value.
Best thing about it: The sheer irreverence of it all. Eating chocolate cake in the bath just sounds like such fun.

phase 4 stereo

DECCA

CARNABY ST.

THE ALAN TEW ORCHESTRA
THIS IS MY SCENE

a phased sitar ending. Wild!

Best thing about it: Imagining just how he explained the final verse, chorus and imminent sitar explosion to his orchestra.

Tiny Tim

Girl and Hey Jude from Girl
ROUNDER CD 9050. Released: 1996.

What the sleeve says: Tiny Tim is one crazy guy who the ladies (well, a lady) loved.

What really happens: The curly haired ukulele-toting eccentric who charted with Tiptoe Through The Tulips in the '60s teams up with roots muso's Brave Combo to produce an album of strange covers. So, alongside Over The Rainbow, New York, New York and Stairway To Heaven which are all delivered in truly camp style, Tim also launches into a cha cha version of Hey Jude and a truly idiosyncratic version of the title track.

Tim's falsetto warble has long since disappeared and it's instead replaced by a mid-range vibrato that's more like Telly Savalas in heat. Girl is delivered as a slow polka and sounds strangely devoid of its Beatles roots.

Best thing about it: The spoken word middle section that sounds like any crazed late night phone prankster might have interpreted the song.

The Alan Tew Orchestra

Penny Lane from This Is My Scene
DECCA PFS 4120. Released: 1967.

What the sleeve says: "This then is where it's at - an overnight success story that has taken 15 years to write; written by a musician who is trying to re-establish that certain essence of artistic quality in the charts that was washed away in the whirlpool of sheer musical "noise" that was unleashed as youth moved to assert itself as a voice in our modern society."

What really happens: Tew, renowned for arrangements for chart-topping acts like John Leyton, Dusty and Paul and Barry Ryan, sees the tide of creativity flowing elsewhere. He dons some winkle-pickers and gets a psychedelic

sleeve together and covers everything from Sinatra (both Nancy and Frank) through to The Monkees, Tom Jones and The Beatles. Particularly, with The Beatles' Penny Lane, which closes the album, he goes completely off-kilter. Sure, he follows the melody for the most part, goes all hammy with a xylophone, adds a drum roll that's all military band-like before adding some heavy chops that take it into new realms of "straightness". To climax though, as it heads into an almost Dambusters-esque break, Tew plays his final joker,

TINY TIM with BRAVE COMBO *Girl*

Unauthorised Version

**Hey Jude from the album
of the same name**
CBS 63642. Released: 1969

What the sleeve says: "Unauthorised Version is a group of seven singers from Oxford University. They are all present or past choral scholars of Maudling College Choir. They are all extremely talented, intelligent and able musicians.

"The relation between the principle of melodic harmony and pop is explored in Hey Jude - counterpoint and horizontal approach to singing is introduced for the first time as opposed to the traditional vertical "block" harmony. The tune appears in each of four parts in counterpoint to one another instead of having a single melody line with others as a less important accompaniment."

What really happens: In comparison to the rest of this "swinging" platter, the title track is slightly straight. The septet do the groovy thing and give Hey Jude a full choral workout but their vocals are almost too polite. Better is their grapple with Shakespeare or their self-penned songs which sound like Burt Bacharach jamming with Pink Floyd in their pubescent 1960's incarnation.

Best thing about it: Girl In A Bus Queue which follows Hey Jude. It's mad.

Caterina Valente

Fool On The Hill from The World Of Caterina Valente
DECCA SPA 192. Released: 1971.

What the sleeve says: I'm not really young enough to be "trendy" but I've got a headband.

What really happens: This French/Spanish vocalist who charted in 1955 in the UK, returned with a penchant for Latin rhythms and a version of Fool On The Hill where she goes scat doolally in the middle. It's mood music with versions of Girl From Ipanema and La Bamba also included from her short-lived faux psychedelic Latin period.

Best thing about it: Caterina can actually sing given half a chance but she struggles on real words and verses, preferring to free-form off into her own world of doo-dahing. The version of Misirlou is far more palatable.

Vanilla Fudge

A medley of I Want To Hold Your Hand, I Feel Fine, Day Tripper and She Loves You from The Beat Goes On
ATCO 33-237. Released: 1968.

What the sleeve says: "This album is fudge, pure. It's like no other album made. Above ground or underground. The music is that if Ludwig Van Beethoven... John Lennon... and Stephen Foster... and Sonny Bono... and Jean Bouchety... and Cole Porter... and Paul McCartney... and Wolfgang Amadeus Mozart."

What really happens: Those crazy Vanilla Fudge guys decided to do a history of the world in music and roped in classical pieces, spoken word nonsense, taped speeches of great leaders and American folk roots songs like Don't Fence Me In with Hound Dog and this Beatles' medley. It's a pompous concept for sure but entertaining in a "Wow! What's happening, man?" kinda way.

Best thing about it: Just that it exists really. The Beatles versions are no great shakes, they do drop into Hello, Goodbye without a credit but the music's purely used for colour really.

Various strange people with orchestras

Eleanor Rigby, Yellow Submarine and Got To Get You Into My Life from Hits A Gogo
CONCERT HALL SVS 2498. Released: 1970.

What the sleeve says: This is going to be dodgy.

What really happens: Various nonentities murder modern pop songs, the likes of which you'd be hard pushed to match. Chris Allen And His Music With Dale Adams give Yellow Submarine the once over and take the song to new depths. Not only does it sound like someone shouts "Piss off" during the talking engine room middle bit, the role of the chirpy captain seems to have been taken by a man whose nine to the wind on the Scotch. Got To Get You Into My Life by Voss, Doc And Mel and Their Orchestra is a lot more straightforward and at least the singer - it may be Voss, it may be Doc, it may be Mel - can belt it out. And finally, there's Eleanor Rigby. It signals the return of Chris Allen, obviously perplexed at the Sub catastrophe as he's jettisoned Dale Adams and the resultant instrumental, with a strange upbeat chop is in the style of northern soul.

Best thing about it: Certainly, it's the version of Yellow Submarine which is just a mental grungefest. However, elsewhere on the album John Francis And The Tramps, groovy guitar and posh accent in tow, do a fine take on The Kinks'

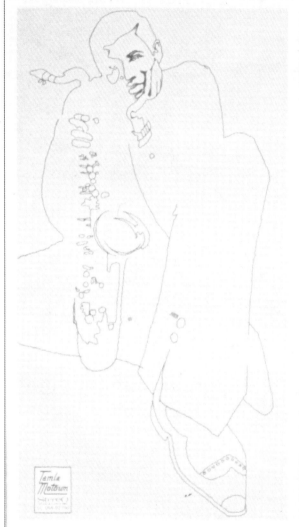

Sunny Afternoon. Everything was so much easier back then. Obviously.

Junior Walker And The All Stars

Something from Rainbow Funk

What the sleeve says: I'm hep with psychedelia. Baby.

What really happens: Rainbow Funk is a great album, with Junior Walker's emotive sax joined by spiritual background vocals and a lead that's wracked with emotion. Elsewhere you get Feelin' Alright, Right On Brothers And Sisters and a top version of Psychedelic Shack. For Something the rhythm is essential, the swaying tambourine and gritty vocal carry proceedings leaving Junior room to stab in with the most emotive of brass bits.

Best thing about it: It's just great.

DIONNE WARWICK
SOULFUL

wand

I'VE BEEN LOVING YOU TOO LONG
PEOPLE GOT TO BE FREE
YOU'VE LOST THAT LOVIN' FEELIN'
PEOPLE GET READY
DO RIGHT WOMAN
I'M YOUR PUPPET
YOU'RE ALL I NEED TO GET BY
WE CAN WORK IT OUT
A HARD DAY'S NIGHT
HEY JUDE
SILENT VOICES
WHAT'S GOOD ABOUT GOODBYE

Dionne Warwick

We Can Work It Out, A Hard Day's Night and Hey Jude from Soulful.
WAND WNS 12. Released: 1971

What the sleeve says: "When you listen to this album you'll hear something that I've wanted to do for a long time. Everyone has their own way of doing things and singing R&B is no different - I had to do it my way. The songs chosen are just some of many I list among my favourites. Happiness, Dionne Warwick."

What really happens: Perhaps best known for her Burt Bacharach balladeering, Dionne has a fine belt-it-out vocal style and her reading of these Beatles songs is extraordinary. We Can Work It Out is treated like an uptempo gospel screecher, with Warwick testifying for all her worth. Elsewhere she covers Penn and Oldham's Do Right Woman and Curtis Mayfield's People Get Ready to truly show her potential, but it's her slow-paced croon on A Hard Day's Night that has all the soul you could ever imagine the song could possess. Perhaps her Hey Jude lacks that kind of conviction but, hey, two out of three ain't bad at all.

Best thing about it: Dionne's bluesy interpretation of A Hard Day's Night.

Elisabeth Welch

Yesterday from This Thing Called Love
TER VIR 8309. RELEASED: 1989.

What the sleeve says: "The popular song is not

a frivolity, but something of vital artistic significance."

What really happens: At 80, this American crooner who'd done Broadway, skipped to England and performed through all manner of styles and situations was roped in to record an album of tunes from her lengthy professional stint. The result included songs from Gershwin, Porter, Sondheim, Mancini, Stynne and co and, nestled in on side one between Porgy and Long Before I Knew You is the only contemporary offering, Lennon and McCartney's Yesterday.

Best thing about it: She sings better than your grandma.

Who knows?

Penny Lane from Hits '67
MUSIC FOR PLEASURE MFP 1089. Released: 1967

What the sleeve says: "For 12/6, 12 Top Hits Superbly Recorded. Can you tell the difference between these and the original sounds?

"Of course, it all started with The Beatles, and their big hit Penny Lane was acknowledged as one of the cleverest conceptions in years. The tune is fascinating but so too are the lyrics which show Lennon and McCartney's tremendous insight into everyday life in their native Liverpool and have a strange melancholy air."

What really happens: Coming after a drab cover of Eidleweiss from The Sound Of Music, the singer given the job of out-Macca-ing Macca

comes on like David Bowie doing a tame Anthony Newley. Lacking is the production, sounds, multi-instruments and, quite frankly, the last bit of puff that reaches the top note on the French horn solo. That aside it plods along, er, ploddingly until the end collides with a totally out of time brass effect.

Best thing about it: The Bowie-styled Newley trying to get his tongue around the line: "The barber shaves another customer" as only John Lennon could.

Who knows again?

Get Back from Top Hits
MUSIC FOR PLEASURE MFP 1319. Released: 1969

What the sleeve says: "As usual John Lennon and Paul McCartney have said 'Get Back' to all other songwriters, with a song that was made up on the roof of Apple's Saville Row headquarters."

What really happens: A strange collection of songs covered unwisely are laid end to end and don't add up to much. From the final salvo of the Sixties, Top Hits revels in real pop pap, with Frank Sinatra's My Way, Bob And Earl's Harlem Shuffle and Jimmy Webb's Galveston next to tunes made famous by Tom Jones, Des O'Connor and Manfred Mann.

Best thing about it: In Beatles' terms it's got to be the half-assed retort of "Get back jojo", if you could be so kind, that is, kind sir.

CHANGES
JOHN WILLIAMS

STANLEY MYERS & ORCHESTRA

melody they do. Mostly they do their own, utilising Jon Anderson and some multi-harmonies to offset their mad "improv". On side one they also add The Byrds' I See You to steady the boat and side two offers Every Little Thing. It's great too. Full of Yes idiosyncrasies but always harking back to the main melody.

Best thing about it: The opening madcap jam that breaks into Ticket To Ride before it evolves into Every Little Thing. Public school eh, it must have been great.

Your Gang

I Call Your Name from The Daily Trip
MERCURY SR 61094. Released: 1968.

What the sleeve says: These guys either think they're in a film, or they're the hippie forerunners of The Village People. The sleeve says: "Most of Your Gang can read music, but prefer not to follow the notes."

What really happens: These spirited West Coasters play new wave jug band music, nod a wink to The Lovin' Spoonful, Tony Hatch and Bob Dylan and close their album with I Call Your Name. An instrumental that veers to the mild side of Dan Hicks before changing gear like a Spike Jones afterthought. Indeed, Your Gang's "strange" credentials remain virtually intact.

Best thing about it: Before the slapstick vaudeville upgear, they offer a pretty neat instrumental.

John Williams

Because from Changes
FLY FLY5. Released: 1971

What the sleeve says: John Williams has lots of pomp mates. Also playing on this musically wide-ranging set is Rick Wakeman, Herbie Flowers and Alan Parker. The tracklisting also reveals that Williams' choice of material includes numbers by Django Rheinhardt and Bach.

What really happens: Williams for the most part soups up arrangements in filmic style - he would of course later go on to work on Star Wars et al. For Because, though, he strips it down and lets his finger style take the melody. It's actually quite an embracing rendition. However, in the confines of the album it's probably his least imaginative arrangement.

Best thing about it: The hammer style of playing and the emotive run on the chorus line.

Yes

Every Little Thing from Yes
ATLANTIC RECORDS 588190. Released: 1969.

What the sleeve says: "At the beginning of 1969 I was asked to pick two groups who I thought would make it the following year. One of my choices was Led Zeppelin, the other was Yes." Claims a pundit of the period.

What really happens: It's the Yes debut. It's complex, hi-falutin', proggy in places but when they need to drop back to a

Beatles Exotica:
The stage
shows, the
films, the
concerto, the
fugues and the
etudes... not to
mention The
Rutles

THE MAGICAL MYSTERY TOUR

So, what have we learnt so far? Beatles ongs can be covered in Spanish! They can be delivered reggae style or in fake Liverpudlian. And they all have their place in history. Yes, people take absolute liberties with the Lennon and McCartney and Harrison catalogues. And a large selection of these people seemingly have no idea what constitutes good taste. Beatles Exotica has become synonymous with an extraordinary series of albums put together by a man called Jim-from London, SE22. He's obsessed with the strange juxtapositions which have been realised by straining musicologists in search of new levels of nirvana through their own particular homage to The Beatles. Or something. As the 1990's closed he'd wracked out three volumes, suitably punctuated with Fabs' comments, poems from masters of the surreal like Stanley Unwin and Frank Sidebottom and covers that in a lot of cases simply beggared belief. Meanwhile, across the Atlantic, the warehouse people at Rhino Records had been collecting all kinds of monstrous covers and releasing them as a series entitled Golden Throats. By Volume Four they had enough to dedicate a whole album to The Beatles. And the extremities of emotions mapped out by Bing Crosby and William Shatner on that album ran the full exotic gamut. With them nothing was sacred. Ditto the use of Beatles music in other media outlets – film, stage shows, TV, etc. In this search for exotica, we also study the culpably kitsch '70s. We have The Beatles' music delivered over World War Two footage, as storytelling vignettes, as a concerto and in pastiche and caricature by The Rutles, who were themselves pastiched by a bunch of indie terrorists further along the line. Welcome to the strangest of the strange...

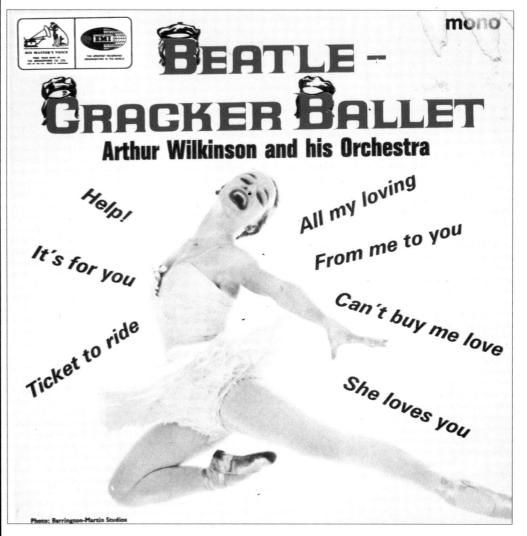

Photo: Barrington-Martin Studios

Back in 1965, the seed for exotic nonsense was spawned in Europe and the USA almost simultaneously. In the UK, Arthur Wilkinson – who was also instrumental in getting The Band Of The Irish Guards to put together a whole album of Beatles' covers – hit on the idea of The Beatlecracker Suite, a classical collision with Lennon and McCartney's songs. Asked to devise some contemporary music for a TV series featuring The Royal Ballet Company he used the ballet standard The Nutcracker Suite and decided to substitute some of The Beatles' material in the style of Tchaikovsky. The resultant EP stayed in the best selling EP Charts, when such things existed, for six months.

Meanwhile, Elektra Records' boss Jac Holzman was flabbergasted at The Beatles' wide ranging success. In his book Follow The Music he recalls: "By the early fall of 1965 the Beatles' songbook was so large that it dominated Top 40 radio. Their music was in the elevators, it was everywhere and from that sprang an idea."
The idea developed into The Baroque Beatles Songbook which utilised the talents of Joshua Rifkin to develop sonatas based around the Beatles' songs.
And so, with Tchaikovsky and Bach in the frame it wasn't long before Fritz Spiegl brought in Wagner and Mozart for his EP Eine Kleine Beatle Musik, a strange string-laden slice of moribund

Drive My Car; Do You Want To Know A secret; We Can Work It Out; I Should Have Known Better; Nowhere Man; You're Going To Lose That Girl; Ticket To Ride; The Word; Eleanor Rigby; Every Little Thing; And Your Bird Can Sing; Get Back; Eight Days A Week; It Won't Be Long; Day Tripper; Wait; Good Day Sunshine; My Sweet Lord; Here Comes The Sun; While My Guitar Gently Weeps; Taxman; A Hard Day's Night; Things We Said Today; If I Fell; You Can't Do That; Please Please Me; From Me To You and I Want To Hold Your Hand.

Before The Australian Doors, Bootleg Beatles et al, Starsound, the brainchild of Dutchman Jaap Eggermont took all kinds of music and recreated it in fastideous detail, like the Top Of The Pops series of albums hadn't really happened. These were versions that actually sounded like the originals.

Great, you might think, but the end result, when grafted to a very tinny disco beat made Starsound's output nothing short of very annoying. Their Beatles medley may have thrilled the working men's clubs in the far north but its incessant chirpiness drove a few mop tops to commit hare kari.

Is it exotic? Exotica? Or just another spectacular cash-in ? Compared to the Exotic Beatles series and, indeed, Rhino Golden Throats, it certainly pales…

The Exotic Beatles

EXOTICA RECORDS PELE 3CD. Released: 1993.

Derek Enright MP: *Yellow Submarine*
Akiko Kanazawa: *Yellow Submarine Ondo*
William Shatner: *Lucy In The Sky With Diamonds*
Dino E I Kings: *I Should Have Known Better (Circa Di Capire)*
Brian Sewell: *I Wanna Be Your Man*
The Wilson Malone Voice Band: *Penny Lane*
Emi Bonilla Y Su Caudro: *She Loves You (Te Quieres)*
Desmond Dekker And The Israelites: *Come Together*
Dickie Henderson: *Step Inside Love*
The 52 Key Verbeek Fairground Organ: *In My Life*
The Metropolitan Police Male Voice Choir: *When I'm 64*
Los Mustang: *Please Please Me*
Les Surfs: *There's A Place (Oh Chagrin)*
OS Vips: *Things We Said Today (Coisas Que*

---

melody which he describes on the sleeve thus: "Eine Kleine Beatle Musik is an historical reconstruction of certain well-loved Merseyside tunes such as La Ci Darem La Mano (I Want To Hold Your Hand) as they might have been written by lesser men like Wolfgang A Mozart or Ludwig Van Beetlehoven."

And to think all this "hep" tomfoolery in '65 would be reduced to the level of Stars On 45 by 1981. Long after they'd hung up their plectrums, pop culture was in the decline and the European response was to invent Starsound. Their soundalike segueways topped the charts throughout Europe and then they turned their attention to "30 tracks made famous by The Beatles".

The damning details and roll call of covers were as follows: It included No Reply; I'll Be Back;

Accontecem)

Edmundo Ros And Catarina Valente: The Fool On The Hill (El Dondo Sur La Collina)
Lefty In The Right: Paperback Writer
The 52 Key Verbeek Fairground Organ: All My Loving
Balsara And His Singing Sitars: I Want To Hold Your Hand
Derek Enright MP: Eleanor Rigby
Sandro: We Can Work It Out (Podemos Solicionato)
The Beatle Barkers: We Can Work It Out
John Otway: I Am The Walrus
The 52 Key Verbeek Fairground Organ: And I Love Her
The Quests: I'll Be Back (Aku Kembali Lagi)
Brian Sewell: Her Majesty
The Moog Beatles: Good Night.

The story: Illuminated with Beatles' comments, reportage news bits, chanting fans and political diatribe, The Exotic Beatles, as the sleevenotes by Louis Phillipe explain, is not another "tour of The Beatles' theme park". Instead you get wild Brazilian punk bands, a theatric Japanese version of Yellow Submarine, eccentric members of the public writing themselves into the lyrics of the Fabs, a crazy thesp or two, a mad art critic whose as camp as he's upper class, and various genre-specific attempts that cover flamenco, tacky early electronica, reggae, shifty samba and Indian raga of sorts. Indeed, The Beatles are delivered on synths, fairground organs and by a choir who attempt to give the songs something The Beatles never dreamed of, a fully half-baked barber shop finish.

Phillipe excuses the fact that the album isn't all about The Beatles. Instead, he reasons, "It's about the thousands of boys who started to go to the hairdresser for a hairdo rather than a haircut." As he rightly continues: "They were not imitators, in the sense that their devotion was so excessive and their skill (generally) so minimal that their act of re-creation had more in common with Andy Warhol's cans of soup than with pale

soundalikes thrown into the market by desperate British record companies." How very true. He finally concludes: "Exoticism also pre-supposes an in-built disdain for common taste, when it's not an assault on its values: Fairground organs and singing sitars and police choirs will probably have to fight for a folding chair in the orchestral pit of Heaven."

And there's enough of it. Lodged between Brian Sewell's ramble on Wanna Be Your Man and the truly off-kilter oompah Brian Wilsonisms of Penny Lane by The Wilson Malone Voice Band,

John and Paul test each other, hammily, on where a bunch of Beatles' covers might emanate from. Half a dozen tunes ring out, all closet Mop Top in a variety of struggling languages. Struggling, that is, to sound as wholesomely Liverpudlian and, well, just plain Beatlesy, as they can.

So, the highlights: Lucy In The Sky With Diamonds is a renowned gem from Star Trek's Captain Kirk (aka William Shatner). He travels to new lands of ambiguous acting, losing all focus on the plot, song and lyrics. Similarly Dickie Henderson takes an off-kilter view of Step

Inside Love and throws a spanner in the works by gruffly waffling through the song in the thinnest of ranges. Dickie's cabaret circuit, TV-friendly delivery is very much the epitome of everything that The Beatles came along and destroyed.

Through the floodgates came the psychedelic meandering of Lefty In The Right and the speeded-up sitar of Balsara And His Singing Sitars to name but two. Sheer madness is also well represented. The MP Derek Enright's overblown examination of the lyrics and his parallels to the classics are as pompous as you like and The Beatle Barkers' howling yap and Brian Sewell's po-faced uncertainty complete the picture.

If there are classics here, they lie quite simply with Desmond Dekker's smoking Come Together, which fuses his roots reggae and everything he ever learned in the rock arena. Next to that it's The Wilson Malone Voice Band for their deconstruction of Lennon and McCartney, which they reshape and remodel into an arrangement that Brian Wilson or indeed Phil Spector might have polished up to something quite potent. Then there's the simple ridiculousness of John Otway's I Am the Walrus which magnifies the song's mesmeric trippy weirdness, making the lyrics sound like they are struggling to escape the song. Otway paints a surreal cartoon of Lennon's daze, which is perfectly offset by a Lennon comment, "Any more for the merry go round?" which is followed by a fairground organ rendition of And I Love Her that underlines the fallibility of their success. The Beatles challenged so much, from the heart of the showbiz industry but ended up with their art being as processed as everything they initially left way behind. That said, without them the spread of simple pop music around the globe might have taken a few centuries longer.

And the sleeve: A pop art beenfeast with portraits of the Fabs by David Oxtoby, Yosuke Kawamura, J Generalic and Jimmy Thomson superimposed with Beatles imagery, memorabilia and paraphernalia. Inside there's beautiful Beatles' wallpaper and fan club facts with homage-driven photo-collages. Neat.

The Exotic Beatles: Part Two

EXOTICA RECORDS PELE 7CD. Released: 1994.

Introduction: Clap And Cheer/We Love You Beatles
The Squirrels: *Let It Be*
Murray The K introduces Joah Valley: *I Saw Her Standing There*
Jimmy Saville introduces Tsunematsu Masatoshi: *Nowhere Man*
The Beatles talk about acid, freedom and trees
Brian Sewell: *Sgt Pepper intro*
Arthur Mullard: *Yesterday*
Fisher And Marks: *Ring Ringo Little Star*
Grupo 15: *Rain (Lluvia)*
Ena Banga: *Can't Buy Me Love*
Geesin's Mahogany Minstrels: *Lady Madonna*
Maurice Chevalier: *Yellow Submarine*
Frank Sidebottom: *Flying*
The Beatle Barkers: *A Hard Day's Night*
The 52 Key Verbeek Fairground Organ: *Yesterday/Hey Jude*
Margarita Pracatan: *From Me To You*
John Lennon on Desert Island Discs
The Velvelettes: *It's For You*
Fisher And Marks: *We Love Rock 'n' Roll*
Johnny Prytko And The Connecticut Hightones: *Ob-La-Di, Ob-La-Da*
The Templeton Twins With Terry Turner And His Bunsen Burners: *Hey Jude*
RAM Peitsch: *Piggies*
Gordon Langford On The Electronic Arp Synthesiser: *Yellow Submarine*
Lol Coxhill with Claire (6), Simon (9), Maddie, Loo (13) and Katie Robertson: *I Am The Walrus*
Klaus Beyer: *Give Peace A Chance (Chant)*
Brian Sewell: *Give Peace A Chance*
The Pestalozzi Children's Village Choir: *Give Peace A Chance (Chant)*
Chiwaki: *A Hard Day's Night*
Lili Ivonova: *The Night Before*
Los Fernandos: *All My Loving*
Klaus Beyer: *The Continuing Story Of Bungalow Bill*
Mae West: *Day Tripper*
Ron Geesin: *Let It Be.*

The story: Volume Two of Exotic Beatles is even more eccentric and exotic than its predecessor. People scream. The Beatles have arrived and

they have a very personal place in everyone's lives. For sleevenote compiler Andy Darling it's an image of his uncle and his uncle's dog delivering their own particular version of A Hard Day's Night which involved a conga-line and the dog howling everytime the Fabs' uttered the immortal words "I've been working like a dog". It's an eduring image. Sort of.

But The Beatles have that affect on people. Their music reaches deep into people's lives and none moreso than Murray The K who's featured here claiming his claim that he was of course the Fifth Beatle. Elsewhere there's quotes and catchphrases which surround some truly strange interpretations of fabdom.

There's Joah Valley, who only supplies his music by mail order to interested parties. Joah's style is strange, his range tinted like he's been forcibly fed through some kind of synthetic pitch shifter. Joah's vocal is disjointed, nervy and not a little bit frightening. According to the sleeve he looks like some kind of religious leader and the fact that you can't buy his stuff in the shops mere-

ly reinforces the image of some strange cult icon locked in his own strange world. Like Bela Lugosi singing Sinatra.

Joah's followed by a strange Japanese trio who make you believe your CD player's broken. The track swirls as Tsunematsu Masatoshi revisit Nowhere Man. Did they mean it to sound like that? Whatever, it proves that the Lennon and McCartney song book is perfect for free form sonic assaults simply because the very basics of each song is so pronounced and perfectly formed.

And around the culture comes the homages. We're all aware of Dora Bryan's All I Want For Christmas Is A Beatle but Fisher And Marks' comic tribute and Frank Sidebottom's strangely moving Flying make the art of loving The Beatles all the more, well, wholesome.

Elsewhere there's more language versions, happy-go-lucky front room organ renditions, a kiddies' choir, bad metal, a polka, the inevitable dog chorus, synthetic doodlings, New Orleans jazz and Maurice Chevalier wholeheartedly deciding to deliver Yellow Submarine like some kind of nationalistic chant.

So, the highlights: I'm not sure if it's an accepted fact that Ron Geesin is a genius but in this company he certainly stands out for his eccentricity. Well, just about. Geesin worked with Pink Floyd but also released a handful of albums under various guises attempting his own concept pieces, mixing and matching musical styles and generally wandering through the form book willy nilly. Here he does exactly the same on Lady Madonna. At times he sounds like a dalek, then he switches into Scottish madman mode, all the while a symphonic noise rattles on with all the tinny insignificance that he can manage. It's plainly odd. As is Frank Sidebottom's adapted ode to the simplicity of the Beatles' Flying. Then there's the ragtime groove of The Templeton Twins with Teddy Turner And His Bunsen Burners. They do Hey Jude in the style of a red-nosed Harry Nilsson, all pastiche and a touch of irony for good measure. Similarly intriguing is the vocal gymnastics of Japanese a capella outfit Chiliwak, who rip it up on A Hard Day's Night. Plaudits about the sheer "terribleness" of Mae West's version of Day Tripper are well known and she proves that her best friend is not timing. Howver, the guitar break is awesome in the style of a Nuggets outtake and her reaction to such a caustic rasp is worth the entrance fee alone.

And the sleeve: A version of the Sgt Pepper's sleeve with a host of dolls and Action Men, characters from comics, Disney and the odd Barbie and Ken, making up the assembled cast. The Beatles are represented by what looks like four Asian looking Mop Tops with painted hair and specially made Pepper's outfits.

The Exotic Beatles: Part Three
EXOTICA RECORDS PELE 14CD. Released: 1999.

Shang Shang Typhoon: *Let It Be*
Cathy Berberian: *Ticket To Ride*
Irvin's 89 Key Marenghi Fairground Organ: *Help!*
David Peel: *With A Little Help From My Friends*
Mrs Yetta Bronstein: *I Want To Hold Your Hand*
Feeling B: *Revolution No 89*
Los Fernandos: *Yellow Submarine*
Frank Sidebottom: *Being For The Benefit Of Mr Kite*
Joah Valley: *In My Life*
Doodles Weaver: *Eleanor Rigby*
Powerillussi: *Lato B (Let It Be)*
Irvin's 89 Key Marenghi Fairground Organ
Klaus Beyer With The Gotz Alsmann Band: *Das Gelbe Underwasserboot (Yellow Submarine)*
The Mirza Men: *Eight Days A week*
The Beatle Barkers: *Love Me Do*
Emi Bonilla: *From Me To You*
Haax: *Gestern Noch (Yesterday)*
The Food: *And Your Hard Bird's Night Thing*
Rafi And Asha: *I Want To Hold Your Hand*
Ena Baga: *World Without Love*
Ogar Grafe: *Eleanor Rigby*
Marty Gold: *Hey Jude.*
The story: And so, to Volume Three and the level of general buffoonery reaches new heights with Morecombe and Wise, Frank Sidebottom and The Vernon Girls all voicing their opinions while organs grind, bier keller tributes run amok and David Peel pledges his allegiance to The Beatles.

In turn Noel Gallagher from Oasis does the same by admitting he's being trying to rip off Ticket To Ride for the last five years.

In the middle of it all there's the now seasonal dog chorus, Jewish humour from Joah Valley and Doodles Weaver and the likes of The Food who reinvent And Your Birds Night Thing in true Pinky And Perky style. Elsewhere Shang Shang Typhoon's glorious Japanese pop version of Let It Be seems like a work of genius placed next to the piano-powered operetta created by Cathy Berberian. She vibrato's through Ticket To Ride, the complete opposite in timing and decorum of Yetta Bronstein who lingers nearby.

Strangely, on volume three, people seem to be troubled by the simplicity and melodic charm of Beatles songs. None moreso than Ogar Graffe who gives Eleanor Rigby a hep reading until he decides to change octave. Ouch!

In the melting pot of inadequacy there's Flamenco madness with a Scally accent from Los Fernandos, Italian a capella from Powerillusi and crazy synth nonsense from Marty Gold, which all provide the perfect offbeat background for the listener to sample the wild Latin rhythms of The Mirza Men. Indeed, those crazy guys from Liverpool are given a heroes welcome wherever they end up.

Sadly the major hoot of an Indian Bollywood-styled version of I Want To Hold Your Hand is spoilt somewhat by poor sound. But the efforts of Rafi And Asha sound truly monumental as they change rhythm, time structure and backing at the snap of a clapperboard. Exquisite it is. So, the highlights: Feeling B's Revolution 89 is a mad indie fuzz fest with bagpipes that rolls in Nowhere Man and I Am The Walrus. It's great, as is Haax's Gestern Noch (Yesterday) which sounds like Slayer with Walter Carlos's electronic bleeps sped up to 78.

Inventiveness is also in good supply with Frank Sidebottom. His love of The Beatles is well known and when he changes the rhythmic scan of For The Benefit Of Mr Kite, a surreal masterpiece is created.

Likewise, friends of the family, David Peel And The Lower East Side provide a moving rendition of With A Little Help From My Friends, hardly a political diatribe but stuffed with attitude nonetheless and Shang Shang Typhoon's Let It Be is one of those helpless oddities that drags you back in to this strange and truly mad world

where The Beatles are everything.
And the sleeve: Another epic it features a space age reading of the Abbey Road crossing and sleevenotes from Martin Kelner whose radio series based on the Exotic album series was put up for an award in Monte Carlo. Attending the ceremony he admits he was shocked to see that people actually took the versions at face value and applauded accordingly. You see, those Beatles, they can do anything.

Golden Throats 4: Celebrities Butcher The Beatles
RHINO RECORDS RS72593 . Released 1997.

George Burns: *In The Beginning/With A Little Help From My Friends*
Joel Grey: *She's Leaving Home*
William Shatner: *Lucy In The Sky With Diamonds*
Telly Savalas: *Something*
Mae West: *Day Tripper*
Bing Crosby: *Hey Jude*
Xaviera Hollander: *Michelle*
Alan Copeland: *Mission Impossible Theme/ Norwegian Wood*
Tennessee Ernie Ford: *Let It Be*
Little Joe (Pesci): *Got To Get You Into My Life*
The Brothers Four: *Revolution*
Noel Harrison: *She's A Woman*
Claudine Longet: *Jealous Guy/Don't Let Me Down*
Theo Bikel: *Piggies*
Jan And Dean: *Norwegian Wood*
George Maharis: *A Hard Day's Night.*

The story: Gary Peterson, a long-term Rhino Records warehouse employee explains the concept in the extensive sleevenotes, revealing his and Pat Sierchio's mutual love of 49 cents albums by washed up celebrities. The two played them to fellow workers and eventually tapes became albums and the Golden Throats series was born. With so many Beatles' covers in the world it was only a matter of time before Beatles' selections were mooted and Butchering The Beatles was born.

The music itself varies from the ham-fisted to the truly magnificent. All of it is at least endearing. Beyond the simple strangeness of George Burns, pre-empting his Sgt Pepper's film appearance, there's Joel Grey, who starred in Cabaret as the MC, throwing his thespy larynx around With A Little Help From My Friends from his album which also, so we're led to believe, includes a cover version of Cream's White Room.

Elsewhere Bing almost can't be bothered with Hey Jude and Tennessee Ernie Ford goes all quasi-religious on Let It Be, while Joe Pesci, who'd later star in Goodfellas and Lethal Weapon, produces the kind of Italian cabaret version of Got To Get You Into My Life that makes the Mafia seem like a good option.

There's sex and sensuality too. Of sorts. Mae West adopts a pick up punk fuzz band called Somebody's Chyldren and delivers Day Tripper in a kitsch but horny way, as latter day call girl turned celeb Xaviera Hollander whispers through Michelle like a phone-sex exponent of girl-on-girl action.

Of course there's the lollipop-sucking Telly Savalas who talks through Something, much in the same way as William Shatner assaults Lucy In The Sky With Diamonds. Except Shatner goes completely am-dram crazy and offers the wordy Spleen prior to LSD, during which, of course, he flips out like we always hoped he would.

It's remarkably strange stuff, begging the question why did people do it and also why did they then release it? The Brothers Four, for instance, have a whole album of slo-mo Beatles' songs but their version of Revolution, which didn't make it to that album is truly remarkable. A song of teenage angst and retribution is delivered like someone reading a shopping list.

Elsewhere there's Claudine Longet. She was Mrs Andy Williams and she possesses the most wispy of featherlite voices. It flutters by Jealous Guy and Don't Let Me Down only hinting at the melody. Nothing more. If that weren't strange enough, then an earful of Noel Harrison's mock cockney jazz and Theo Bikel's ragged version of Piggies set up the album perfectly for George Maharis's Vegas set closer on A Hard Day's Night.

So, the highlights: From the sleevenotes it seems that the Rhino team have a down on Alan Copeland's strange fusion of the instrumental backing track to Mission: Impossible and the vocals from Norwegian Wood but, without a doubt, it was the Fat Boy Slim supermix of the day. It's actually really good as is Jan And Dean's version of the Wood epic. They steal all of The Beach Boys' Pet Sounds tricks, in a tit for tat move after the Wilson's stole their surf franchise, and make a quality Phil Spector-esque production of it.

And the sleeve: The sleeve is a take on the Fabs' Beatles' covers with the celeb selection destroying dolls of our heroes. Inside, each song is explained and Gary Peterson declares that if "Yoko or Pete Best or Mal Evans or Neil Aspinall was the fifth Beatle, then what about Murry The K" concluding that we're all the fifth Beatle, "You, me and Bing Crosby. Even William Shatner." Well, you can't argue with that.

The Beatles' music, then, has been subject to all sorts of interpretations over the years. And, in the course of wallowing in the glorious underbelly of Beatific entertainment, imagine the joy of discovering The Ides Of March's beautiful Symphony For Eleanor. The Ides had been a garagey, psychedelic pop rock outfit of some note on the Chicago scene of the late '60s but by the time 1970 rolled around they'd inherited a brass section and charted in the UK with their excellent Vehicle single. The long-deleted album of the same name saw them flesh out their brass rock sound and it closed with a lengthy take on Eleanor Rigby which was built into an uplifting collection of cross melodies and shrieking trumpets.

With nous and imagination the '70s were sure, then, to add more grandiose levels of culture and refinement to The Beatles' music. Weren't they? The Ides had decreed it after all! But, alas, a string of pomp exotica extravaganzas took the Fabs into new realms of strangeness during that decade. It was a period when anything went. Witness the Willy Russell stage play John, Paul, George, Ringo And Bert, or The Beatles music in a film which featured footage of Hitler, or a two-act examination of Beatlemania. Not to mention the arrival of The Rutles, Rostal And Schaeffer's Beatles Concerto and Peter Frampton and The Bee Gees' bizarre Sgt Pepper's film.

John, Paul, George, Ringo And Bert

By Willy Russell. Original Cast Recording with Barabara Dickson.

RSO 2394 141. Released: 1974

I Should Have Known Better by the cast
*Your Mother Should Know by **Barbara Dickson***
*Ooee Boppa by **Tiny Tina And The Titular Three***
*With A Little Help From My Friends by **Barbara Dickson***
*Penny Lane by **Barbara Dickson***
*In The Bleak Midwinter by **Barbara Dickson***
*Here Comes The Sun by **Barbara Dickson***
*The Long And Winding Road by **Barbara Dickson***
Clap And Cheer by the cast
*Help! By **Barbara Dickson***
*Lucy In The Sky With Diamonds by **Barbara Dickson***
*You Never Give Me Your Money/Carry That Weight by **Barbara Dickson***
*We Can Work It Out by **Barbara Dickson***
*I Will Be Your Love by **Leroy Lover (Bert)***
*A Day In The Life by **Barbara Dickson***
The story: A Robert Stigwood-produced, Willy

Russell-written tale of young love between Tiny Tina and Leroy Lover (Bert) set to a mish-mash of rock 'n' roll, Beatlesy take-offs and emotional readings of the Beatles canon by Barbara Dickson, John, Paul, George, Ringo And Bert was a way-back-then precursor to Ally McBeal with a barrage of songs thrown in for mood and scene setting. The most remarkable thing about this Liverpool Everyman Theatre production is that Bernard Hill (Yosser Hughes in Boys From The Blackstuff and the captain in Titanic) plays Paul McCartney. Beyond that all your left with is some confusing scores, a few off-stage noises and Dickson doing it her way.

The sleeve: An illustration of The Beatles in Pepper's garb with Bert along for good measure. And just how exotic is that? Not really. Barbara Dickson is soulful but the arrangements are – as in Ally McBeal – hardly inspiring weird or, indeed, wonderful.

All This And World War II
Original Soundtrack
RIVA RECORDS RVLP2. Released: 1976.

The Magical Mystery Tour by **Ambrosia**

Lucy In The Sky With Diamonds by **Elton John**
Golden Slumbers/Carry That Weight by **The Bee Gees**
I Am The Walrus by **Leo Sayer**
She's Leaving Home by **Bryan Ferry**
Lovely Rita by **Roy Wood**
When I'm 64 by **Keith Moon**
Get Back by **Rod Stewart**
Let It Be by **Leo Sayer**
Yesterday by **David Essex**
With A Little Help From My Friends by **Jeff Lynne**
Because by **Lynsey De Paul**
She Came In Through The Bathroom Window by **The Bee Gees**
Michelle by **Richard Cocciante**
We Can Work It Out by **The Four Seasons**
The Fool On The Hill by **Helen Reddy**
Maxwell's Silver Hammer by **Frankie Laine**
Hey Jude by **The Brothers Johnson**
Polythene Pam by **Roy Wood**
Sun King by **The Bee Gees**
Getting Better by **Status Quo**
The Long And Winding Road by **Leo Sayer**
Help by **Henry Gross**
A Day In The Life by **Frankie Valli**
Come Together by **Tina Turner**
You Never Give Me Your Money by **Wil Malone and Lou Reizner**
The End by **The London Symphony Orchestra**

The story: The sleeve has a footnote which thanks the "greatest record companies in the world" for their help in creating this album and "not causing world war three".

This Lou Reizner production was a movie extravaganza directed by Susan Winslow which included newsreel footage of the second world war with a soundtrack by a host of celebs covering Beatles' songs. Why? We may never know. "Beatles' "significance" is pushed to breaking point in this bizarre documentary that juxtaposes their songs with World War II footage."

claims the book Rock On Film and who are we to argue? "Helen Reddy sings Fool On The Hill while Hitler relaxes at Bertchtesgaden. Rod Stewart husks Get Back while Nazi troops goosestep."

The concept itself is bizarre to say the least and the collection of versions are strange enough in themselves. Some work. Some don't. There's the oft-played standards by Elton, Rod and Tina but Leo Sayer's brace of songs are simply perverse in their fleeting innocence . Roy Wood struggles with the tempo on Lovely Rita, Keith Moon is the archetypal fool on the hill on When I'm 64 and Jeff Lynne sounds like he's trying to be the most un-Beatlesy he can on a complicated With A Little Help From My Friends that goes all ELO as he breaks into Nowhere Man. Elsewhere The Bee Gees are strangely tame, Lynsey de Paul is as wispy as a butterfly and Frankie Laine sounds like your crazy uncle trying to do karaoke.

Certainly Rod holds his rockin' end up well but most of these takes just seem plain uncomfortable. If proof were ever needed, catch the full force of the madness that is the vocoded Lou Reizner murdering You Never Give Me Your Money.

The sleeve: Soldiers with guitars. Hey, that's funny.

And just how exotic is that? Pretty darn exotic I'd say.

Beatlemania
Recorded Live At The Winter Garden Theatre. Not The Beatles, an incredible simulation.
ARISTA AL 8501. Released: 1978.

The Coming: I Want To Hold Your Hand, She Loves You.
Making It: Help!, Can't Buy Me Love, Day Tripper.
Listening: Yesterday, Eleanor Rigby, Nowhere Man.
Tripping: Strawberry Fields Forever, Penny Lane, Magical Mystery Tour.
Dropping Out: Lady Madonna, The Fool On The Hill, Got To Get You Into My Life, Michelle, Get Back
Flower Power: All You Need Is Love.
Bottoming Out: Revolution, Hey Jude.
Moving On: I Am The Walrus, The Long And Winding Road, Let it Be.

The story: According to the sleeve: "Beatlemania has arrived! A multi-media and live musical celebration of The Sixties. A crew of over 40 designers, researchers, photographers, film editors, programmers and technicians worked to create the visual atmosphere, setting the tone for the excitement and colour of that tumultuous decade. A new concept in Broadway entertainment, Beatlemania has been refereed to as one of the most "Ambitious theatrical audio-visual productions to date", by critics, theatre buffs and audio-visual experts alike. The production's two hour non-stop visual montage is produced by over 10,000 separate slides, which are programmed through 28 channel computer-type programmers."

So, what you get on vinyl, is a play in two acts (it's a double album) split into, The Coming, Making It, Listening, Tripping, Dropping Out, Flower Power, Bottoming Out and Moving On. I'd like to say that you get a fantastic journey through the integral disintegration of one of the world's greatest groups... but you don't. On vinyl you get a series of copycat versions and fake crowd noise and "atmospherics". There's little in the way of soul and the cast are trying so hard to sound like the real thing that they mostly just miss the mood.

The sleeve pontificates over the assassination of Martin Luther King, before delving into style setting, social reasoning and various other pertinent issues of the day and their associated paraphernalia. It's just an idea that's run wildly our of control. Still, it must make sense to someone. Mustn't it?

The sleeve: Like a Broadway film poster with a few pix of the lads and the stage set inside.

And just how exotic is that? Not enough by any stretch of the imagination.

The Rutles

WARNER BROTHERS HS 3151. Released: 1978.

Hold My Hand, Number One, With A Girl Like You, I Must Be In Love, Ouch!, Living In Hope, Love Life, Nevertheless, Good Times Roll, Doubleback Alley, Cheese And onions, Another Day, Piggy In The Middle, Let's Be Natural.

The story: The brainchild of Neil Innes of The Bonzo Dog Doodah Band, The Rutles were the subject of a spoof TV rockumentary called All You Need Is Cash which carefully followed The Beatles' career and parodied their huge success, from Reeperbaun shows, royal performances, US tours, films, psychedelia and the whole she bang through to the group's demise. So, Help! Became Ouch!, A Hard Day's Night became A Hard Day's Rut, Let It Be is Let It Rot, etc, etc. With cameos from Jagger and Paul Simon and the quartet renamed Ron Nasty (Innes as Lennon), Stig O'Hara (Harrison), Dirk McQuickly (Monty Python's Eric Idle as Macca) and Barry Wom (Ringo), the attention to detail in the TV show is amazing and the rewriting of Beatles' tunes is unnerving. Quite rightly it created a cult sensation in its own right.

The sleeve: The perfect pastiche.

And just how exotic is that? Pretty darn exotic. So much so that it also spawned Rutles Highway Revisited, a compilation of Rutles' covers which included: Cheese And Onion by Galaxie 500, Hold My Hand by The Pussywillows, Good Times Roll by Lida Husik, Another Day by Dogbowl, Piggy In The Middle by Das Damen, I Must Be In Love by Syd Straw, Ouch! By Peter Stampfel, Love Life by Bongwater and Doubleback Alley by King Missile, among many others.

Sgt Pepper's Lonely Hearts Club Band

RSO 1598. Released: 1978.

The Long And Winding Road by **Peter Frampton**
A Day In The Life by **Barry Gibb, The Bee Gees**
Golden Slumbers by **Peter Frampton**
Carry That Weight by **The Bee Gees**
Got To Get You Into My Life by **Earth, Wind And Fire**
Nowhere Man by **The Bee Gees**
Maxwell's Silver Hammer by **Steve Martin**
Get Back by **Billy Preston**
Polythene Pam by **The Bee Gees**
Oh! Darling by **Robin Gibb**

Because by **Alice Cooper, The Bee Gees**
Fixing A Hole by **George Burns**
She Came In Through The Bathroom Window by **Peter Frampton and The Bee Gees**
Sgt Pepper's Lonely Hearts Club Band (reprise) by **Peter Frampton and The Bee Gees**
Getting Better by **Peter Frampton, The Bee Gees**

With A Little Help From My Friends by **Peter Frampton and The Bee Gees**
Come Together by **Aerosmith**
Being For The Benefit Of Mr Kite by **Maurice Gibb, Peter Frampton, George Burns and The Bee Gees**
Here Comes The Sun by **Sandy Farina**
Sgt Pepper's Lonely Hearts Club Band by **Paul Nicholas and The Bee Gees**
Good Morning, Good Morning by **Paul Nicholas, Peter Frampton and The Bee Gees**
I Want You (She's So Heavy) by **The Bee Gees, Dianne Steinberg, Paul Nicholas, Donald Pleasance, Stargard**
Mean Mr Mustard by **Frankie Howerd**
She's Leaving Home by **The Bee Gees, Jay MacIntosh, John Wheeler**
Lucy In the Sky With Diamonds by **Dianne Steinberg, Stargard**
Strawberry Fields Forever by **Sandy Farina**
You Never Give Me Your Money by **Paul Nicholas, Dianne Steinberg**
When I'm 64 by **Frankie Howerd, Sandy Farina**

The story: Another Robert Stigwood special, this time the great man honed in on Sgt Pepper's and decided that it/they were worth a film in their own right. Without the Fabs taking part, the quartet comprised of The Bee Gees (signed to his label) and Peter Frampton.

"Many notables, including Wilson Pickett appear in this flop," reports Rockin' Reels. "You know it's going to be bad when Strawberry Fields, an English girls school, becomes a person. Anyway it contains valiant if not half-bad efforts of singing The Beatles' songs as good as The Beatles did."

With George Martin along to help, the audio production is fair enough and there are some fine performances coaxed out of a cast of many. But just the roll call of ego's was probably scary enough to make it a difficult birth. And, as the story strayed from Sgt Pepper's to Yellow Submarine and beyond, a few baddies and the inevitable chase scene were added in search of a cohesive plot.

There are some musical highs, of course, and they certainly include: I Want You (She's So Heavy) by the strangest of conglomerations which include The Bee Gees, Dianne Steinberg, Paul Nicholas, Donald Pleasance and Stargard. Also of note is Earth With And Fire's Got To Get You Into My Life and Billy Preston's Get Back.

But, of course, there are also the lows. And the pretty darn terrible list most certainly includes Frampton's tortured take on The Long And Winding Road. Beyond that there's just some plain odd stuff, like Frankie Howerd's synthetic Mean Mr Mustard, George Burns struggling with Fixing A Hole, Alice Cooper trying to be officially evil on Because and the sub-disco operetta of She's Leaving Home. And don't even mention Steve Martin destroying Maxwell's Silver Hammer.

The sleeve: A logo-friendly cover reveals a host of scenes from the film. Hey, this is Hollywood.

And just how exotic is that? In a budget-busting mad idea way it was pretty exotic.

The Beatles Concerto
By Rostal And Schaefer, Ron Goodwin and The Royal Liverpool Philharmonic Orchestra

PARLOPHONE PAS 10014. Released: 1979.

The Beatles Concerto
1st Movement: Maestoso – Allegro moderato. She Loves You; Eleanor Rigby; Yesterday; All My Loving; Hey Jude.
2nd Movement: Andante espressivo. Here, There And Everywhere; Something.
3rd Movement: Presto. Can't Buy Me Love; The Long And Winding Road.
Six Beatles Impressions: Fool On The Hill; Lucy In The Sky With Diamonds; Michelle; Maxwell's Silver Hammer; Here Comes The Sun; A Hard Day's Night.

The story: This is orchestral music, let's not be flippant, let's go right past the formalities and study the sleevenotes by George Martin: "The arrival of The Beatles in 1962 heralded a collation of creativity unprecedented in English popular music, embracing the best talents far wider than their own group. Their success broke all kinds of barriers, and when the shocked establishment managed to hear the music through the "noise" they realised that genuinely original music of lasting beauty was being created.

"Now, 17 years later, we have the happy assembly of the talents of the brilliant young duo-pianists Peter Rostal and Paul Schaeffer, the tasteful writing of John Rutter, and the Royal Liverpool Philharmonic Orchestra under the superb direction of Ron Goodwin.

"Anyone who admits to liking the great piano concertos of Grieg, Rachmaninov, or Tchaikovsky cannot fail to enjoy The Beatles' concerto – a true composition in classical form."

The result is back to square one. It's 1965 all over again with Rostal And Schaeffer giving it full Eine Kleine Nutcracker and Baroque Beatlesisms. Crazy. Again, we must ask, what have we learnt? Mmmmm. Can I get back to you on that one?

The sleeve: An inexplicable caped figure trolls off in a psychedelic swirl. What relevance this has is hard to say.

And just how exotic is that? In a Liberace was nice kind of way? Pretty exotic.

THEY CAME IN THROUGH THE BATHROOM WINDOW

Beyond the obvious pleasure dome of Beatles pastiche, cover and tribute, another world of post-69 Beatledom exists. Inspiration and perspiration has made pop music a well known if over-used tag. While today it stands for something quite different from what it did back in the early '60s. Now the natural descendants of Beatles-styled creativity are more likely to be heralded as cult icons rather than pop commodities. These children of melody may not have covered their songs, but they've certainly interpreted The Beatles' wares. Their arrival was almost inevitable, from the day John, Paul, George and Ringo stepped off the plane in New York.

In America, Beatlemania changed everything. Sinatra was out. Presley was floundering. Chirpy Brits ruled the roost. The Fabs' electric zip was followed by a torrent of UK acts and the likes of Herman's Hermits made their Britpop bigger over there than in the

UK. During the invasion, The Byrds' new electric roots and Brian Wilson's Beach Boys' productions were America's saving grace. And, amid the hub-bub legions of imitators took the triad's not dissimilar gameplans and tried to create their own version of a bankable pop sound. The early '70s saw Badfinger's Beatles-esque quaintness also hailed over the Atlantic and home-grown American acts like Big Star and The Raspberries began to emulate their inspiration. In a natural food chain, they beget The Rubinoos, Greg Khin, Dwight Twilley, The Shoes, The Plimsouls and a variety of other groovily-named wannabes. However, commercial success was not on the agenda. Cult status loomed instead. And, even in the hands of touted artistes, the cusp of Beatles, Big Star, Badfinger, Beach Boys and Byrds creativity couldn't be made lucrative, as former Merry Go Round vocalist Emmit Rhodes found in 1970. Much ado surrounded his debut album and the eventual failure of its beautifully-appointed songs and intricate layered production dismayed him, his label and indeed everyone else. He reacted by growing a futile beard and becoming a recluse.

Even old pro's, like The Nazz's Todd Rundgren couldn't get all the bits in the right order. His Something Anything from 1972 was a masterpiece that spawned a minor hit single in I Saw The Light, but, for whatever reason, the set remained something of an acquired taste. Certainly, Rundgren avoided the beard option, but with mass adulation AWOL he turned the volume up to 11 and melody was confined to the doldrums.

The mid-'70s saw the arrival of major rumours. The Beatles were indeed back together again and masquerading as Klaatu. According to Malcolm Atkinson, who runs a Klaatu site on the web, the story goes like this: "Rumours emerged in 1973 that The Beatles had reformed under an assumed name, Klaatu and in 1976, Capitol released an anonymous album by the group. They remained obscure until 1977, when Charlie Parker, a DJ on WDRC in Providence, Rhode Island, played one of the tracks on his show. Hundreds of listeners phoned, convinced he had played a new Beatles record.

An article by Steve Smith in the Providence Journal claimed that Klaatu was the Beatles. He suggested there were some 150 clues and pieces of evidence which pointed to a 'Klaatu Konspiracy'. These included...

1 A University of Miami voice print test on Klaatu and McCartney recordings which proved the lead vocalist was the same.
2 An Australian disc jockey with evidence to show that the 'Klaatu' album was an unreleased Beatles album called 'Sun' (the cover for 'Klaatu' depicts a smiling sun)
3 Playing 'Sub Rosa Subway' backwards, using a low speed frequency ocillator and filters revealed the message 'Its us, its the Beeeeetles!'
4 On the cover of his 'Goodnight Vienna' album, Ringo Starr's head was shown superimposed on the body of a character from the film The Day The Earth Stood Still. The character's name? Klaatu. The connection was strenthened by Apple promotional material for 'Goodnight Vienna', which said 'Don't Forget - Klaatu Barada Nikto'

"There was no biographical info on the cover of the album, while the group's manager, Frank Davis, when asked directly if Klaatu were the Beatles, refused to confirm or deny the rumour. Likewise, Capitol, far from denying the allegations, went so far as to circulate the Providence Journal article, and within eight weeks, the album had sold 300,000 copies."

Klaatu were in fact Canadian session musicians. And even with a huge press campaign and consequential sales they couldn't manage to make post Beatles pop work. However their first couple of albums are pretty cool.

Picking up on Emmit Rhodes, Todd and Klaatu, a natural line back to Badfinger and The Beatles and if you swing it forward, the roadway heads straight to today's so-called power pop elite of Myracle Brah, Cotton Mather et al.

But don't take my word for it. Starting in 1970, here's the natural linneage that makes today's American Beatle-esque music so wildly evocative and so immensely enjoyable...

Emitt Rhodes
Emitt Rhodes
PROBE SPBA 6256.
Released 1970

He was a one man band weened on The Beatles whose clean cut songs and boy next door image gradually faded as he became exasperated when the hits failed to materialise. His debut was full of classic multi-layered pop harmonies and subsequent albums confirmed his genius status but he disappeared into the ether and grew a beard at the last.

The Raspberries
The Raspberries
CAPITOL E-ST 11036.
Released: 1972

Fronted by Eric Carmen, The Raspberries are the missing link between The Beatles and anything Jeff Lynne ever thinks about doing. Carmen's wandering vocal, echoey double harmonies and the group's standard rock phrasing make their songs beautiful and wholesome, just on the sugary side of Big Star, with plenty of muscle when needed.

Big Star
Radio City
STAX/BIG BEAT CDWIK 910. Released: 1973

Big Star had debuted a year previous with a chunkier guitar sound than The Raspberries but by 1973 they'd become chirpier and cheekier. Versatile indeed, they were able to produce both Lennon-essque rockers and Macca-styled smoochers and Radio City was them at their best. It also includes the awesome September Gurls.

The Dwight Twilley Band
Sincerely
SHELTER ISA 5012.
Released: 1976

Twilley followed the Big Star blueprint of Beatlesy pop too, fleshing it out on occasion, adding Byrdsian phrasing when needed and ending up as an all-round pop icon into the bargain. Revived and revisited in the late '90s his legendary status is assured. Nice haircut too.

Klaatu
Klaatu
EMI E-ST 11542. Released 1976

The would-be/could-be Beatles' debut is a tremendous collection of spacey pop music chocfull with melody and effects. Opening with the Carpenters-approved Calling Occupants From Interplanetary Space and dipping into the Beach Boys' bag to widen their sound, Klaatu – Beatles scam forgotten – are truly special.

The Flamin' Groovies
Shake Some Action
PHILIPS 6370 804. Released: 1976

The Flamin' Groovies returned their American interpretation of The Beatles' pop vision on the cusp of the punk revolution in the UK. Their stylish sound was hip and the title track is awesome but their pent-up verve was never really appreciated by the pogo-ing Brits even if their tight suits were worth millions.

The Plimsouls
The Plimsouls
PLANET P13. Released: 1981

Harking back to an earlier Beatles' incarnation with their chiming guitars and layered harmonies, The Plimsouls come complete with groggy Lennon vocals. From the school of sub-Tom Petty Byrds-flavoured Beatles-friendly combos list - and that's not an easy tag to live up to.

The Shoes
Silhouette
DEMON FIEND 19. Released 1984.

Despite the chunky electronic keyboards in places, The Shoes rely and fully maintain their chirpy melodies and neat harmonies. Adding a taste of Byrds jangle and some heartfelt vocals to their Fab roots they're hummably gorgeous. And the charm of their long deleted Present Tense album still pervades.

The Pursuit Of Happiness
Love Junk
CHRYSALIS CHR 1675.
Released: 1989

In the late '80s The Pursuit Of Happiness were being preened by Chrysalis for rock stardom, but lank-haired front man Moe Berg had a penchant for pop and chart success was on his mind. Todd Rundgren was brought in for their debut album which spawned the awesome single I'm An Adult Now.

Jellyfish
Bellybutton
CHARISMA CDCUS 3. Released: 1990

Quite simply they loved Macca, they even covered Jet live, and added an almost prog rock enormity to their songs and those classic Beatles melody lines. Bellybutton was just a phenomenal experience, its arrangements and pacing almost draining, a real rollercoaster of sound and emotion.

Matthew Sweet
Girlfriend
ZOO PD 90644.
Released: 1991

In the world of the under-rated singer/songwriter, Matthew Sweet is king. In Japan he's huge and 1991's Girlfriend explains why. In the style of Emmit Rhodes, Sweet mixes all the main ingredients, adding a touch of sadness for his ballads and enough double-tracked vocals to pluck at every heartstring.

The Posies
Frosting On The Beater
GEFFEN GFLD 19298. Released: 1993

One more for the list of lost heroes, The Posies strayed too close to rock flamboyance and burned out. But on songs like Flavor Of The Month from 1993's Frosting On The Beater, their harmony style and keen sense of minor-chord melody are nothing short of compulsive in a truly Beatlesy way.

20/20
Four Day Tornado
OGLIO OGL 89100-2. Released: 1995

Good time, Flamin' Groovies-styled Beatlesisms from these key figures in the '90s power pop movement whose Yellow Pills tune is a standard of the genre (and the name of a subsequent fanzine). 20/20 sound like what The Beatles would have sounded like if George had had an upper hand.

Wondermints
Wondermints
BIG DEAL 9033-2. Released: 1996

Back in 1996, this superb debut presented the group as a space-age meeting of The Beach Boys and The Beatles. The eclectic brew is further spiced with classic Bacharach and Brill building couplets accompanied when necessary by Byrds' jangle, Jellyfish's dramatic depth and a few love songs to boot.

Cotton Mather
Kontiki
COPPER CPR 2249.
Released: 1997

Cotton Mather's second album is staggering level. Certainly the Lennon/McCartney duel vocal is in evi-dence, but it's the clever post-grunge guitar shapes that add to the White Album/Abbey Road era sound. The uptempo drive and the pure joy that Cotton Mather exude make this totally moreish.

Myracle Brah
Life On Planet Eartsnop
NOT LAME NL-044.
Released: 1998

Love Nut mainman Andy Bopp knocks out 20 pop gems from the lost song book of Badfinger, Big Star, The La's - whoever. Life On Planet Eartsnop rattles with exuberant tambourine but possesses a batch of truly uplifting melodies all underpinned by Bopp's bittersweet Lennon impersonation. Two more albums have already followed.

Supremium
Lucky
POP SQUAD 003. Released: 2000

Rockier, in the style of Revolver-era Fabs with John on the mike and a touch of The Byrds on hand for effect, Supremium are a truly infectious, highly whitsleable and hummalongable set of songsmiths. All the classic hooks are here and all you want them to do is throw in an ooh and aah for the full effect.

Other key players include the venerable Tommy Keene, a veteran in such a young scene whose Songs From The Film (Matador) is awesome. Not to mention former Jellyfish man Jason Falkner's excellent Nigel Godrich-produced solo album Can You Still Feel? (Elektra), various Australian and Finnish and Swedish combos and a host of emerging new acts.
One glance at the Not Lame catalogue (Box 2266, Ft Collins, Colorado 80522-2266, USA. www.not-lame.com) with its 1,000 plus releases tells you how big this burgeoning scene is becoming. Add to the above: Fountains Of Wayne, Semisonic, The Velvet Crush, The Scruffs, Odds and The Idle Jets and the flexible friend will be taking some beating.

I, Me, Moog

DIG A PONY

Every time I go to meet my friend who works across the other side of London we go through this ritual of meeting near Newman Passage, a tight lane beside a pub renowned for its pies, near Charlotte Street. Sometimes it's not even on our way to anywhere but our pilgrimage to the site is essential.

Every time we get there my friend stops. He collects himself and a moment of stiff upper lip Britishness comes over him. He knows I know why this is happening but he always insists on telling me the same thing.

"I always get a bit emotional about Newman Passage," he says. "The Fabs."

What he's referring to is a scene in A Hard Day's Night where The Beatles are hiding from marauding fans in a pub. It's that pub. At the end of Newman Passage. Then they ran off down the lane. And, unlike Abbey Road, there's not even a bit of pro-Fab graffiti, just a few butterflies in our stomachs because we're walking the same streets that they walked a mere 35 years before. Undoubtedly everyone who's wandered into a studio to lay down some Lennon, McCartney or Harrison must have experienced the same tingling sensations – with the possible exception of The Beatle Barkers of course.

Everyone wants to be a Beatle and to experience that adrenalin rush. Just check out the popularity and, indeed, the authenticity of The Bootleg Beatles. And, imagine the scene when Don Was rounded up five new wave heroes in 1994 to be the playing arm of the Backbeat band from the movie of the same name. The electricity created by The Afghan Whigs' Greg Dulli, cult producer Don Fleming, Sonic Youth's Thurston Moore, The Foo Fighters' Dave Grohl and REM's Mike Mills must have been phenomenal.

Even the loosest of connections seems to turn people's heads. Check out the pastiches of the Meet The Beatles sleeve from Roogalator, Genesis and closet Beatles' fans The Residents. The latter's debut album featured a defaced Beatles' sleeve, the perfect foil for their defaced music and, without doubt, the easiest way for them to gain a large audience at the drop of a felt pen.

Without doubt, some heinous crimes have been committed in the name of the Beatles. Even their own label, Parlophone, seem to show little remorse at times. Back in 1982, for whatever reason, they cobbled together a roughly edited selection of Beatles songs used in movies to promote the album Reel Music. The Beatles' Movie Medley shoe-horned Magical Mystery Tour, All You Need Is Love, You've Got To Hide Your Love Away, I Should Have Known Better, A Hard Day's Night, Ticket To Ride and Get Back into three minutes and 56 seconds, illustrating that you don't even have to be The Original Brasso band, or Billy And The Pepperpots to juggle the crown jewels clumsily.

Certainly, the parade of pretenders that make up this book are by turn intriguing and eccentric and now with the arrival of the internet we're fortunate enough to be able to see and in some cases hear yet more Beatles-related nonsense, starting with The Accordion Beatles.

Based at Domenic's Accordion Beatles Page, you can actually download nervous accordion versions of Beatles' songs by this Canadian eccentric. The Tornoto Star is obviously proud of Dom. This is their reporter Peter Krivel's take on the local boy made good… well, goodish.

"The Beatles and accordion music. What more could you want? If you put yourself in that category, then visit the site for Toronto marketing man Domenic Amatucci. He's been captivating audiences in TTC subway stations with his squeezebox renditions of such favourites as In My Life, Please Please Me, All My Loving, A Little Help From My Friends and I Saw Her Standing There.

And now he brings the best of his music to http://home.ican.net/~domenic/accordion.html where you can download examples of his prowess."

And what did Yahoo magazine make of it?

"It's not that we're powerful fans of the squeeze box, or that we haven't come to terms with the Fab Four's break up and subsequent ageing. We like this page just for being its non-commercial, non-glitzy self. Proprietor Domenic builds Web pages for a living and plays accordion in the subways of Toronto for the joy of it. These pleasant (and yes, well-played) clips are fun."

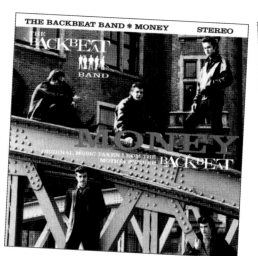

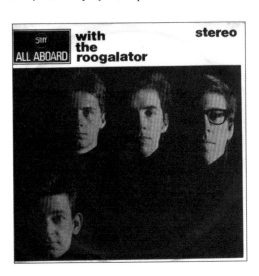

Yeah. Really. Nearly as much fun as The Beagles' Can't Buy Me Love on Hit Records. In the process of putting this book together I came across this 45 and was willing it to be another slice of dog-related Beatles mayhem. Sadly not though. It was just another cash-in for short-sighted punters (that's me) who misread "The Beagles" as "The Beatles". The version itself is a stodgy copy that lacks swing and real passion, a sour note to go out on. But in collecting these chestnuts there's always going to be some indeterminate rubbish lurking.

And after so much attention to people's detailed dissection of The Beatles' back catalogue you'd be forgiven for being confused – I know I have been by the sheer audacity of some of the perpetrators. Whatever, here's the top 30 Beatles covers as voted for by me. I couldn't narrow it down any more than that. I'll leave that up to you…

1 A Day In The Life by The Leo Chauliac Orchestra Crazy psychedelic cover, bowler hats and dishointed swishing strings.

2 And I Love Her by Smokey Robinson Moody and evocative as only Smokey can be, adding an extra turn of wry charm to the song.

3 Come Together by Desmond Dekker Haunting, frightening with a pounding rhythm.

4 Day Tripper/We Can Work It Out by Fever Tree They took psychedelics, rolled their eyes and sneaked inside both songs.

5 Don't Let Me Down by Dillard And Clark Beautiful blue-eyed soul from the late Gene Clark.

6 Eight Days A Week by Alma Cogan Allegedly with The Beatles in the studio, she sings her heart out and completely re-designs the song.

7 For The Benefit Of Mr Kite by Frank Sidebottom He wears a papier mache head and sings with a peg on his nose. But he loves The Beatles.

8 Here, There And Everywhere by Emmylou Harris She sand with Gram Parsosn then went out on her own. Her stock-in-trade is country and she breathes high and lonseome emotion into every couplet.

9 I Am The Walrus by Spooky Tooth A formative evil-sounding grind that sounds like it's powered by a giant metallic key. Ouch!

10 I Call Your Name by The Mamas And The Papas Mama Cass at her squeeky best with every ounce of passion squished into the verses.

11 I Me Mine by Laibach More eveil than the Tooth? A Gothic monstrosity of great power and beauty.

12 I'm Happy Just To Dance With You by The Cyrkle Unhinged psychedelic where time doesn't seem to matter. Neither does timing for that matter.

13 It's Getting Better by The Wedding Present Frenetic post-post-punk rattles from David Gedge and co which sounds like they're simply racing to see who can finish first.

14 I'm Down by The Beastie Boys I heard this when I interviewed the group in a hotel room in North London. I couldn't believe how audacious and emotive they'd made this unsung gem sound. The Beatles refused permission for its release.

15 I've Just Seen A Face by The Dillards From my childhood and cosmic country roots. A fresh-faced and boy-next-door paced classic.

16 I Want You (She's So Heavy) by The Bee Gees, Dianne Steinberg, Paul Nicholas, Donald Pleasance and Stargard Plainly bizarre and the arrival of Donald Pleasance just makes it even more surreal.

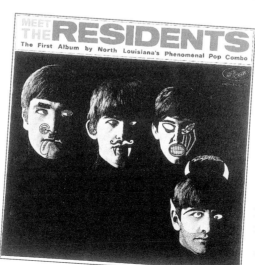

17 Lucy In The Sky With Diamonds by William Shatner He's the greatest when it comes to over-acting and he doesn't dissapoint on this tortured masterpiece.

18 Mission: Impossible/Norwegian Wood by Alan Copeland A dancefloor friendly remix before such things existed. Awesome.

19 Norwegian Wood by The Buddy Rich Big Band Walloping his drums into submission and exploding into action just because he can, Buddy Rich's horn-laden screamer is like a crazed anthem for the would-be beats.

20 Please Please Me by Keely Smith Nightclubbing balladeering with a smouldering jazz arrangement.

21 She Came In Thru the Bathroom Window by Joe Cocker He shouts, he hollers, he pulls all the right faces.

22 She's A Woman by Jose Feliciano Wild strumming, shades and gritty yeahs, yeah, yeahs.

23 Strawberry Fields Forever by Todd Rundgren Under rated songwriter with a bent for Spector-esque productions and a gorgeous nasal singing style.

24 Symphony For Eleanor by The Ides Of March A rewriting of history with pumping brass and prog rock tendencies.

25 The Fool On The Hill by Sergio Mendes And Brasil '66 Groovy sambas with lots of bababadadadahs.

26 The Royale Beatleworks Musicke, MBE 1963 including Ouverture: I Want To Hold Your Hand by Joshua Rifkin Forsooth it is the classics like never before.

27 With A Little Help From My Friends by David Peel And The Lower East Side A revolution in the air, from the streets of New York with plenty of pathos.

28 Within You, Without You by Rainer Ptacek Ambient strumming, moody bottleneck and a slide into the netherworld.

29 World Without Love by Alan Haven One of my Dad's favourites. An organist who would go down very well at the Tower in Blackpool, doing it to the Fabs.

30 Yesterday by The Carmen Cavallaro Camp It's just strange for the sake of it, a collission of styles and playing. A masterpiece no less.

So, that all seems pretty conclusive, doesn't it? Plainly, The Beatles were fab. They changed everything. Everyone pinched their songs. The world is littered with cover versions, the majority of which are sub-standard. However, between the cracks there's a wealth of Godsent takes and many bizarre offerings lurk.

Of course, I've tried repeatedly to conclude this tome. To put a final analysis in. The synopsise (if such a word exists) but new angles arrive daily... and today was no exception. Imagine the utter thrill - the butterfly and stomach miss-match - when I purloigned Moog Plays Beatles - which has one of the most fantastic sleeves ever, featuring an inexplicably naked pair of claymation models. Wallace And Gromit, look out!

Marty Gold
Moog Plays The Beatles
AVCO EMBASSY 6466 001. Released: 1970

Eleanor Rigby; Norwegian Wood; Day Tripper; Yesterday, get Back, Penny Lane; Lucy In The Sky With Diamonds; Michelle; Hey Jude; In My Life; The Fool On The Hill; Good Night.

The music: In 1970 the synthesiser was new and the musician's union were still complaining that it would take away people's jobs in orchestra's. No-one realised its potential and Marty Gold who recorded these Beatles' tunes was no exception. None of the machine's versatility is troubled here, as Marty opts to use his Moog for a collection of "other worldly" noises that play out his chosen selection of songs. Actually that's absolutely fine though as what he does play is some of the kitschest music that you're likely to hear. Ever. It is the sound of an age stuck in time grasping in a very futile way at the future. Excellent.

The sleeve: I'm speechless. It's so ace.

The sleevenotes: "Moog plays The Beatles" Yet less than a decade ago, this would have sounded like a preposterous title, for nobody knew that what either a Moog or a Beatle was. Now, of course, we all know The Beatles. And, record by record, we are learning more about the Moog.

Classic Beatles cut: It's all absolutely brilliant, like there's a mad scientist at the controls who's desperate to add swirlingand farting noises to the proceedings whenever possible. Priceless, however, is In My Life which was undoubtedly recorded on the moon.

THE ELECTRONIC MUSIC OF MARTY GOLD

HELP AND ENTHUSIASM: Q magazine, Mojo magazine, The Beatles Covers List (their archive gave me reassurance that I was heading in the right direction and set me on a mission to find things I never even knew existed), Jac Holzman (his book Follow The Music is fab) and Jim Phelan (his Exotic Beatles series is a brilliant place to start).

Then, of course, there's The Accordion Beatles, Frank's Vinyl Museum, Jim Yoakum, Cool And Strange Music Magazine, Acker Bilk, Dave Santer, Phil Bowen, Tim Rice, Parlophone Records, Apple Records and Rodney Dillard.

Plus a load of shops and mags, like Record And Tape Exchange Notting Hill, Stigmata Records in Geneva, Escridiscos in Madrid, Laibach, some dodgy bloke at Glastonbury Festival, Music And Video Exchange, Soho, Daddy Kool Records, Happenstance magazine, Rhythm Records in Camden, Minus Zero in Notting Hill and Tower Records.

And Johnny Vaughan (his incensed enthusiasm over Beatles Go Bossa thrust this whole thing forward), Katherine Allen (she gave me a copy of the reggae covers album), Tor Records in Glastonbury, a junk shop in Brampton, Jumble sale in Pewsey, Oxfam in Goodge Street, Cancer Research in Carlisle.

Not to mention Joe Cocker (his facial expressions at Woodstock to With A Little Help From My Friends will always stay with me), The Cyrkle (crazy psychedelics), the boot sale in Marlborough, Bucketful Of Brains magazine, Sound Choice in Reading, Pet Sounds in Newcastle, The Residents, Mark Ellen, Genesis and Steve Davis.

Also June Carswell (she saw Help! six times in the first week), Aunt Mimi (she inspired John), Auntie Ella (she inspired me), David Black, Gary and Nick, Drummond Base, the new pop labels Parasol, Ginger, Pop Squad and the Not Lamers.

Plus The Beastie Boys, Sean Body at Helter Skelter, Kevin Donald Taylor, Howard Johnson, record hunters Phil Alexander and Paul rees and Paul Trynka and his withering expression.

CARRY THAT WEIGHT

SLEEVES AND ARTWORK CREDITS: Pye International (P5,96), Reprise Records (P5,67,104), Raven Records (P6), Jim Phelan (P8, 9,11,126,127,128), CBS Records (P8,49,95,118), Straight (P9), Red Rocket magazine (P10), Cherry Red (P11), Parlophone (P14,17,18,21, 22, 25,27, 29,31,33,34,38,39,94,134), Apple Records (P35, 37), Atlantic Records (P40,122), Springboard Records (P42), RCA (P42,49,50,51,111), Studio 2 (P43), Pickwick (P43), Music For Pleasure (P44,53,71,77,93, 112,113,121), EMI (P44,54,59,80,93, 97,124,125,136), A&M (P45,97,101,111,115), GNP (P45), Stax (P46), Columbia (P46,50,98,100,125), Decca (P47,92,105,109,116,118), Elektra (P47,63, 101), Concert Hall (P48), Stereo Plus (P48), K-Tel (P51,59,80), Emporio (P51,65,88), Konga (P52), Fontana (P52,55,115,116), Stereo Gold Award (P52), Music Joy (P54), Hallmark (P54), Mute (P56), Polydor (P57,99,105,106), Philips (P57,101,103,109), DJM (P58,115), Wyncote (P58), See For Miles (P59), Music Digital (P60), Castle Communications (P60), Penny Farthing (P60,61), Capitol (P62,103,109), Studio Two (P62), Mercury Records (P64,122), Stereo Gold (P64), Disky (P65), Auto Pilot Records (P65), Arc (P66), American (P66),World Record Club (P67), Windmill (P68), Sydney Thompson Records (P67), Tring (P70), Atlantic Jazz (P72), Skyline Records (P72), Sequel (P75,100,109), Tower (P76), Planeta (P76), Connoisseur (P78), Echo (P78), Tamla Motown (P79,114,119), Dino Entertainment (P81), RMM (P82), Concert Gold (P83,107), NYC (P84), Windham Hill (P84), Bluenote (P85), Dressed To Kill (P85), Pop God (P86), NME (P87), Tribute Records (P89), Trojan (P88,89), Embassy (P90), Fierce Recordings (P93), Shimmydisc (P94), Coronet (P95), Command (P96), Atco (P98,118), Columbia UK (P98), London (P99), Contour (P102), Uni (P102), Rykodisc (P104), Homestead (P105), MCA (P105), Pye Golden Guinea (P106), Warner Bros (P107,132), RCA (P109,113), Fidelio (P111), Mint (P112), Chevron (P113), HMV (P112), Pickwick (P114), Sunset (P114), Island (P16), Fire Records (P116), Rounder (P117), Concert Hall (P119), Wand (P120), TER (P121), Fly (P122), Rhino (P129), RSO (P130), Riva (P131), Arista (P131), RSO (P133), Probe (PT37), Shelter (P137), Big Beat (P137), Planet (P137), Chrysalis (P137), Charisma (P138), Zoo (P138), Geffen (P138), Copper (P138), Big Beat (P137), Oglio (P130), Not Lame (P138), Stiff (P140), Virgin (p140), Ralph (P140),Hit (P140), Avco (P142).

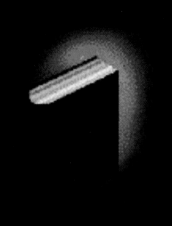

THE BLACK BOOK COMPANY

**PO BOX 2030
PEWSEY
SN9 5QZ
ENGLAND**

**TELEPHONE
44 (0) 1672 564929
FAX
44 (0) 1672 564433
EMAIL
dhende7730@aol.com
INTERNET
www.blackbookco.com**

The regular guys:
**Dave Henderson
Howard Johnson
Keith Drummond
David Black
Gary Perry
Nick Clode
Karyn Hansell**

DISTRIBUTION UK
Turnaround 44 (0) 181
329 3009

**DISTRUBUTION
AUSTRALIA**
Tower Books (02) 9975
5566

"Revolver's been
turned over."

Actually, we're just mad about music. The Black Book Company is obsessed with songs, sounds, riffs and legends. Apocryphal tales, rock 'n' roll lifestyles, eccentrics, lunatics and cool grooves. From Dylan to the Fabs, Kurt, Curtis and The Bar-Kays to Curtis, Otis and Neil, it's our one true love.

Thanks for buying The Beatles Uncovered. We're currently planning revelatory investigations into offbeat and ridiculous vinyl, the legend of Glastonbury Festival and a rites-of-passage analogy of Neil Young. After that it's the concept album. Help!

For now you can check out our back pages on Bob, AC/DC and the art of Leaving The 20th Century. Hope you enjoyed the ride...

Touched By The Hand Of Bob

EPIPHANAL BOB DYLAN EXPERIENCES FROM A BUICK SIX
by Dave Henderson. PUBLISHED: June 1, 1999
Paperback, heavyweight matt finish, fully illustrated.
ISBN: 1-902799-00-3

Like remembering how you heard about the assassination of John Lennon, the world and their Walkman all have a story about their experience with Bob Dylan.

Dave Henderson delves deep into Dylanland, discovering Fatwa-invoking fanatics, rune-juggling astrologers, hi-brow intellectuals and a bizarre circus of followers. Touched By The Hand Of Bob follows Dylan's miracle-strewn journey, meeting the people who covered his songs, copied his haircut and grabbed at the hem of his frock coat. They walk among us...

WHAT THE PAPERS SAID:

TIME OUT " A rule of thumb. You can never have too many Dylan books. Best of the most recent bunch is Dave Henderson's Touched By The Hand Of Bob. Henderson entertainingly delves into the 'psyche of Bob';s faithful'. All aspects of Bob's mixed up legend are rifled, explored, documented and exposed in what is a genuinely compelling, funny and fantastic book."

Q MAGAZINE "Dave Henderson has opted for a fan's eye view of what it means to have been metaphorically nuzzled by the great man. It's a brisk volume filled with bite-sized anecdotes, remembrances and the odd critical opinion; ideal for dipping into."

UNCUT MAGAZINE "What we get here is a trot through Dylan's career as seen through the eyes of numerous witnesses, both contemporary and modern. There are quotes from stars and the unknown and several endearing tales of people meeting Dylan and instantly making complete prats of themselves. Enormously enjoyable: Dylan book of the year!"

MOJO MAGAZINE "This is a real ragbag of a book- fans recalling epiphanic Bob moments, as well as discographies, cuttings and other fascinating odds and ends - which makes it one of the more enjoyable Dylan books of late."

BEAT SCENE MAGAZINE "There are elements of Nick Hornby's Fever Pitch here even, and more relevantly, High Fidelity. Henderson concedes his record collector passions but strives for meaning to it all and tries to elicit some sane answers from everyone he meets who shares this predeliction for Bob Dylan. A massive treasure chest of Dylan stuff to absorb and written with a lot of spark."

RECORD COLLECTOR "Touched By The Hand of Bob captures the bizarre intoxication of being a Dylan fan, in an era which has chosen to ignore everything for which he stands. Whether you lost your virginity to Nashville Skyline or sacrificed friendships, marriages or faithful dogs in your devotion to Dylan's art, anyone who has been touched by Bob's apparently sweaty hands will recognise themselves or their close friends in Henderson's anthology of neurosis and nostalgia."

You can order books published by the Black Book Company direct from us

You can order copies of our titles for £10.50 each (including post and packing in the UK and within the EC). For overseas orders, please add £1 (outside of EC but within Europe) or £3 (USA, Canada and Australia). If you'd like to order more than one copy, please add £1 per additional copy. Make cheques payable to THE BLACK BOOK COMPANY LTD.

If you'd like to order in bulk (over five copies), then please fax us at +44 (0) 1672 564433

IF YOU'D LIKE TO GET ON OUR MAILING LIST for news on upcoming projects, then send your details by fax +44 (0) 1672 564433

or email dhende7730@aol.com or write to us at **THE BLACK BOOK COMPANY BOX 2030PEWSEY SN9 5QZ NGLAND** or visit our website **www.blackbookco.com**

Get Your Jumbo Jet Out Of My Airport

RANDOM NOTES FOR AC/DC OBSESSIVES
by Howard Johnson. PUBLISHED: June 1, 1999
Pbk, hweight matt finish, fully illustrated. ISBN: 1-902799-01-1

When AC/DC vocalist Bon Scott died in 1980 few could have envisaged that 19 years later the group would still be one of the world's biggest rockacts. Why are they still so popular on the back of a few boogie chords and a schoolboy uniform?

Get Your Jumbo Jet Out Of My Airport is the first book ever to fully document the group's massive appeal. From the obsessive owners of 500 bootlegs to the record company execs and producers who have brought AC/DC to the world, Howard Johnson has interviewed them all. The result is a collection of the finest anecdotes and most revealing tales, revealing why AC/DC remain so special, so important and so influential. Delivering one of the most revealing pictures of the band ever, with a wealth of previously unseen pictures, this is a work of frankly lunatic devotion.

WHAT THE PAPERS SAID:
Q MAGAZINE "Johnson's teenage confessions offer a stark but welcome contrast to those of most thirtysomething journalists fixated with The Clash. "I had records by The Scorpions, UFO and Journey." he crows, while stapling together 1,000 copies of Phoenix, the north's premier heavy metal fanzine. The result is an irresistible read but, perhaps for like-minded souls only."

RECORD COLLECTOR MAGAZINE "Howard Johnson provides an informative, entertaining text, while allowing it to be a framework for more juicy material, care of fanzine writers, video extras, journalists, ex-AC/DC members and, most importantly, the fan obsessives. On the whole, this is a wow!"

Leaving The 20th Century

LAST WORDS ON ROCK 'N' ROLL
by Dave Henderson and Howard Johnson
PUBLISHED: November 1, 1999
ISBN 1-902799-02-X
Paperback, 196-pages, fully-illustrated

Tribute albums, fond memories, conventions and super fandom reach new levels when the icon of your idealism dies. In Leaving The 20th Century, Dave Henderson and Howard Johnson have collected a moving collection of rock 'n' roll obituaries, inked by the fans, the famous and the familiar.

As we head for the year 2000, Leaving The 20th Century looks at the people who built modern music and the effect their spiralling from the planet has had. From Elvis Presley, Kurt Cobain, Keith Moon, Buddy Holly, Clarence White, Tim Buckley, Jerry Garcia, Tim Hardin, Brian Jones, Freddie Mercury, Pete Ham, Sterling Morrison, Marvin Gaye, Ian Curtis, Frank Sinatra, Tupac Shakur, Joe Meek, Michael Hutchence, Nico, Sam Cooke, Randy Rhoads, John Lennon, Jeff Buckley, Richard Manuel and Sid Vicious to Tiny Tim and The Singing Nun.

WHAT THE PAPERS SAID:
Q MAGAZINE: "Henderson and Johnson have created a treasure trove of fulsome, often obscure rock eulogies from the music press, heartbroken fan obsessives and scarily obsessive websites."

TIME OUT MAGAZINE: "Eminentlybrowsable and thoroughly researched, it is a fascinating work that manages to tread a fine line between good fun and bad taste. It makes for a fine read."

Fontana

45

1

RECORDING FIRST
PUBLISHED 1963

UNAUTHORISED PUBLIC PERFORMANCE,

TF 427
267310 TF
267310 TF

Flamingo Music

ALL I WANT FOR CHRISTMAS IS A BEATLE
(Gladys Benton)
DORA BRYAN
with accompaniment directed by
JOHNNY GREGORY